THE
COMPLETE
PROSE OF
WOODY
ALLEN

THE COMPLETE PROSE OF WOODY ALLEN

Without Feathers
Getting Even
Side Effects

WINGS BOOKS
NEW YORK

This edition was originally published in separate volumes under the titles:
Without Feathers, copyright © 1972, 1973, 1974, 1975 by Woody Allen.
Getting Even, copyright © 1966, 1967, 1968, 1969, 1970, 1971 by Woody Allen.
Side Effects, copyright © 1975, 1976, 1977, 1979, 1980 by Woody Allen.

This edition is published by Wings Books,
distributed by Random House Value Publishing, Inc.,
201 East 50th St., New York, New York 10022,
by arrangement with Random House, Inc.

Random House
New York • Toronto • London • Sydney • Auckland
http://www.randomhouse.com/

Printed and bound in the United States of America

Library of Congress Cataloging-in-Publication Data
Allen, Woody.
[Selections. 1991]
The complete prose of Woody Allen / Woody Allen.
p. cm.
Contents: Without feathers—Getting even—Side effects.
ISBN 0-517-07229-7
I. Title.
PS3551.L44A6 1991
818´.5407—dc20 91-28866
CIP

Book design by Clair Moritz

14 13 12 11 10 9 8 7

CONTENTS

WITHOUT FEATHERS

"Hope is the thing with feathers . . ."
—Emily Dickinson

CONTENTS

Selections from the Allen Notebooks

Following are excerpts from the hitherto secret private journal of Woody Allen, which will be published post-humously or after his death, which ever comes first.

GETTING through the night is becoming harder and harder. Last evening, I had the uneasy feeling that some men were trying to break into my room to shampoo me. But why? I kept imagining I saw shadowy forms, and at 3 A.M. the underwear I had draped over a chair resembled the Kaiser on roller skates. When I finally did fall asleep, I had that same hideous nightmare in which a woodchuck is trying to claim my prize at a raffle. Despair.

I believe my consumption has grown worse. Also my asthma. The wheezing comes and goes, and I get dizzy more and more frequently. I have taken to violent choking and fainting. My room is damp and I have perpetual chills and palpitations of the heart. I noticed, too, that I am out of napkins. Will it never stop?

Idea for a story: A man awakens to find his parrot has been made Secretary of Agriculture. He is consumed with

7

8 jealousy and shoots himself, but unfortunately the gun is the type with a little flag that pops out, with the word "Bang" on it. The flag pokes his eye out, and he lives—a chastened human being who, for the first time, enjoys the simple pleasures of life, like farming or sitting on an air hose.

Thought: Why does man kill? He kills for food. And not only food: frequently there must be a beverage.

Should I marry W.? Not if she won't tell me the other letters in her name. And what about her career? How can I ask a woman of her beauty to give up the Roller Derby? Decisions . . .

Once again I tried committing suicide—this time by wetting my nose and inserting it into the light socket. Unfortunately, there was a short in the wiring, and I merely caromed off the icebox. Still obsessed by thoughts of death, I brood constantly. I keep wondering if there is an afterlife, and if there is will they be able to break a twenty?

I ran into my brother today at a funeral. We had not seen one another for fifteen years, but as usual he produced a pig bladder from his pocket and began hitting me on the head with it. Time has helped me understand him better. I finally realized his remark that I am "some loathsome vermin fit only for extermination" was said more out of compassion than anger. Let's face it: he was always much brighter than me—wittier, more cultured, better educated. Why he is still working at McDonald's is a mystery.

Idea for story: Some beavers take over Carnegie Hall and perform *Wozzeck*. (Strong theme. What will be the structure?)

Good Lord, why am I so guilty? Is it because I hated my father? Probably it was the veal-parmigian' incident. Well, what *was* it doing in his wallet? If I had listened to him, I would be blocking hats for a living. I can hear him now: "To block hats—that is everything." I remember his reaction when I told him I wanted to write. "The only writing you'll do is in collaboration with an owl." I still have no idea what he meant. What a sad man! When my first play, *A Cyst for Gus,* was produced at the Lyceum, he attended opening night in tails and a gas mask.

Today I saw a red-and-yellow sunset and thought, How insignificant I am! Of course, I thought that yesterday, too, and it rained. I was overcome with self-loathing and contemplated suicide again—this time by inhaling next to an insurance salesman.

Short story: A man awakens in the morning and finds himself transformed into his own arch supports. (This idea can work on many levels. Psychologically, it is the quintessence of Kruger, Freud's disciple who discovered sexuality in bacon.)

How wrong Emily Dickinson was! Hope is not "the thing with feathers." The thing with feathers has turned out to be my nephew. I must take him to a specialist in Zurich.

I have decided to break off my engagement with W. She doesn't understand my writing, and said last night that my *Critique of Metaphysical Reality* reminded her of *Airport.* We quarreled, and she brought up the subject of children again, but I convinced her they would be too young.

10

Do I believe in God? I did until Mother's accident. She fell on some meat loaf, and it penetrated her spleen. She lay in a coma for months, unable to do anything but sing "Granada" to an imaginary herring. Why was this woman in the prime of life so afflicted—because in her youth she dared to defy convention and got married with a brown paper bag on her head? And how can I believe in God when just last week I got my tongue caught in the roller of an electric typewriter? I am plagued by doubts. What if everything is an illusion and nothing exists? In that case, I definitely overpaid for my carpet. If only God would give me some clear sign! Like making a large deposit in my name at a Swiss bank.

Had coffee with Melnick today. He talked to me about his idea of having all government officials dress like hens.

Play idea: A character based on my father, but without quite so prominent a big toe. He is sent to the Sorbonne to study the harmonica. In the end, he dies, never realizing his one dream—to sit up to his waist in gravy. (I see a brilliant second-act curtain, where two midgets come upon a severed head in a shipment of volleyballs.)

While taking my noon walk today, I had more morbid thoughts. What is it about death that bothers me so much? Probably the hours. Melnick says the soul is immortal and lives on after the body drops away, but if my soul exists without my body I am convinced all my clothes will be loose-fitting. Oh, well . . .

Did not have to break off with W. after all, for as luck would have it, she ran off to Finland with a professional circus geek. All for the best, I suppose, although I had another of those attacks where I start coughing out of my ears.

Last night, I burned all my plays and poetry. Ironically, as I was burning my masterpiece, *Dark Penguin*, the room caught fire, and I am now the object of a lawsuit by some men named Pinchunk and Schlosser. Kierkegaard was right.

Examining Psychic
Phenomena

THERE is no question that there is an unseen world. The problem is, how far is it from midtown and how late is it open? Unexplainable events occur constantly. One man will see spirits. Another will hear voices. A third will wake up and find himself running in the Preakness. How many of us have not at one time or another felt an ice-cold hand on the back of our neck while we were home alone? (Not me, thank God, but some have.) What is behind these experiences? Or in front of them, for that matter? Is it true that some men can foresee the future or communicate with ghosts? And after death is it still possible to take showers?

Fortunately, these questions about psychic phenomena are answered in a soon to be published book, *Boo!*, by Dr. Osgood Mulford Twelge, the noted parapsychologist and professor of ectoplasm at Columbia University. Dr. Twelge has assembled a remarkable history of supernatural incidents that covers the whole range of psychic phenomena,

15

from thought transference to the bizarre experience of two brothers on opposite parts of the globe, one of whom took a bath while the other suddenly got clean. What follows is but a sampling of Dr. Twelge's most celebrated cases, with his comments.

Apparitions

On March 16, 1882, Mr. J. C. Dubbs awoke in the middle of the night and saw his brother Amos, who had been dead for fourteen years, sitting at the foot of his bed flicking chickens. Dubbs asked his brother what he was doing there, and his brother said not to worry, he was dead and was only in town for the weekend. Dubbs asked his brother what it was like in "the other world," and his brother said it was not unlike Cleveland. He said he had returned to give Dubbs a message, which was that a dark-blue suit and Argyle socks are a big mistake.

At that point, Dubbs's servant girl entered and saw Dubbs talking to "a shapeless, milky haze," which she said reminded her of Amos Dubbs but was a little better-looking. Finally, the ghost asked Dubbs to join him in an aria from *Faust*, which the two sang with great fervor. As dawn rose, the ghost walked through the wall, and Dubbs, trying to follow, broke his nose.

This appears to be a classic case of the apparition phenomenon, and if Dubbs is to be believed, the ghost returned again and caused Mrs. Dubbs to rise out of a chair and hover over the dinner table for twenty minutes until she dropped into some gravy. It is interesting to note that spirits have a tendency to be mischievous, which A. F. Childe, the British mystic, attributes to a marked feeling of inferiority they have over being dead. "Apparitions" are often associated with individuals who have suffered an unusual demise. Amos Dubbs, for instance, had died

under mysterious circumstances when a farmer accidentally planted him along with some turnips.

Spirit Departure

Mr. Albert Sykes reports the following experience: "I was
sitting having biscuits with some friends when I felt my
spirit leave my body and go make a telephone call. For
some reason, it called the Moscowitz Fiber Glass Company. My spirit then returned to my body and sat for
another twenty minutes or so, hoping nobody would suggest charades. When the conversation turned to mutual
funds, it left again and began wandering around the city. I
am convinced that it visited the Statue of Liberty and then
saw the stage show at Radio City Music Hall. Following
that, it went to Benny's Steak House and ran up a tab of
sixty-eight dollars. My spirit then decided to return to my
body, but it was impossible to get a cab. Finally, it walked
up Fifth Avenue and rejoined me just in time to catch the
late news. I could tell that it was reentering my body, because I felt a sudden chill, and a voice said, 'I'm back. You
want to pass me those raisins?'

"This phenomenon has happened to me several times
since. Once, my spirit went to Miami for a weekend, and
once it was arrested for trying to leave Macy's without
paying for a tie. The fourth time, it was actually my body
that left my spirit, although all it did was get a rubdown
and come right back."

Spirit departure was very common around 1910, when
many "spirits" were reported wandering aimlessly around
India searching for the American Consulate. The phenomenon is quite similar to transubstantiation, the process
whereby a person will suddenly dematerialize and re-
materialize somewhere else in the world. This is not a bad
way to travel, although there is usually a half-hour wait for

luggage. The most astonishing case of transubstantiation was that of Sir Arthur Nurney, who vanished with an audible *pop* while he was taking a bath and suddenly appeared in the string section of the Vienna Symphony Orchestra. He stayed on as the first violinist for twenty-seven years, although he could only play "Three Blind Mice," and vanished abruptly one day during Mozart's Jupiter Symphony, turning up in bed with Winston Churchill.

Precognition

Mr. Fenton Allentuck describes the following precognitive dream: "I went to sleep at midnight and dreamed that I was playing whist with a plate of chives. Suddenly the dream shifted, and I saw my grandfather about to be run over by a truck in the middle of the street, where he was waltzing with a clothing dummy. I tried to scream, but when I opened my mouth the only sound that came out was chimes, and my grandfather was run over.

"I awoke in a sweat and ran to my grandfather's house and asked him if he had plans to go waltzing with a clothing dummy. He said of course not, although he had contemplated posing as a shepherd to fool his enemies. Relieved, I walked home, but learned later that the old man had slipped on a chicken-salad sandwich and fallen off the Chrysler Building."

Precognitive dreams are too common to be dismissed as pure coincidence. Here a man dreams of a relative's death, and it occurs. Not everyone is so lucky. J. Martinez, of Kennebunkport, Maine, dreamed he won the Irish Sweepstakes. When he awoke, his bed had floated out to sea.

Trances

Sir Hugh Swiggles, the skeptic, reports an interesting séance experience:

> We attended the home of Madame Reynaud, the noted medium, where we were all told to sit around the table and join hands. Mr. Weeks couldn't stop giggling, and Madame Reynaud smashed him on the head with a Ouija board. The lights were turned out, and Madame Reynaud attempted to contact Mrs. Marple's husband, who had died at the opera when his beard caught fire. The following is an exact transcript:

MRS. MARPLE: What do you see?

MEDIUM: I see a man with blue eyes and a pinwheel hat.

MRS. MARPLE: That's my husband!

MEDIUM: His name is . . . Robert. No . . . Richard . . .

MRS. MARPLE: Quincy.

MEDIUM: Quincy! Yes, that's it!

MRS. MARPLE: What else about him?

MEDIUM: He is bald but usually keeps some leaves on his head so nobody will notice.

MRS. MARPLE: Yes! Exactly!

MEDIUM: For some reason, he has an object . . . a loin of pork.

MRS. MARPLE: My anniversary present to him! Can you make him speak?

MEDIUM: Speak, spirit. Speak.

QUINCY: Claire, this is Quincy.

MRS. MARPLE: Oh, Quincy! Quincy!

QUINCY: How long do you keep the chicken in when you're trying to broil it?

MRS. MARPLE: That voice! It's him!

MEDIUM: Everybody concentrate.

MRS. MARPLE: Quincy, are they treating you okay?

QUINCY: Not bad, except it takes four days to get your cleaning back.

MRS. MARPLE: Quincy, do you miss me?

QUINCY: Huh? Oh, er, sure. Sure, kid. I got to be going. . . .

MEDIUM: I'm losing it. He's fading. . . .

I found this séance to pass the most stringent tests of credulity, with the minor exception of a phonograph, which was found under Madame Reynaud's dress.

There is no doubt that certain events recorded at séances are genuine. Who does not recall the famous incident at Sybil Seretsky's, when her goldfish sang "I Got Rhythm"—a favorite tune of her recently deceased nephew? But contacting the dead is at best difficult, since most deceased are reluctant to speak up, and those that do seem to hem and haw before getting to the point. The author has actually seen a table rise, and Dr. Joshua Fleagle, of Harvard, attended a séance in which a table not only rose but excused itself and went upstairs to sleep.

Clairvoyance

One of the most astounding cases of clairvoyance is that of the noted Greek psychic, Achille Londos. Londos realized he had "unusual powers" by the age of ten, when he could lie in bed and, by concentrating, make his father's false teeth jump out of his mouth. After a neighbor's husband had been missing for three weeks, Londos told them to look in the stove, where the man was found knitting. Londos could concentrate on a person's face and force the image to come out on a roll of ordinary Kodak film, although he could never seem to get anybody to smile.

In 1964, he was called in to aid police in capturing the Düsseldorf Strangler, a fiend who always left a baked Alaska on the chests of his victims. Merely by sniffing a handkerchief, Londos led police to Siegfried Lenz, handyman at a school for deaf turkeys, who said he was the strangler and could he please have his handkerchief back.

Londos is just one of many people with psychic powers. C. N. Jerome, the psychic, of Newport, Rhode Island, claims he can guess any card being thought of by a squirrel.

Prognostication

Finally, we come to Aristonidis, the sixteenth-century count whose predictions continue to dazzle and perplex even the most skeptical. Typical examples are:

"Two nations will go to war, but only one will win."

(Experts feel this probably refers to the Russo-Japanese War of 1904–05—an astounding feat of prognostication, considering the fact that it was made in 1540.)

"A man in Istanbul will have his hat blocked, and it will be ruined."

(In 1860, Abu Hamid, Ottoman warrior, sent his cap out to be cleaned, and it came back with spots.)

"I see a great person, who one day will invent for mankind a garment to be worn over his trousers for protection while cooking. It will be called an 'abron' or 'aprone.' "

(Aristonidis meant the apron, of course.)

"A leader will emerge in France. He will be very short and will cause great calamity."

(This is a reference either to Napoleon or to Marcel

Lumet, an eighteenth-century midget who instigated a plot to rub béarnaise sauce on Voltaire.)

"In the New World, there will be a place named California, and a man named Joseph Cotten will become famous."

(No explanation necessary.)

A Guide to Some of the Lesser Ballets

Dmitri

The ballet opens at a carnival. There are refreshments and rides. Many people in gaily colored costumes dance and laugh, to the accompaniment of flutes and woodwinds, while the trombones play in a minor key to suggest that soon the refreshments will run out and everybody will be dead.

Wandering around the fairgrounds is a beautiful girl named Natasha, who is sad because her father has been sent to fight in Khartoum, and there is no war there. Following her is Leonid, a young student, who is too shy to speak to Natasha but places a mixed-green salad on her doorstep every night. Natasha is moved by the gift and wishes she could meet the man who is sending it, particularly since she hates the house dressing and would prefer Roquefort.

The two strangers accidentally meet when Leonid,

trying to compose a love note to Natasha, falls out of the Ferris wheel. She helps him up, and the two dance a pas de deux, after which Leonid tries to impress her by rolling his eyes until he has to be carried to the comfort station. Leonid offers profuse apologies and suggests that the two of them stroll to Tent No. 5 and watch a puppet show—an invitation that confirms in Natasha's mind the idea that she is dealing with an idiot.

The puppet show, however, is enchanting, and a large, amusing puppet named Dmitri falls in love with Natasha. She realizes that although he is only sawdust, he has a soul, and when he suggests checking into a hotel as Mr. and Mrs. John Doe, she is excited. The two dance a pas de deux, despite the fact that she just danced a pas de deux and is perspiring like an ox. Natasha confesses her love for Dmitri and swears that the two of them will always be together, even though the man who works his strings will have to sleep on a cot in the parlor.

Leonid, outraged at being thrown over for a puppet, shoots Dmitri, who doesn't die but appears on the roof of the Merchants Bank, drinking haughtily from a bottle of Air Wick. The action becomes confused, and there is much rejoicing when Natasha fractures her skull.

The Sacrifice

A melodic prelude recounts man's relation to the earth and why he always seems to wind up buried in it. The curtain rises on a vast primitive wasteland, not unlike certain parts of New Jersey. Men and women sit in separate groups and then begin to dance, but they have no idea why and soon sit down again. Presently a young male in the prime of life enters and dances a hymn to fire. Suddenly it is discovered he is *on* fire, and after being put out he slinks off. Now the stage becomes dark, and Man challenges Nature—a stirring encounter during which Nature is bitten on the hip, with the result that for the next six months the temperature never rises above thirteen degrees.

Scene 2 opens, and Spring still has not come, although it is late August and no one is quite sure when to set the clocks ahead. The elders of the tribe meet and decide to propitiate Nature by sacrificing a young girl. A maiden is selected. She is given three hours to report to the outskirts of town, where she is told they are having a weenie roast. When the girl appears that night, she asks where all the frankfurters are. She is ordered by the elders to dance herself to death. She pleads pathetically, telling them that she is not that good a dancer. The villagers insist, and, as the music builds relentlessly, the girl spins in a frenzy, achieving sufficient centrifugal force to hurl her silver fillings across a football field. Everyone rejoices, but too soon, for not only does Spring fail to come but two of the elders get subpoenaed in a mail-fraud charge.

The Spell

The overture begins with the brass in a joyous mood, while underneath, the double basses seem to be warning us, "Don't listen to the brass. What the hell does brass know?" Presently, the curtain rises on Prince Sigmund's palace, magnificent in its splendor and rent-controlled. It is the Prince's twenty-first birthday, but he grows despondent as he opens his gifts because most of them turn out to be pajamas. One by one, his old friends pay their respects, and he greets them with a handshake or a slap on the back, depending on which way they are facing. He reminisces with his oldest friend, Wolfschmidt, and they vow that if either of them grows bald the other will wear a toupee. The ensemble dances in preparation for the hunt until Sigmund says, "What hunt?" No one is quite sure, but the revelry has gone too far, and when the check comes there is much anger.

Bored with life, Sigmund dances his way down to the shore of the lake, where he stares at his perfect reflection for forty minutes, annoyed at not having brought his shaving equipment. Suddenly he hears the flutter of wings, and a group of wild swans flies across the moon; they take the first right and head back to the Prince. Sigmund is astounded to see that their leader is part swan and part woman—unfortunately, divided lengthwise. She enchants Sigmund, who is careful not to make any poultry jokes. The two dance a pas de deux that ends when Sigmund throws his back out. Yvette, the Swan Woman, tells Sigmund that she is under a spell cast by a magician named Von Epps, and that because of her appearance it is nearly impossible to get a bank loan. In an especially difficult solo, she explains, in dance language, that the only way to lift Von Epp's curse is for her lover to go to secretarial school and learn shorthand. This is odious to Sigmund, but he swears he will. Suddenly Von Epps appears, in the form of yesterday's laundry, and spirits Yvette away with him as the first act ends.

As Act II begins, it is a week later, and the Prince is about to be married to Justine, a woman he had completely forgotten about. Sigmund is torn by ambivalent feelings because he still loves the Swan Woman, but Justine is very beautiful, too, and has no major drawbacks like feathers or a beak. Justine dances seductively around Sigmund, who seems to be debating whether to go through with the marriage or find Yvette and see if the doctors can come up with anything. Cymbals crash and Von Epps, the Magician, enters. Actually, he was not invited to the wedding, but he promises not to eat much. Furious, Sigmund pulls his sword and stabs Von Epps through the heart. This casts a pall on the party, and Sigmund's mother commands the chef to wait a few minutes before bringing out the roast beef.

Meanwhile, Wolfschmidt, acting on Sigmund's behalf,

has found the missing Yvette—not a difficult task, he explains, "because how many half women, half swans are there hanging around Hamburg?" Despite Justine's imploring, Sigmund rushes off to Yvette. Justine runs after him and kisses him, as the orchestra strikes a minor chord and we realize Sigmund has his leotards on inside out. Yvette weeps, explaining that the only way to lift the spell is for her to die. In one of the most moving and beautiful passages in any ballet, she runs headlong into a brick wall. Sigmund watches her body change from a dead swan to a dead woman and realizes how bittersweet life can be, particularly for fowl. Grief-stricken, he decides to join her, and after a delicate dance of mourning he swallows a barbell.

The Predators

This celebrated electronic ballet is perhaps the most dramatic of all modern dances. It begins with an overture of contemporary sounds—street noises, ticking clocks, a dwarf playing "Hora Staccato" on a comb and tissue paper. The curtain then rises on a blank stage. For several minutes, nothing happens; eventually, the curtain falls and there is an intermission.

Act II begins with a hush as some young men dance on, pretending to be insects. The leader is a common housefly, while the others resemble a variety of garden pests. They move sinuously to the dissonant music, in search of an immense buttered roll, which gradually appears in the background. They are about to eat it when they are interrupted by a procession of women who carry a large can of Raid. Panic-stricken, the males try to escape, but they are put into metal cages, with nothing to read. The women dance orgiastically around the cages, preparing to devour the males the minute they can find some soy sauce. As the females prepare to dine, one young girl notices a forlorn male, with drooping antennae. She is drawn to him, and the two dance slowly to French horns as he whispers in her ear, "Don't eat me." The two fall in love, and make elaborate plans for a nuptial flight, but the female changes her mind and devours the male, preferring instead to move in with a roommate.

A Day in the Life of a Doe

Unbearably lovely music is heard as the curtain rises, and we see the woods on a summer afternoon. A fawn dances on and nibbles slowly at some leaves. He drifts lazily through the soft foliage. Soon he starts coughing and drops dead.

The Scrolls

SCHOLARS will recall that several years ago a shepherd, wandering in the Gulf of Aqaba, stumbled upon a cave containing several large clay jars and also two tickets to the ice show. Inside the jars were discovered six parchment scrolls with ancient incomprehensible writing which the shepherd, in his ignorance, sold to the museum for $750,000 apiece. Two years later the jars turned up in a pawnshop in Philadelphia. One year later the shepherd turned up in a pawnshop in Philadelphia and neither was claimed.

Archaeologists originally set the date of the scrolls at 4000 B.C., or just after the massacre of the Israelites by their benefactors. The writing is a mixture of Sumerian, Aramaic, and Babylonian and seems to have been done by either one man over a long period of time, or several men who shared the same suit. The authenticity of the scrolls is currently in great doubt, particularly since the word "Oldsmobile" appears several times in the text, and the

34

few fragments that have finally been translated deal with familiar religious themes in a more than dubious way. Still, excavationist A. H. Bauer has noted that even though the fragments seem totally fraudulent, this is probably the greatest archeological find in history with the exception of the recovery of his cuff links from a tomb in Jerusalem. The following are the translated fragments.

ONE . . . And the Lord made an bet with Satan to test Job's loyalty and the Lord, for no apparent reason to Job, smote him on the head and again on the ear and pushed him into an thick sauce so as to make Job sticky and vile and then He slew a tenth part of Job's kine and Job calleth out: "Why doth thou slay my kine? Kine are hard to come by. Now I am short kine and I'm not even sure what kine are." And the Lord produced two stone tablets and snapped them closed on Job's nose. And when Job's wife saw this she wept and the Lord sent an angel of mercy who anointed her head with a polo mallet and of the ten plagues, the Lord sent one through six, inclusive, and Job was sore and his wife angry and she rent her garment and then raised the rent but refused to paint.

And soon Job's pastures dried up and his tongue cleaved to the roof of his mouth so he could not pronounce the word "frankincense" without getting big laughs.

And once the Lord, while wreaking havoc upon his faithful servant, came too close and Job grabbed him around the neck and said, "Aha! Now I got you! Why art thou giving Job a hard time, eh? Eh? Speak up!"

And the Lord said, "Er, look—that's my neck you have . . . Could you let me go?"

But Job showed no mercy and said, "I was doing very well till you came along. I had myrrh and fig trees in abundance and a coat of many colors with two pairs of pants of many colors. Now look."

And the Lord spake and his voice thundered: "Must I

who created heaven and earth explain my ways to thee? What hath thou created that thou doth dare question me?"

"That's no answer," Job said. "And for someone who's supposed to be omnipotent, let me tell you, 'tabernacle' has only one *l*." Then Job fell to his knees and cried to the Lord, "Thine is the kingdom and the power and glory. Thou hast a good job. Don't blow it."

Two . . . And Abraham awoke in the middle of the night and said to his only son, Isaac, "I have had an dream where the voice of the Lord sayeth that I must sacrifice my only son, so put your pants on." And Isaac trembled and said, "So what did you say? I mean when He brought this whole thing up?"

"What am I going to say?" Abraham said. "I'm standing there at two A.M. in my underwear with the Creator of the Universe. Should I argue?"

"Well, did he say why he wants me sacrificed?" Isaac asked his father.

But Abraham said, "The faithful do not question. Now let's go because I have a heavy day tomorrow."

And Sarah who heard Abraham's plan grew vexed and said, "How doth thou know it was the Lord and not, say, thy friend who loveth practical jokes, for the Lord hateth practical jokes and whosoever shall pull one shall be delivered into the hands of his enemies whether they can pay the delivery charge or not." And Abraham answered, "Because I know it was the Lord. It was a deep, resonant voice, well modulated, and nobody in the desert can get a rumble in it like that."

And Sarah said, "And thou art willing to carry out this senseless act?" But Abraham told her, "Frankly yes, for to question the Lord's word is one of the worst things a person can do, particularly with the economy in the state it's in."

And so he took Isaac to a certain place and prepared to

sacrifice him but at the last minute the Lord stayed Abraham's hand and said, "How could thou doest such a thing?"

And Abraham said, "But thou said—"

"Never mind what I said," the Lord spake. "Doth thou listen to every crazy idea that comes thy way?" And Abraham grew ashamed. "Er—not really . . . no."

"I jokingly suggest thou sacrifice Isaac and thou immediately runs out to do it."

And Abraham fell to his knees, "See, I never know when you're kidding."

And the Lord thundered, "No sense of humor. I can't believe it."

"But doth this not prove I love thee, that I was willing to donate mine only son on thy whim?"

And the Lord said, "It proves that some men will follow any order no matter how asinine as long as it comes from a resonant, well-modulated voice."

And with that, the Lord bid Abraham get some rest and check with him tomorrow.

THREE . . . And it came to pass that a man who sold shirts was smitten by hard times. Neither did any of his merchandise move nor did he prosper. And he prayed and said, "Lord, why hast thou left me to suffer thus? All mine enemies sell their goods except I. And it's the height of the season. My shirts are good shirts. Take a look at this rayon. I got button-downs, flare collars, nothing sells. Yet I have kept thy commandments. Why can I not earn a living when mine younger brother cleans up in children's ready-to-wear?"

And the Lord heard the man and said, "About thy shirts . . ."

"Yes, Lord," the man said, falling to his knees.

"Put an alligator over the pocket."

"Pardon me, Lord?"

"Just do what I'm telling you. You won't be sorry."

And the man sewed on to all his shirts a small alligator symbol and lo and behold, suddenly his merchandise moved like gangbusters, and there was much rejoicing while amongst his enemies there was wailing and gnashing of teeth, and one said, "The Lord is merciful. He maketh me to lie down in green pastures. The problem is, I can't get up."

Laws and Proverbs

Doing abominations is against the law, particularly if the abominations are done while wearing a lobster bib.

The lion and the calf shall lie down together but the calf won't get much sleep.

Whosoever shall not fall by the sword or by famine, shall fall by pestilence so why bother shaving?

The wicked at heart probably know something.

Whosoever loveth wisdom is righteous but he that keepeth company with fowl is weird.

My Lord, my Lord! What hast Thou done, lately?

Lovborg's Women Considered

PERHAPS no writer has created more fascinating and complex females than the great Scandinavian playwright Jorgen Lovborg, known to his contemporaries as Jorgen Lovborg. Tortured and embittered by his agonizing relationships with the opposite sex, he gave the world such diverse and unforgettable characters as Jenny Angstrom in *Geese Aplenty* and Mrs. Spearing in *A Mother's Gums*. Born in Stockholm in 1836, Lovborg (originally Lövborg, until, in later years he removed the two dots from above the *o* and placed them over his eyebrows) began writing plays at the age of fourteen. His first produced work, brought to the stage when he was sixty-one, was *Those Who Squirm*, which drew mixed notices from the critics, although the frankness of the subject matter (cheese fondling) caused conservative audiences to blush. Lovborg's work can be divided into three periods. First came the series of plays dealing with anguish, despair, dread, fear, and loneliness (the comedies); the second group focused on social change (Lovborg was instrumental in bringing about safer methods of weighing herring); finally, there were the six great tragedies written just before his death, in Stockholm, in 1902, when his nose fell off, owing to tension.

Lovborg's first outstanding female character was Hedvig Moldau in *I Prefer to Yodel*, the playwright's ironic indictment of penmanship among the upper classes. Hedvig is aware that Greger Norstad has used substandard mortar to roof the henhouse, and when it collapses on Klavar Akdal, causing him to go blind and bald on the same night, she is racked with remorse. The obligatory scene follows:

HEDVIG: So—it collapsed.

DR. RORLUND *(after a long pause):* Yes. It fell down on Akdal's face.

HEDVIG: *(ironically):* What was he doing in the henhouse?

DR. RORLUND: He liked the hens. Oh, not all the hens, I'll grant you. But certain ones. *(Significantly)* He had his favorites.

HEDVIG: And Norstad? Where was he during the . . . accident?

DR. RORLUND: He smeared his body with chives and jumped into the reservoir.

HEDVIG *(to herself):* I'll never marry.

DR. RORLUND: What's that?

HEDVIG: Nothing. Come, Doctor. It's time to launder your shorts . . . to launder everybody's shorts. . . .

Hedvig, one of the first really "modern" women, can only sneer when Dr. Rorlund suggests she run up and down in place until Norstad consents to have his hat blocked. She bears close resemblance to Lovborg's own sister Hilda, a neurotic, domineering woman married to a quick-tempered Finnish seaman, who eventually harpooned her. Lovborg worshiped Hilda, and it was her influence that broke him of the habit of speaking to his cane.

The second great "heroine" in Lovborg's work appears in his drama of lust and jealousy *While We Three Hemorrhage*. Moltvick Dorf, the anchovy trainer, learns that his father's unmentionable disease has been inherited by his brother Eyeowulf. Dorf goes to court, claiming the disease is rightfully his, but Judge Manders upholds Eyeowulf's claim. Netta Holmquist, the beautiful and arrogant actress, tries to persuade Dorf to blackmail Eyeowulf by threatening to tell authorities that he once forged a penguin's signature on some insurance policies. Then, in Act II, Scene 4:

DORF: Oh, Netta. All is lost! Lost!

NETTA: For a weak man, perhaps, but not if one had—courage.

DORF: Courage?

NETTA: To tell Parson Smathers he can never hope to walk again and that for the rest of his life he must skip everywhere.

DORF: Netta! I couldn't!

NETTA: Ha! Of course not! I should have known.

DORF: Parson Smathers trusts Eyeowulf. They shared a piece of chewing gum once. Yes, before I was born. Oh, Netta . . .

NETTA: Stop whining. The bank will never extend the mortgage on Eyeowulf's pretzel. And he's already eaten half of it.

DORF: Netta, what are you suggesting?

NETTA: Nothing a thousand wives would not do for their husbands. I mean to soak Eyeowulf in brine.

DORF: Pickle my own brother?

NETTA: Why not? What do you owe him?

DORF: But such drastic measures! Netta, why not let him keep Father's unmentionable disease? Perhaps we could compromise. Perhaps he would let me have the symptoms.

NETTA: Compromise, ha! Your middle-class mentality makes me sick! Oh, Moltvick, I'm so bored by this marriage! Bored by your ideas, your ways, your conversations. And your habit of wearing feathers to dinner.

DORF: Oh! Not my feathers, too!

NETTA *(contemptuously):* I am going to tell you something now that only I and your mother know. You are a dwarf.

DORF: *What?*

NETTA: Everything in the house has been made to scale. You are only forty-eight inches tall.

DORF: Don't, don't! The pains are returning!

NETTA: Yes, Moltvick!

DORF: My kneecaps—they're throbbing!

NETTA: What a weakling.

DORF: Netta, Netta, open the shutters . . .

NETTA: I'll close them.

DORF: Light! Moltvick needs light . . .

To Lovborg, Moltvick represented the old, decadent, dying Europe. Netta, on the other hand, was the new—the vibrant, cruel Darwinian force of nature, which was to blow through Europe for the next fifty years and find its deepest expression in the songs of Maurice Chevalier. The relationship between Netta and Moltvick mirrored Lovborg's marriage to Siri Brackman, an actress who served as a constant inspiration to him throughout the eight hours their marriage lasted. Lovborg remarried several times after that, but always to department-store mannequins.

Clearly, the most fully realized woman in all of Lovborg's plays was Mrs. Sanstad in *Mellow Pears*, Lovborg's last naturalistic drama. (After *Pears*, he experimented with an Expressionist play in which all the characters were named Lovborg, but it failed to win approval, and for the remaining three years of his life he could not be coaxed out of the hamper.) *Mellow Pears* ranks with his greatest works, and the final exchange between Mrs. Sanstad and her son's wife, Berte, is perhaps more pertinent today than ever:

BERTE: Do say you like the way we furnished the house! It was so hard, on a ventriloquist's salary.

MRS. SANSTAD: The house is—serviceable.

BERTE: What! Only serviceable?

MRS. SANSTAD: Whose idea was the red satin elk?

BERTE: Why, your son's. Henrick is a born decorator.

MRS. SANSTAD (*suddenly*): Henrick is a fool!

BERTE: No!

MRS. SANSTAD: Did you know that he did not know what snow was until last week?

BERTE: You're lying!

MRS. SANSTAD: My precious son. Yes, Henrick—the same man who went to prison for mispronouncing the word "diphthong."

BERTE: No!

MRS. SANSTAD: Yes. And with an Eskimo in the room at the time!

BERTE: I don't want to hear about it!

MRS. SANSTAD: But you will, my little nightingale! Isn't that what Henrick calls you?

BERTE (*crying*): He calls me nightingale! Yes, and sometimes thrush! And hippo!

(*Both women weep unashamedly.*)

46

MRS. SANSTAD: Berte, dear Berte! . . . Henrick's earmuffs are not his own! They are owned by a corporation.

BERTE: We must help him. He must be told he can never fly by flapping his arms.

MRS. SANSTAD *(suddenly laughing):* Henrick knows everything. I told him your feelings about his arch supports.

BERTE: So! You tricked me!

MRS. SANSTAD: Call it what you will. He's in Oslo now.

BERTE: Oslo!

MRS. SANSTAD: With his geranium . . .

BERTE: I see. I . . . see. *(She wanders through the French doors upstage.)*

MRS. SANSTAD: Yes, my little nightingale, he is out of your clutches at last. By this time next month, he will realize his lifelong dream—to fill his hat with cinders. And you thought you'd keep him cooped up here! No! Henrick is a wild creature, a thing of nature! Like some wonderful mouse—or a tick. *(A shot is heard. Mrs. Sanstad runs into the next room. We hear a scream. She returns, pale and shaken.)* Dead . . . She's lucky. I . . . must go on. Yes, night is falling . . . falling rapidly. So rapidly, and I still have all those chickpeas to rearrange.

Mrs. Sanstad was Lovborg's revenge on his mother. Also a critical woman, she began life as a trapeze artist with the circus; his father, Nils Lovborg, was the human cannonball. The two met in midair and were married before touching ground. Bitterness slowly crept into the marriage, and by the time Lovborg was six years old his parents exchanged gunfire daily. This atmosphere took its toll on a sensitive youngster like Jorgen, and soon he began to suffer the first of his famous "moods" and "anxieties," rendering him for some years unable to pass a roast chicken without tipping his hat. In later years, he told friends that he was tense all during the writing of *Mellow Pears* and on several occasions believed he heard his mother's voice asking him directions to Staten Island.

The Whore
of Mensa

ONE thing about being a private investigator, you've got to learn to go with your hunches. That's why when a quivering pat of butter named Word Babcock walked into my office and laid his cards on the table, I should have trusted the cold chill that shot up my spine.

"Kaiser?" he said, "Kaiser Lupowitz?"

"That's what it says on my license," I owned up.

"You've got to help me. I'm being blackmailed. Please!"

He was shaking like the lead singer in a rumba band. I pushed a glass across the desk top and a bottle of rye I keep handy for nonmedicinal purposes. "Suppose you relax and tell me all about it."

"You . . . you won't tell my wife?"

"Level with me, Word. I can't make any promises."

He tried pouring a drink, but you could hear the clicking sound across the street, and most of the stuff wound up in his shoes.

"I'm a working guy," he said. "Mechanical maintenance. I build and service joy buzzers. You know—those little fun gimmicks that give people a shock when they shake hands?"

"So?"

"A lot of your executives like 'em. Particularly down on Wall Street."

"Get to the point."

"I'm on the road a lot. You know how it is—lonely. Oh, not what you're thinking. See, Kaiser, I'm basically an intellectual. Sure, a guy can meet all the bimbos he wants. But the really brainy women—they're not so easy to find on short notice."

"Keep talking."

"Well, I heard of this young girl. Eighteen years old. A Yassar student. For a price, she'll come over and discuss any subject—Proust, Yeats, anthropology. Exchange of ideas. You see what I'm driving at?"

"Not exactly."

"I mean, my wife is great, don't get me wrong. But she won't discuss Pound with me. Or Eliot. I didn't know that when I married her. See, I need a woman who's mentally stimulating, Kaiser. And I'm willing to pay for it. I don't want an involvement—I want a quick intellectual experience, then I want the girl to leave. Christ, Kaiser, I'm a happily married man."

"How long has this been going on?"

"Six months. Whenever I have that craving, I call Flossie. She's a madam, with a master's in comparative lit. She sends me over an intellectual, see?"

So he was one of those guys whose weakness was really bright women. I felt sorry for the poor sap. I figured there must be a lot of jokers in his position, who were starved for a little intellectual communication with the opposite sex and would pay through the nose for it.

"Now she's threatening to tell my wife," he said.

"Who is?"

"Flossie. They bugged the motel room. They got tapes of me discussing *The Waste Land* and *Styles of Radical Will*, and, well, really getting into some issues. They want ten grand or they go to Carla. Kaiser, you've got to help me! Carla would die if she knew she didn't turn me on up here."

The old call-girl racket. I had heard rumors that the boys at headquarters were on to something involving a group of educated women, but so far they were stymied.

"Get Flossie on the phone for me."

"What?"

"I'll take your case, Word. But I get fifty dollars a day, plus expenses. You'll have to repair a lot of joy buzzers."

"It won't be ten Gs' worth, I'm sure of that," he said with a grin, and picked up the phone and dialed a number. I took it from him and winked. I was beginning to like him.

Seconds later, a silky voice answered, and I told her what was on my mind. "I understand you can help me set up an hour of good chat," I said.

"Sure, honey. What do you have in mind?"

"I'd like to discuss Melville."

"*Moby Dick* or the shorter novels?"

"What's the difference?"

"The price. That's all. Symbolism's extra."

"What'll it run me?"

"Fifty, maybe a hundred for *Moby Dick*. You want a comparative discussion—Melville and Hawthorne? That could be arranged for a hundred."

"The dough's fine," I told her and gave her the number of a room at the Plaza.

"You want a blonde or a brunette?"

"Surprise me," I said, and hung up.

I shaved and grabbed some black coffee while I checked over the Monarch College Outline series. Hardly an hour had passed before there was a knock on my door. I opened it, and standing there was a young redhead who was packed into her slacks like two big scoops of vanilla ice cream.

"Hi, I'm Sherry."

They really knew how to appeal to your fantasies. Long straight hair, leather bag, silver earrings, no make-up.

"I'm surprised you weren't stopped, walking into the hotel dressed like that," I said. "The house dick can usually spot an intellectual."

"A five-spot cools him."

"Shall we begin?" I said, motioning her to the couch.

She lit a cigarette and got right to it. "I think we could start by approaching *Billy Budd* as Melville's justification of the ways of God to man, *n'est-ce pas?*"

"Interestingly, though, not in a Miltonian sense." I was bluffing. I wanted to see if she'd go for it.

"No. *Paradise Lost* lacked the substructure of pessimism." She did.

"Right, right. God, you're right," I murmured.

"I think Melville reaffirmed the virtues of innocence in a naïve yet sophisticated sense—don't you agree?"

I let her go on. She was barely nineteen years old, but already she had developed the hardened facility of the pseudo-intellectual. She rattled off her ideas glibly, but it was all mechanical. Whenever I offered an insight, she faked a response: "Oh, yes, Kaiser. Yes, baby, that's deep. A platonic comprehension of Christianity—why didn't I see it before?"

We talked for about an hour and then she said she had to go. She stood up and I laid a C-note on her.

"Thanks, honey."

"There's plenty more where that came from."

"What are you trying to say?"

I had piqued her curiosity. She sat down again.

"Suppose I wanted to—have a party?" I said.

"Like, what kind of party?"

"Suppose I wanted Noam Chomsky explained to me by two girls?"

"Oh, wow."

"If you'd rather forget it . . ."

"You'd have to speak with Flossie," she said. "It'd cost you."

Now was the time to tighten the screws. I flashed my private-investigator's badge and informed her it was a bust.

"What!"

"I'm fuzz, sugar, and discussing Melville for money is an 802. You can do time."

"You louse!"

"Better come clean, baby. Unless you want to tell your story down at Alfred Kazin's office, and I don't think he'd be too happy to hear it."

She began to cry. "Don't turn me in, Kaiser," she said. "I needed the money to complete my master's. I've been turned down for a grant. *Twice.* Oh, Christ."

It all poured out—the whole story. Central Park West upbringing, Socialist summer camps, Brandeis. She was every dame you saw waiting in line at the Elgin or the Thalia, or penciling the words "Yes, very true" into the margin of some book on Kant. Only somewhere along the line she had made a wrong turn.

"I needed cash. A girl friend said she knew a married guy whose wife wasn't very profound. He was into Blake. She couldn't hack it. I said sure, for a price I'd talk Blake with him. I was nervous at first. I faked a lot of it. He didn't care. My friend said there were others. Oh, I've been busted before. I got caught reading *Commentary* in a parked car, and I was once stopped and frisked at Tanglewood. Once more and I'm a three-time loser."

"Then take me to Flossie."

She bit her lip and said, "The Hunter College Book Store is a front."

"Yes?"

"Like those bookie joints that have barbershops outside for show. You'll see."

I made a quick call to headquarters and then said to her, "Okay, sugar. You're off the hook. But don't leave town."

She tilted her face up toward mine gratefully. "I can get you photographs of Dwight Macdonald reading," she said.

"Some other time."

I walked into the Hunter College Book Store. The salesman, a young man with sensitive eyes, came up to me. "Can I help you?" he said.

"I'm looking for a special edition of *Advertisements for Myself*. I understand the author had several thousand gold-leaf copies printed up for friends."

"I'll have to check," he said. "We have a WATS line to Mailer's house."

I fixed him with a look. "Sherry sent me," I said.

"Oh, in that case, go on back," he said. He pressed a button. A wall of books opened, and I walked like a lamb into that bustling pleasure palace known as Flossie's.

Red flocked wallpaper and a Victorian décor set the tone. Pale, nervous girls with black-rimmed glasses and blunt-cut hair lolled around on sofas, riffling Penguin Classics provocatively. A blonde with a big smile winked at me, nodded toward a room upstairs, and said, "Wallace Stevens, eh?" But it wasn't just intellectual experiences— they were peddling emotional ones, too. For fifty bucks, I learned, you could "relate without getting close." For a hundred, a girl would lend you her Bartók records, have dinner, and then let you watch while she had an anxiety attack. For one-fifty, you could listen to FM radio with twins. For three bills, you got the works: A thin Jewish brunette would pretend to pick you up at the Museum of Modern Art, let you read her master's, get you involved in a screaming quarrel at Elaine's over Freud's conception of women, and then fake a suicide of your choosing—the perfect evening, for some guys. Nice racket. Great town, New York.

"Like what you see?" a voice said behind me. I turned and suddenly found myself standing face to face with the business end of a .38. I'm a guy with a strong stomach, but this time it did a back flip. It was Flossie, all right. The voice was the same, but Flossie was a man. His face was hidden by a mask.

"You'll never believe this," he said, "but I don't even have a college degree. I was thrown out for low grades."

"Is that why you wear that mask?"

"I devised a complicated scheme to take over *The New York Review of Books*, but it meant I had to pass for Lionel Trilling. I went to Mexico for an operation. There's a doctor in Juarez who gives people Trilling's features—for a price. Something went wrong. I came out looking like Auden, with Mary McCarthy's voice. That's when I started working the other side of the law."

Quickly, before he could tighten his finger on the trigger, I went into action. Heaving forward, I snapped my elbow across his jaw and grabbed the gun as he fell back. He hit the ground like a ton of bricks. He was still whimpering when the police showed up.

"Nice work, Kaiser," Sergeant Holmes said. "When we're through with this guy, the F.B.I. wants to have a talk with him. A little matter involving some gamblers and an annotated copy of Dante's *Inferno*. Take him away, boys."

Later that night, I looked up an old account of mine named Gloria. She was blond. She had graduated *cum laude*. The difference was she majored in physical education. It felt good.

The Early Essays

Following are a few of the early essays of Woody Allen.
There are no late essays, because he ran out of observations.
Perhaps as Allen grows older he will understand more of
life and will set it down, and then retire to his bedroom and
remain there indefinitely. Like the essays of Bacon, Allen's
are brief and full of practical wisdom, although space does
not permit the inclusion of his most profound statement,
"Looking at the Bright Side."

On Seeing a Tree in Summer

Of all the wonders of nature, a tree in summer is perhaps
the most remarkable, with the possible exception of a
moose singing "Embraceable You" in spats. Consider the
leaves, so green and leafy (if not, something is wrong).
Behold how the branches reach up to heaven as if to say,
"Though I am only a branch, still I would love to collect
Social Security." And the varieties! Is this tree a spruce or
poplar? Or a giant redwood? No, I'm afraid it's a stately
elm, and once again you've made an ass of yourself. Of
course, you'd know all the trees in a minute if you were
nature's creature the woodpecker, but then it would be too
late and you'd never get your car started.

But why is a tree so much more delightful than, say, a
babbling brook? Or anything that babbles, for that matter?
Because its glorious presence is mute testimony to an intelligence far greater than any on earth, certainly in the

present Administration. As the poet said, "Only God can make a tree"—probably because it's so hard to figure out how to get the bark on.

Once a lumberjack was about to chop down a tree, when he noticed a heart carved on it, with two names inside. Putting away his axe, he sawed down the tree instead. The point of that story escapes me, although six months later the lumberjack was fined for teaching a dwarf Roman numerals.

On Youth and Age

The true test of maturity is not how old a person is but how he reacts to awakening in the midtown area in his shorts. What do years matter, particularly if your apartment is rent-controlled? The thing to remember is that each time of life has its appropriate rewards, whereas when you're dead it's hard to find the light switch. The chief problem about death, incidentally, is the fear that there may be no afterlife—a depressing thought, particularly for those who have bothered to shave. Also, there is the fear that there is an afterlife but no one will know where it's being held. On the plus side, death is one of the few things that can be done as easily lying down.

Consider, then: Is old age really so terrible? Not if you've brushed your teeth faithfully! And why is there no buffer to the onslaught of the years? Or a good hotel in downtown Indianapolis? Oh, well.

In short, the best thing to do is behave in a manner befitting one's age. If you are sixteen or under, try not to go bald. On the other hand, if you are over eighty, it is extremely good form to shuffle down the street clutching a brown paper bag and muttering, "The Kaiser will steal my string." Remember, everything is relative—or should be. If it's not, we must begin again.

On Frugality

As one goes through life, it is extremely important to conserve funds, and one should never spend money on anything foolish, like pear nectar or a solid-gold hat. Money is not everything, but it is better than having one's health. After all, one cannot go into a butcher shop and tell the butcher, "Look at my great suntan, and besides I never catch colds," and expect him to hand over any merchandise. (Unless, of course, the butcher is an idiot.) Money is better than poverty, if only for financial reasons. Not that it can buy happiness. Take the case of the ant and the grasshopper: The grasshopper played all summer, while the ant worked and saved. When winter came, the grasshopper had nothing, but the ant complained of chest pains. Life is hard for insects. And don't think mice are having any fun, either. The point is, we all need a nest egg to fall back on, but not while wearing a good suit.

Finally, let us bear in mind that it is easier to spend two dollars than to save one. And for God's sake don't invest money in any brokerage firm in which one of the partners is named Frenchy.

On Love

Is it better to be the lover or the loved one? Neither, if your cholesterol is over six hundred. By love, of course, I refer to romantic love—the love between man and woman, rather than between mother and child, or a boy and his dog, or two headwaiters.

The marvelous thing is that when one is in love there is an impulse to sing. This must be resisted at all costs, and care must also be taken to see that the ardent male doesn't "talk" the lyrics of songs. To be loved, certainly, is different from being admired, as one can be admired from afar but to really love someone it is essential to be in the same room with the person, crouching behind the drapes.

To be a really good lover, then, one must be strong and yet tender. How strong? I suppose being able to lift fifty pounds should do it. Bear in mind also that to the lover the loved one is always the most beautiful thing imaginable, even though to a stranger she may be indistinguishable from an order of smelts. Beauty is in the eye of the beholder. Should the beholder have poor eyesight, he can ask the nearest person which girls look good. (Actually, the prettiest ones are almost always the most boring, and that is why some people feel there is no God.)

"The joys of love are but a moment long," sang the troubadour, "but the pain of love endures forever." This was almost a hit song, but the melody was too close to "I'm a Yankee Doodle Dandy."

On Tripping Through a Copse and Picking Violets

This is no fun at all, and I would recommend almost any other activity. Try visiting a sick friend. If this is impossible, see a show or get into a nice warm tub and read. Anything is better than turning up in a copse with one of those vacuous smiles and accumulating flowers in a basket. Next thing you know, you'll be skipping to and fro. What are you going to do with the violets once you get them, anyhow? "Why, put them in a vase," you say. What a stupid answer. Nowadays you call the florist and order by phone. Let *him* trip through the copse, he's getting paid for it. That way, if an electrical storm comes up or a beehive is chanced upon, it will be the florist who is rushed to Mount Sinai.

Do not conclude from this, incidentally, that I am

insensitive to the joys of nature, although I have come to the conclusion that for sheer fun it is hard to beat forty-eight hours at Foam Rubber City during the high holidays. But that is another story.

A Brief, Yet Helpful, Guide to Civil Disobedience

IN perpetrating a revolution, there are two requirements: someone or something to revolt against and someone to actually show up and do the revolting. Dress is usually casual and both parties may be flexible about time and place but if either faction fails to attend, the whole enterprise is likely to come off badly. In the Chinese Revolution of 1650 neither party showed up and the deposit on the hall was forfeited.

The people or parties revolted against are called the "oppressors" and are easily recognized as they seem to be the ones having all the fun. The "oppressors" generally get to wear suits, own land, and play their radios late at night without being yelled at. Their job is to maintain the "status quo," a condition where everything remains the same although they may be willing to paint every two years.

When the "oppressors" become too strict, we have what is known as a police state, wherein all dissent is forbidden, as is chuckling, showing up in a bow tie, or referring to the mayor as "Fats." Civil liberties are greatly curtailed in a police state, and freedom of speech is unheard of, although one is allowed to mime to a record. Opinions critical of the government are not tolerated, particularly about their dancing. Freedom of the press is also curtailed and the ruling party "manages" the news, permitting the citizens to hear only acceptable political ideas and ball scores that will not cause unrest.

The groups who revolt are called the "oppressed" and can generally be seen milling about and grumbling or claiming to have headaches. (It should be noted that the oppressors never revolt and attempt to become the oppressed as that would entail a change of underwear.)

Some famous examples of revolutions are:

THE FRENCH REVOLUTION, in which the peasants seized power by force and quickly changed all locks on the palace doors so the nobles could not get back in. Then they had a large party and gorged themselves. When the nobles finally recaptured the palace they were forced to clean up and found many stains and cigarette burns.

THE RUSSIAN REVOLUTION, which simmered for years and suddenly erupted when the serfs finally realized that the Czar and the Tsar were the same person.

It should be noted that after a revolution is over, the "oppressed" frequently take over and begin acting like the "oppressors." Of course by then it is very hard to get them on the phone and money lent for cigarettes and gum during the fighting may as well be forgotten about.

Methods of Civil disobedience:

HUNGER STRIKE. Here the oppressed goes without food until his demands are met. Insidious politicians will often leave biscuits within easy reach or perhaps some cheddar cheese, but they must be resisted. If the party in power can get the striker to eat, they usually have little trouble putting down the insurrection. If they can get him to eat and also lift the check, they have won for sure. In Pakistan, a hunger strike was broken when the government produced an exceptionally fine veal cordon bleu which the masses found was too appealing to turn down, but such gourmet dishes are rare.

The problem with the hunger strike is that after several days one can get quite hungry, particularly since sound trucks are paid to go through the street saying, "Um . . . what nice chicken—umm . . . some peas . . . umm . . ."

A modified form of the Hunger Strike for those whose political convictions are not quite so radical is giving up chives. This small gesture, when used properly, can greatly influence a government, and it is well known that Mahatma Gandhi's insistence on eating his salads untossed shamed the British government into many concessions. Other things besides food one can give up are: whist, smiling, and standing on one foot and imitating a crane.

Sɪᴛ-ᴅᴏᴡɴ Sᴛʀɪᴋᴇ. Proceed to a designated spot and then sit down, but sit all the way down. Otherwise you are squatting, a position that makes no political point unless the government is also squatting. (This is rare, although a government will occasionally crouch in cold weather.) The trick is to remain seated until concessions are made, but as in the Hunger Strike, the government will try subtle means of making the striker rise. They may say, "Okay, everybody up, we're closing." Or, "Can you get up for a minute, we'd just like to see how tall you are?"

Dᴇᴍᴏɴsᴛʀᴀᴛɪᴏɴ ᴀɴᴅ Mᴀʀᴄʜᴇs. The key point about a demonstration is that it must be seen. Hence the term "demonstration." If a person demonstrates privately in his own home, this is not technically a demonstration but merely "acting silly" or "behaving like an ass."

A fine example of a demonstration was the Boston Tea Party, where outraged Americans disguised as Indians dumped British tea into the harbor. Later, Indians disguised as outraged Americans dumped actual British into the harbor. Following that, the British disguised as tea, dumped each other into the harbor. Finally, German mercenaries clad only in costumes from *The Trojan Women* leapt into the harbor for no apparent reason.

When demonstrating, it is good to carry a placard stating one's position. Some suggested positions are: (1) lower taxes, (2) raise taxes, and (3) stop grinning at Persians.

Miscellaneous methods of Civil Disobedience:

Standing in front of City Hall and chanting the word "pudding" until one's demands are met.

Tying up traffic by leading a flock of sheep into the shopping area.

Phoning members of "the establishment" and singing "Bess, You Is My Woman Now" into the phone.

Dressing as a policeman and then skipping.

Pretending to be an artichoke but punching people as they pass.

Match Wits
with Inspector Ford

The Case of the Murdered Socialite

Inspector Ford burst into the study. On the floor was the body of Clifford Wheel, who apparently had been struck from behind with a croquet mallet. The position of the body indicated that the victim had been surprised in the act of singing "Sorrento" to his goldfish. Evidence showed there had been a terrible struggle that had twice been interrupted by phone calls, one a wrong number and one asking if the victim was interested in dance lessons.

Before Wheel had died, he had dipped his finger into the inkwell and scrawled out a message: "Fall Sale Prices Drastically Reduced—Everything Must Go!"

"A businessman to the end," mused Ives, his manservant, whose elevator shoes, curiously enough, made him two inches shorter.

The door to the terrace was open and footprints led from there, down the hall and into a drawer.

"Where were you when it happened, Ives?"

"In the kitchen. Doing the dishes." Ives produced some suds from his wallet to corroborate his story.

"Did you hear anything?"

"He was in there with some men. They were arguing over who was the tallest. I thought I heard Mr. Wheel start yodeling and Mosley, his business partner, began yelling, 'My God, I'm going bald!' Next thing I knew, there was a harp glissando and Mr. Wheel's head came rolling out onto the lawn. I heard Mr. Mosley threaten him. He said if Mr. Wheel touched his grapefruit again, he would not co-sign a bank loan for him. I think he killed him."

"Does the terrace door open from the inside or from the outside?" Inspector Ford asked Ives.

"From the outside. Why?"

"Exactly as I suspected. I now realize it was you, not Mosley, who killed Clifford Wheel."

How Did Inspector Ford Know?

Because of the layout of the house, Ives could not have sneaked up behind his employer. He would have had to sneak up in front of him, at which time Mr. Wheel would have stopped singing "Sorrento" and used the mallet on Ives, a ritual they had gone through many times.

A Curious Riddle

Apparently, Walker was a suicide. Overdose of sleeping pills. Still, something seemed amiss to Inspector Ford. Perhaps it was the position of the body. Inside the TV set, looking out. On the floor was a cryptic suicide note. "Dear Edna, My woolen suit itches me, and so I have decided to take my own life. See that our son finishes all his push-ups. I leave you my entire fortune, with the exception of my porkpie hat, which I hereby donate to the planetarium.

Please don't feel sorry for me, as I enjoy being dead and much prefer it to paying rent. Goodbye, Henry. P.S. This may not be the time to bring it up, but I have every reason to believe that your brother is dating a Cornish hen."

Edna Walker bit her lower lip nervously. "What do you make of it, Inspector?"

Inspector Ford looked at the bottle of sleeping pills on the night table. "How long had your husband been an insomniac?"

"For years. It was psychological. He was afraid that if he closed his eyes, the city would paint a white line down him."

"I see. Did he have any enemies?"

"Not really. Except for some gypsies who ran a tearoom on the outskirts of town. He insulted them once by putting on a pair of earmuffs and hopping up and down in place on their sabbath."

Inspector Ford noticed a half-finished glass of milk on the desk. It was still warm. "Mrs. Walker, is your son away at college?"

"I'm afraid not. He was expelled last week for immoral conduct. It came as quite a surprise. They caught him trying to immerse a dwarf in tartar sauce. That's one thing they won't tolerate at an Ivy League school."

"And one thing I won't tolerate is murder. Your son is under arrest."

*Why Did Inspector Ford Suspect
Walker's Son Had Killed Him?*

Mr. Walker's body was found with cash in his pockets. A man who was going to commit suicide would be sure to take a credit card and sign for everything.

The Stolen Gem

The glass case was shattered and the Bellini Sapphire was missing. The only clues left behind at the museum were a blond hair and a dozen fingerprints, all pinkies. The guard explained that he had been standing there when a black-clad figure crept up behind him and struck him over the head with some notes for a speech. Just before losing consciousness, he thought he had heard a man's voice say, "Jerry, call your mother," but he could not be sure. Apparently, the thief had entered through the skylight and walked down the wall with suction shoes, like a human fly. The museum guards always kept an enormous fly swatter for just such occasions, but this time they had been fooled.

"Why would anyone want the Bellini Sapphire?" the museum curator asked. "Don't they know it's cursed?"

"What's this about a curse?" Inspector Ford was quick to ask.

"The sapphire was originally owned by a sultan who died under mysterious circumstances when a hand reached out of a bowl of soup he was eating and strangled him. The next owner was an English lord who was found one day by his wife growing upside down in a window box. Nothing was heard of the stone for a while; then it turned up years later in the possession of a Texas millionaire, who was brushing his teeth when he suddenly caught fire. We purchased the sapphire only last month, but the curse seemed to be working still, because shortly after we obtained it, the entire board of trustees at the museum formed a conga line and danced off a cliff."

"Well," Inspector Ford said, "it may be an unlucky jewel, but it's valuable, and if you want it back, go to Handleman's Delicatessen and arrest Leonard Handleman. You'll find that the sapphire is in his pocket."

The previous day, Leonard Handleman had remarked, "Boy, if I had a large sapphire, I could get out of the delicatessen business."

The Macabre Accident

"I just shot my husband," wept Cynthia Freem as she stood over the body of the burly man in the snow.

"How did it happen?" asked Inspector Ford, getting right to the point.

"We were hunting. Quincy loved to hunt, as did I. We got separated momentarily. The bushes were overgrown. I guess I thought he was a woodchuck. I blasted away. It was too late. As I was removing his pelt, I realized we were married."

"Hmm," mused Inspector Ford, glancing at the footprints in the snow. "You must be a very good shot. You managed to plug him right between the eyebrows."

"Oh, no, it was lucky. I'm really quite an amateur at that sort of thing."

"I see." Inspector Ford examined the dead man's possessions. In his pocket there was some string, also an apple from 1904 and instructions on what to do if you wake up next to an Armenian.

"Mrs. Freem, was this your husband's first hunting accident?"

"His first fatal one, yes. Although once in the Canadian Rockies, an eagle carried off his birth certificate."

"Did your husband wear a toupee?"

"Not really. He would usually carry it with him and produce it if challenged in an argument. Why?"

"He sounds eccentric."

"He was."

"Is that why you killed him?"

How Did Inspector Ford Know
It Was No Accident?

An experienced hunter like Quincy Freem would never have stalked deer in his underwear. Actually, Mrs. Freem had bludgeoned him to death at home while he was playing the spoons and had tried to make it look like a hunting accident by dragging his body to the woods and leaving a copy of *Field & Stream* nearby. In her haste, she had forgotten to dress him. Why he had been playing the spoons in his underwear remains a mystery.

The Bizarre Kidnapping

Half-starved, Kermit Kroll staggered into the living room of his parents' home, where they waited anxiously with Inspector Ford.

"Thanks for paying the ransom, folks," Kermit said. "I never thought I'd get out of there alive."

"Tell me about it," the inspector said.

"I was on my way downtown to have my hat blocked when a sedan pulled up and two men asked me if I wanted to see a horse that could recite the Gettysburg Address. I said sure and got in. Next thing, I'm chloroformed and wake up somewhere tied to a chair and blindfolded."

Inspector Ford examined the ransom note. "Dear Mom and Dad, Leave $50,000 in a bag under the bridge on Decatur Street. If there is no bridge on Decatur Street, please build one. I am being treated well, given shelter and good food, although last night the clams casino were overcooked. Send the money quickly, because if they don't hear from you within several days, the man who now makes up my bed will strangle me. Yours, Kermit. P.S. This is no joke. I am enclosing a joke so you will be able to tell the difference."

"Do you have any idea at all as to where you were being held?"

"No, I just kept hearing an odd noise outside the window."

"Odd?"

"Yes. You know the sound a herring makes when you lie to it?"

"Hmm," reflected Inspector Ford. "And how did you finally escape?"

"I told them I wanted to go to the football game but I only had a single ticket. They said okay, as long as I kept the blindfold on and promised to return by midnight. I complied, but during the third quarter, the Bears had a big lead, so I left and made my way back here."

"Very interesting," Inspector Ford said. "Now I know this kidnapping was a put-up job. I believe you're in on it and are splitting the money."

How Did Inspector Ford Know?

Although Kermit Kroll did still live with his parents, they were eighty and he was sixty. Actual kidnappers would never abduct a sixty-year-old child, as it makes no sense.

The Irish Genius

VISCOUS AND SONS had announced publication of *The Annotated Poems of Sean O'Shawn*, the great Irish poet, considered by many to be the most incomprehensible and hence the finest poet of his time. Abounding in highly personal references, an understanding of O'Shawn's work requires an intimate knowledge of his life, which, according to scholars, not even he had.

Following is a sample from this fine book.

Beyond Ichor

Let us sail. Sail with
Fogarty's chin to Alexandria,
While the Beamish Brothers
Hurry giggling to the tower,
Proud of their gums.
A thousand years passed since
Agamemnon said, "Don't open
The gates, who the hell needs
A wooden horse that size?"

What is the connection? Only
That Shaunnesy, with dying
Breath, refused to order an
Appetizer with his meal although
He was entitled to it.
And brave Bixby, despite his
Resemblance to a woodpecker,
Could not retrieve his underwear
From Socrates without a ticket.
Parnell had the answer, but no
One would ask him the question.
No one but old Lafferty, whose
Lapis lazuli practical joke caused
A whole generation to take
Samba lessons.
True, Homer was blind and that
Accounted for why he dated those
Particular women.
But Aegnus and the Druids bear
Mute testimony to man's quest
For free alterations.
Blake dreamed of it too, and
O'Higgins who had his suit
Stolen while he was still in it.
Civilization is shaped like a
Circle and repeats itself, while
O'Leary's head is shaped like
A trapezoid.
Rejoice! Rejoice! And call your
Mother once in a while.

Let us sail. O'Shawn was fond of sailing, although he
had never done it on the sea. As a boy he dreamed of
becoming a ship's captain but gave it up when someone
explained to him what sharks were. His older brother
James, however, did go off and join the British Navy,

though he was dishonorably discharged for selling cole-slaw to a bosun.

Fogarty's chin. Undoubtedly a reference to George Fo-garty, who convinced O'Shawn to become a poet and assured him he would still be invited to parties. Fogarty published a magazine for new poets and although its cir-culation was limited to his mother, its impact was interna-tional.

Fogarty was a fun-loving, rubicund Irishman whose idea of a good time was to lie down in the public square and imitate a tweezers. Eventually he suffered a nervous breakdown and was arrested for eating a pair of pants on Good Friday.

Fogarty's chin was an object of great ridicule because it was tiny to the point of nonexistence, and at Jim Kelly's wake, he told O'Shawn, "I'd give anything for a larger chin. If I don't find one soon I'm liable to do something rash." Fogarty, incidentally, was a friend of Bernard Shaw's and was once permitted to touch Shaw's beard, provided he would go away.

Alexandria. References to the Middle East appear throughout O'Shawn's work, and his poem that begins "To Bethlehem with suds . . ." deals caustically with the hotel business seen through the eyes of a mummy.

The Beamish Brothers. Two half-wit brothers who tried to get from Belfast to Scotland by mailing each other.

Liam Beamish went to Jesuit school with O'Shawn but was thrown out for dressing like a beaver. Quincy Beamish was the more introverted of the two and kept a furniture pad on his head till he was forty-one.

The Beamish Brothers used to pick on O'Shawn and usually ate his lunch just before he did. Still, O'Shawn remembers them fondly and in his best sonnet, "My love is like a great, great yak," they appear symbolically as end tables.

The tower. When O'Shawn moved out of his parent's

home, he lived in a tower just south of Dublin. It was a very low tower, standing about six feet, or two inches shorter than O'Shawn. He shared this residence with Harry O'Connel, a friend with literary pretension, whose verse play *The Musk Ox*, closed abruptly when the cast was chloroformed.

O'Connel was a great influence on O'Shawn's style and ultimately convinced him that every poem need not begin, "Roses are red, violets are blue."

Proud of their gums. The Beamish Brothers had unusually fine gums. Liam Beamish could remove his false teeth and eat peanut brittle, which he did every day for sixteen years until someone told him there was no such profession.

Agamemnon. O'Shawn was obsessed with the Trojan War. He could not believe an army could be so stupid as to accept a gift from its enemy during wartime. Particularly when they got close to the wooden horse and heard giggling inside. This episode seems to have traumatized the young O'Shawn and throughout his entire life he examined every gift given him very carefully, going so far as to shine a flashlight into a pair of shoes he received on his birthday and calling out, "Anybody in there? Eh? Come on out!"

Shaunnesy. Michael Shaunnesy, an occult writer and mystic, who convinced O'Shawn there would be a life after death for those who saved string.

Shaunnesy also believed the moon influenced actions and that to take a haircut during a total eclipse caused sterility. O'Shawn was very much taken with Shaunnesy and devoted much of his life to occult studies, although he never achieved his final goal of being able to enter a room through the keyhole.

The moon figures heavily in O'Shawn's later poems, and he told James Joyce that one of his greatest pleasures was to immerse his arm in custard on a moonlit night.

The reference to Shaunnesy's refusing an appetizer

probably refers to the time the two men dined together in Innesfree and Shaunnesy blew chickpeas through a straw at a fat lady when she disagreed with his views on embalming.

Bixby. Eamon Bixby. A political fanatic who preached ventriloquism as a cure for the world's ills. He was a great student of Socrates but differed from the Greek philosopher in his idea of the "good life," which Bixby felt was impossible unless everybody weighed the same.

Parnell had the answer. The answer O'Shawn refers to is "Tin," and the question is "What is the chief export of Bolivia?" That no one asked Parnell the question is understandable, although he was challenged once to name the largest fur-bearing quadruped extant and he said, "Chicken," for which he was severely criticized.

Lafferty. John Millington Synge's podiatrist. A fascinating character who had a passionate affair with Molly Bloom until he realized she was a fictional character.

Lafferty was fond of practical jokes and once with some corn meal and egg, he breaded Synge's arch supports. Synge walked peculiarly as a result, and his followers imitated him, hoping that by duplicating his gait, they too would write fine plays. Hence the lines: "caused/A whole generation to take/Samba lessons."

Homer was blind. Homer was a symbol for T. S. Eliot, whom O'Shawn considered a poet of "immense scope but very little breadth."

The two men met in London at rehearsals of *Murder in the Cathedral* (at that time entitled *Million Dollar Legs*). O'Shawn persuaded Eliot to abandon his sideburns and give up any notion he might have of becoming a Spanish dancer. Both writers then composed a manifesto stating the aims of the "new poetry," one of which was to write fewer poems that dealt with rabbits.

Aegnus and the Druids. O'Shawn was influenced by Celtic mythology, and his poem that begins, "Clooth na bare, na bare, na bare . . ." tells how the gods of ancient Ireland transformed two lovers into a set of the Encyclopaedia Britannica.

Free alterations. Probably refers to O'Shawn's wish to "alter the human race," whom he felt were basically depraved, especially jockeys. O'Shawn was definitely a pessimist, and felt that no good could come to mankind until they agreed to lower their body temperature from 98.6, which he felt was unreasonable.

Blake. O'Shawn was a mystic and, like Blake, believed in unseen forces. This was confirmed for him when his brother Ben was struck by lightning while licking a postage stamp. The lightning failed to kill Ben, which O'Shawn attributed to Providence, although it took his brother seventeen years before he could get his tongue back in his mouth.

O'Higgins. Patrick O'Higgins introduced O'Shawn to Polly Flaherty, who was to become O'Shawn's wife after a courtship of ten years in which the two did nothing more than meet secretly and wheeze at each other. Polly never realized the extent of her husband's genius and told intimates she thought he would be most remembered not for his poetry but for his habit of emitting a piercing shriek just before eating apples.

O'Leary's head. Mount O'Leary, where O'Shawn proposed to Polly just before she rolled off. O'Shawn visited her in the hospital and won her heart with his poem "On the Decomposing of Flesh."

Call your mother. On her deathbed, O'Shawn's mother Bridget, begged her son to abandon poetry and become a vacuum-cleaner salesman. O'Shawn couldn't promise and suffered from anxiety and guilt the rest of his life, although at the International Poetry Conference in Geneva, he sold W. H. Auden and Wallace Stevens each a Hoover.

Fabulous Tales
and Mythical Beasts

(The following is a sample of some of world literature's more imaginative creations that I am anthologizing in a four-volume set that Remainder and Sons plans to publish pending the outcome of the Norwegian shepherds' strike.)

The Nurk

The nurk is a bird two inches long that has the power of speech but keeps referring to itself in the third person, such as, "He's a great little bird, isn't he?"

Persian mythology holds that if a nurk appears on the window sill in the morning a relative will either come into money or break both legs at a raffle.

Zoroaster was said to have received a nurk as a gift on his birthday, although what he really needed was some gray slacks. The nurk also appears in Babylonian mythology, but here he is much more sarcastic and is always saying, "Ah, come off it."

Some readers may be acquainted with a lesser-known opera by Holstein called *Taffelspitz,* in which a mute girl falls in love with a nurk, kisses it, and they both fly around the room till the curtain falls.

The Flying Snoll

A lizard with four hundred eyes, two hundred for distance and two hundred for reading. According to legend, if a man gazes directly into the face of the snoll he immediately loses his right to drive in New Jersey.

Also legendary is the snoll's graveyard, the location of which is unknown even to snolls, and should a snoll drop dead he must remain where he is until picked up.

In Norse mythology, Loki attempts to find the snoll's graveyard but chances upon some Rhine maidens bathing instead and somehow winds up with trichinosis.

• • • • •

The Emperor Ho Sin had a dream in which he beheld a palace greater than his for half the rent. Stepping through the portals of the edifice, Ho Sin suddenly found that his body became young again, although his head remained somewhere between sixty-five and seventy. Opening a door, he found another door, which led to another; soon he realized he had entered a hundred doors and was now out in the backyard.

Just when Ho Sin was on the verge of despair, a nightingale perched on his shoulder and sang the most beautiful song he'd ever heard and then bit him on the nose.

Chastened, Ho Sin looked into a mirror and instead of seeing his own reflection, he saw a man named Mendel Goldblatt who worked for the Wasserman Plumbing Company and who accused him of taking his overcoat.

From this Ho Sin learned the secret of life, and it was "Never to yodel."

When the emperor awoke he was in a cold sweat and couldn't recall if he dreamed the dream or was now in a dream being dreamt by his bail bondsman.

The Frean

The frean is a sea monster with the body of a crab and the head of a certified public accountant.

Freans are said to possess fine singing voices which drive sailors mad when they hear them, particularly on Cole Porter tunes.

Killing a frean is bad luck: in a poem by Sir Herbert Figg, a sailor shoots one and his boat suddenly founders in a storm, causing the crew to seize the captain and jettison his false teeth in hopes of staying afloat.

The Great Roe

The great roe is a mythological beast with the head of a lion and the body of a lion, though not the same lion. The roe is reputed to sleep for a thousand years and then suddenly rise in flames, particularly if it was smoking when it dozed off.

Odysseus was said to have awakened a roe after six hundred years but found it listless and grouchy, and it begged to remain in bed just two hundred more years.

The appearance of a Roe is generally considered unlucky and usually precedes a famine or news of a cocktail party.

• • • • •

A wise man in India bet a magician that he could not fool him, whereupon the magician tapped the wise man on the head and changed him into a dove. The dove then flew out the window to Madagascar and had his luggage forwarded.

The wise man's wife, who had witnessed this, asked the magician if he could also change things to gold, and if so, could he change her brother to three dollars in cash so the whole day shouldn't be a total loss.

96

The magician said that in order to learn that trick one must journey to the four corners of the earth, but that one should go in the off-season, as three of the corners are usually booked.

The woman thought a moment and then set out on a pilgrimage to Mecca, forgetting to turn off her stove. Seventeen years later she returned, having spoken with the High Lama, and immediately went on welfare.

(The above is one of a series of Hindu myths that explain why we have wheat. Author.)

The Weal

A large white mouse with the lyrics to "Am I Blue?" printed on its stomach.

The weal is unique amongst rodents in that it can be picked up and played like an accordion. Similar to the weal is the lunette, a small squirrel that can whistle and knows the mayor of Detroit personally.

· · · · ·

Astronomers talk of an inhabited planet named Quelm, so distant from earth that a man traveling at the speed of light would take six million years to get there, although they are planning a new express route that will cut two hours off the trip.

Since the temperature on Quelm is thirteen hundred below, bathing is not permitted and the resorts have either closed down or now feature live entertainment.

Because of its remoteness from the center of the solar system, gravity is nonexistent on Quelm and having a large sit-down dinner takes a great deal of planning.

In addition to all these obstacles on Quelm, there is no oxygen to support life as we know it, and what creatures do exist find it hard to earn a living without holding down two jobs.

Legend has it, however, that many billions of years ago the environment was not quite so horrible—or at least no worse than Pittsburgh—and that human life existed. These humans—resembling men in every way except perhaps for a large head of lettuce where the nose normally is—were to a man philosophers. As philosophers they relied heavily on logic and felt that if life existed, somebody must have caused it, and they went looking for a dark-haired man with a tattoo who was wearing a Navy pea jacket.

When nothing materialized, they abandoned philosophy and went into the mail-order business, but postal rates went up and they perished.

But Soft . . .
Real Soft

Ask the average man who wrote the plays entitled *Hamlet, Romeo and Juliet, King Lear,* and *Othello,* and in most cases he'll snap confidently back with, "The Immortal Bard of Stratford on Avon." Ask him about the authorship of the Shakespearean sonnets and see if you don't get the same illogical reply. Now put these questions to certain literary detectives who seem to crop up every now and again over the years, and don't be surprised if you get answers like Sir Francis Bacon, Ben Jonson, Queen Elizabeth and possibly even the Homestead Act.

The most recent of these theories is to be found in a book I have just read that attempts to prove conclusively that the real author of Shakespeare's works was Christopher Marlowe. The book makes a very convincing case, and when I got through reading it I was not sure if Shakespeare was Marlowe or Marlowe was Shakespeare or what. I know this, I would not have cashed checks for either one of them—and I like their work.

Now, in trying to keep the above mentioned theory in perspective, my first question is: if Marlowe wrote Shakespeare's works, who wrote Marlowe's? The answer to this lies in the fact that Shakespeare was married to a woman named Anne Hathaway. This we know to be factual. However, under the new theory, it is actually Marlowe who was married to Anne Hathaway, a match which caused Shakespeare no end of grief, as they would not let him in the house.

One fateful day, in a jealous rage over who held the lower number in a bakery, Marlowe was slain—slain or whisked away in disguise to avoid charges of heresy, a most serious crime punishable by slaying or whisking away or both.

It was at this point that Marlowe's young wife took up the pen and continued to write the plays and sonnets we all know and avoid today. But allow me to clarify.

We all realize Shakespeare (Marlowe) borrowed his plots from the ancients (moderns); however, when the time came to return the plots to the ancients he had used them up and was forced to flee the country under the assumed name of William Bard (hence the term "immortal bard") in an effort to avoid debtor's prison (hence the term "debtor's prison"). Here Sir Francis Bacon enters into the picture. Bacon was an innovator of the times who was working on advanced concepts of refrigeration. Legend has it he died attempting to refrigerate a chicken. Apparently the chicken pushed first. In an effort to conceal Marlowe from Shakespeare, should they prove to be the same person, Bacon had adopted the fictitious name Alexander Pope, who in reality was Pope Alexander, head of the Roman Catholic Church and currently in exile owing to the invasion of Italy by the Bards, last of the nomadic hordes (the Bards give us the term "immortal bard"), and years before had galloped off to London, where Raleigh awaited death in the tower.

The mystery deepens for, as this goes on, Ben Jonson stages a mock funeral for Marlowe, convincing a minor poet to take his place for the burial. Ben Jonson is not to be confused with Samuel Johnson. He was Samuel Johnson. Samuel Johnson was not. Samuel Johnson was Samuel Pepys. Pepys was actually Raleigh, who had escaped from the tower to write *Paradise Lost* under the name of John Milton, a poet who because of blindness accidentally escaped to the tower and was hanged under the name of Jonathan Swift. This all becomes clearer when we realize that George Eliot was a woman.

Proceeding from this then, King Lear is not a play by Shakespeare but a satirical revue by Chaucer, originally titled "Nobody's Parfit," which contains in it a clue to the man who killed Marlowe, a man known around Elizabethan times (Elizabeth Barret Browning) as Old Vic. Old Vic became more familiar to us later as Victor Hugo, who wrote *The Hunchback of Notre Dame,* which most students of literature feel is merely *Coriolanus* with a few obvious changes. (Say them both fast.)

We wonder then, was not Lewis Carroll caricaturing the whole situation when he wrote *Alice in Wonderland?* The March Hare was Shakespeare, the Mad Hatter, Marlowe, and the Dormouse, Bacon—or the Mad Hatter, Bacon, and the March Hare, Marlowe—or Carroll, Bacon, and the Dormouse, Marlowe—or Alice was Shakespeare—or Bacon—or Carroll was the Mad Hatter. A pity Carroll is not alive today to settle it. Or Bacon. Or Marlowe. Or Shakespeare. The point is, if you're going to move, notify your post office. Unless you don't give a hoot about posterity.

If the Impressionists Had Been Dentists

(A fantasy exploring the
transposition of temperament)

Dear Theo,

Will life never treat me decently? I am wracked by despair! My head is pounding! Mrs. Sol Schwimmer is suing me because I made her bridge as I felt it and not to fit her ridiculous mouth! That's right! I can't work to order like a common tradesman! I decided her bridge should be enormous and billowing, with wild, explosive teeth flaring up in every direction like fire! Now she is upset because it won't fit in her mouth! She is so bourgeois and stupid, I want to smash her! I tried forcing the false plate in but it sticks out like a star burst chandelier. Still, I find it beautiful. She claims she can't chew! What do I care whether she can chew or not! Theo, I can't go on like this much longer! I asked Cézanne if he would share an office with me, but he is old and infirm and unable to hold the instruments and they must be tied to his wrists but then he lacks accuracy and once inside a mouth, he knocks out more teeth than he saves. What to do?

Vincent

Dear Theo,

I took some dental X-rays this week that I thought were good. Degas saw them and was critical. He said the composition was bad. All the cavities were bunched in the lower left corner. I explained to him that's how Mrs. Slotkin's mouth looks, but he wouldn't listen! He said he hated the frames and mahogany was too heavy. When he left, I tore them to shreds! As if that was not enough, I attempted some root-canal work on Mrs. Wilma Zardis, but halfway through I became despondent. I realized suddenly that root-canal work is not what I want to do! I grew flushed and dizzy. I ran from the office into the air where I could breathe! I blacked out for several days and woke up at the seashore. When I returned, she was still in the chair. I completed her mouth out of obligation but I couldn't bring myself to sign it.

Vincent

Dear Theo,

Once again I am in need of funds. I know what a burden I must be to you, but who can I turn to? I need money for materials! I am working almost exclusively with dental floss now, improvising as I go along, and the results are exciting! God! I have not even a penny left for Novocaine! Today I pulled a tooth and had to anesthetize the patient by reading him some Dreiser. Help.

Vincent

Dear Theo,

Have decided to share offices with Gauguin. He is a fine dentist who specializes in bridgework, and he seems to like me. He was very complimentary about my work on Mr. Jay Greenglass. If you recall, I filled his lower seven, then despised the filling and tried to remove it. Greenglass was adamant and we went to court. There was a legal question of ownership, and on my lawyer's advice, I

cleverly sued for the whole tooth and settled for the filling.
Well, someone saw it lying in the corner of my office and
he wants to put it in a show! They are already talking
about a retrospective!

Vincent

Dear Theo,
I think it is a mistake to share offices with Gauguin. He is a
disturbed man. He drinks Lavoris in large quantities.
When I accused him, he flew into a rage and pulled my
D.D.S. off the wall. In a calmer moment, I convinced him
to try filling teeth outdoors and we worked in a meadow
surrounded by greens and gold. He put caps on a Miss
Angela Tonnato and I gave a temporary filling to Mr. Louis
Kaufman. There we were, working together in the open
air! Rows of blinding white teeth in the sunlight! Then
a wind came up and blew Mr. Kaufman's toupee into
the bushes. He darted for it and knocked Gauguin's instruments to the ground. Gauguin blamed me and tried to
strike out but pushed Mr. Kaufman by mistake, causing
him to sit down on the high-speed drill. Mr. Kaufman
rocketed past me on a fly, taking Miss Tonnato with him.
The upshot, Theo, is that Rifkin, Rifkin, Rifkin
and Meltzer have attached my earnings. Send whatever
you can.

Vincent

Dear Theo,
Toulouse-Lautrec is the saddest man in the world. He
longs more than anything to be a great dentist, and he has
real talent, but he's too short to reach his patients' mouths
and too proud to stand on anything. Arms over his head,
he gropes around their lips blindly, and yesterday, instead
of putting caps on Mrs. Fitelson's teeth, he capped her
chin. Meanwhile, my old friend Monet refuses to work on

anything but very, very large mouths and Seurat, who is quite moody, has developed a method of cleaning one tooth at a time until he builds up what he calls "a full, fresh mouth." It has an architectural solidity to it, but is it dental work?

Vincent

Dear Theo,
I am in love. Claire Memling came in last week for an oral prophylaxis. (I had sent her a postcard telling her it had been six months since her last cleaning even though it had been only four days.) Theo, she drives me mad! Wild with desire! Her bite! I've never seen such a bite! Her teeth come together perfectly! Not like Mrs. Itkin's, whose lower teeth are forward of her uppers by an inch, giving her an underbite that resembles that of a werewolf! No! Claire's teeth close and meet! When this happens you know there is a God! And yet she's not too perfect. Not so flawless as to be uninteresting. She has a space between lower nine and eleven. Ten was lost during her adolescence. Suddenly and without warning it developed a cavity. It was removed rather easily (actually it fell out while she was talking) and was never replaced. "Nothing could replace lower ten," she told me. "It was more than a tooth, it had been my life to that point." The tooth was rarely discussed as she got older and I think she was only willing to speak of it to me because she trusts me. Oh, Theo, I love her. I was looking down into her mouth today and I was like a nervous young dental student again, dropping swabs and mirrors in there. Later I had my arms around her, showing her the proper way to brush. The sweet little fool was used to holding the brush still and moving her head from side to side. Next Thursday I will give her gas and ask her to marry me.

Vincent

Dear Theo,
Gauguin and I had another fight and he has left for Tahiti! He was in the midst of an extraction when I disturbed him. He had his knee on Mr. Nat Feldman's chest with the pliers around the man's upper right molar. There was the usual struggle and I had the misfortune to enter and ask Gauguin if he had seen my felt hat. Distracted, Gauguin lost his grip on the tooth and Feldman took advantage of the lapse to bolt from the chair and race out of the office. Gauguin flew into a frenzy! He held my head under the X-ray machine for ten straight minutes and for several hours after I could not blink my eyes in unison. Now I am lonely.

Vincent

Dear Theo,
All is lost! Today being the day I planned to ask Claire to marry me, I was a bit tense. She was magnificent in her white organdy dress, straw hat, and receding gums. As she sat in the chair, the draining hook in her mouth, my heart thundered. I tried to be romantic. I lowered the lights and tried to move the conversation to gay topics. We both took a little gas. When the moment seemed correct, I looked her directly in the eye and said, "Please rinse." And she laughed! Yes, Theo! She laughed at me and then grew angry! "Do you think I could rinse for a man like you!? What a joke!" I said, "Please, you don't understand." She said, "I understand quite well! I could never rinse with anyone but a licensed orthodontist! Why, the thought I would rinse here! Get away from me!" And with that she ran out weeping. Theo! I want to die! I see my face in the mirror and I want to smash it! Smash it! Hope you are well.

Vincent

Dear Theo,

Yes, it's true. The ear on sale at Fleishman Brothers Novelty Shop is mine. I guess it was a foolish thing to do but I wanted to send Claire a birthday present last Sunday and every place was closed. Oh, well. Sometimes I wish I had listened to father and become a painter. It's not exciting but the life is regular.

Vincent

112

No Kaddish for Weinstein

WEINSTEIN lay under the covers, staring at the ceiling in a depressed torpor. Outside, sheets of humid air rose from the pavement in stifling waves. The sound of traffic was deafening at this hour, and in addition to all this his bed was on fire. Look at me, he thought. Fifty years old. Half a century. Next year, I will be fifty-one. Then fifty-two. Using this same reasoning, he could figure out his age as much as five years in the future. So little time left, he thought, and so much to accomplish. For one thing, he wanted to learn to drive a car. Adelman, his friend who used to play dreidel with him on Rush Street, had studied driving at the Sorbonne. He could handle a car beautifully and had already driven many places by himself. Weinstein had made a few attempts to steer his father's Chevy but kept winding up on the sidewalk.

He had been a precocious child. An intellectual. At twelve, he had translated the poems of T. S. Eliot into English, after some vandals had broken into the library

and translated them into French. And as if his I.Q. did not
isolate him enough, he suffered untold injustices and per-
secutions because of his religion, mostly from his parents.
True, the old man was a member of the synagogue, and his
mother, too, but they could never accept the fact that their
son was Jewish. "How did it happen?" his father asked,
bewildered. My face looks Semitic, Weinstein thought
every morning as he shaved. He had been mistaken several times for Robert Redford, but on each occasion it was
by a blind person. Then there was Feinglass, his other boyhood friend: A Phi Beta Kappa. A labor spy, ratting on the
workers. Then a convert to Marxism. A Communist agita-
tor. Betrayed by the Party, he went to Hollywood and became the offscreen voice of a famous cartoon mouse.
Ironic.

Weinstein had toyed with the Communists, too. To
impress a girl at Rutgers, he had moved to Moscow and
joined the Red Army. When he called her for a second
date, she was pinned to someone else. Still, his rank of
sergeant in the Russian infantry would hurt him later
when he needed a security clearance in order to get the
free appetizer with his dinner at Longchamps. Also, while
at school he had organized some laboratory mice and led
them in a strike over work conditions. Actually, it was not
so much the politics as the poetry of Marxist theory that
got him. He was positive that collectivization could work if
everyone would learn the lyrics to "Rag Mop." "The with-
ering away of the state" was a phrase that had stayed with
him, ever since his uncle's nose had withered away in Saks
Fifth Avenue one day. What, he wondered, can be learned
about the true essence of social revolution? Only that it
should never be attempted after eating Mexican food.

The Depression shattered Weinstein's Uncle Meyer,
who kept his fortune under the mattress. When the market
crashed, the government called in all mattresses, and
Meyer became a pauper overnight. All that was left for

him was to jump out the window, but he lacked the nerve and sat on a window sill of the Flatiron Building from 1930 to 1937.

"These kids with their pot and their sex," Uncle Meyer was fond of saying. "Do they know what it is to sit on a window sill for seven years? There you see life! Of course, everybody looks like ants. But each year Tessie—may she rest in peace—made the Seder right out there on the ledge. The family gathered round for Passover. Oy, nephew! What's the world coming to when they have a bomb that can kill more people than one look at Max Rifkin's daughter?"

Weinstein's so-called friends had all knuckled under to the House Un-American Activities Committee. Blotnick was turned in by his own mother. Sharpstein was turned in by his answering service. Weinstein had been called by the committee and admitted he had given money to the Russian War Relief, and then added, "Oh, yes, I bought Stalin a dining-room set." He refused to name names but said if the committee insisted he would give the heights of the people he had met at meetings. In the end he panicked and instead of taking the Fifth Amendment, took the Third, which enabled him to buy beer in Philadelphia on Sunday.

Weinstein finished shaving and got into the shower. He lathered himself, while steaming water splashed down his bulky back. He thought, Here I am at some fixed point in time and space, taking a shower. I, Isaac Weinstein. One of God's creatures. And then, stepping on the soap, he slid across the floor and rammed his head into the towel rack. It had been a bad week. The previous day, he had got a bad haircut and was still not over the anxiety it caused him. At first the barber had snipped judiciously, but soon Weinstein realized he had gone too far. "Put some back!" he screamed unreasonably.

"I can't," the barber said. "It won't stick."

"Well, then give it to me, Dominic! I want to take it with me!"

"Once it's on the floor of the shop it's mine, Mr. Weinstein."

"Like hell! I want my hair!"

He blustered and raged, and finally felt guilty and left. Goyim, he thought. One way or another, they get you.

Now he emerged from the hotel and walked up Eighth Avenue. Two men were mugging an elderly lady. My God, thought Weinstein, time was when one person could handle that job. Some city. Chaos everyplace. Kant was right: The mind imposes order. It also tells you how much to tip. What a wonderful thing, to be conscious! I wonder what the people in New Jersey do.

He was on his way to see Harriet about the alimony payments. He still loved Harriet, even though while they were married she had systematically attempted to commit adultery with all the *R*'s in the Manhattan telephone directory. He forgave her. But he should have suspected something when his best friend and Harriet took a house in Maine together for three years, without telling him where they were. He didn't *want* to see it—that was it. His sex life with Harriet had stopped early. He slept with her once on the night they first met, once on the evening of the first moon landing, and once to test if his back was all right after a slipped disc. "It's no damn good with you, Harriet," he used to complain. "You're too pure. Every time I have an urge for you I sublimate it by planting a tree in Israel. You remind me of my mother." (Molly Weinstein, may she rest in peace, who slaved for him and made the best stuffed derma in Chicago—a secret recipe until everyone realized she was putting in hashish.)

For lovemaking, Weinstein needed someone quite opposite. Like LuAnne, who made sex an art. The only trouble was she couldn't count to twenty without taking her shoes off. He once tried giving her a book on existentialism, but she ate it. Sexually, Weinstein had always felt inadequate. For one thing, he felt short. He was five-four in his stocking feet, although in someone else's stocking feet he could be as tall as five-six. Dr. Klein, his analyst, got him to see that jumping in front of a moving train was more hostile than self-destructive but in either case would ruin the crease in his pants. Klein was his third analyst. His first was a Jungian, who suggested they try a Ouija board. Before that, he attended "group," but when it came time for him to speak he got dizzy and could only recite the names of all the planets. His problem was women, and he knew it. He was impotent with any woman who finished college with higher than a B-minus average. He felt most at home with graduates of typing school, although if the woman did over sixty words a minute he panicked and could not perform.

Weinstein rang the bell to Harriet's apartment, and suddenly she was standing before him. Swelling to maculate giraffe, as usual, thought Weinstein. It was a private joke that neither of them understood.

"Hello, Harriet," he said.

"Oh, Ike," she said. "You needn't be so damn self-righteous."

She was right. What a tactless thing to have said. He hated himself for it.

"How are the kids, Harriet?"

"We never had any kids, Ike."

"That's why I thought four hundred dollars a week was a lot for child support."

She bit her lip, Weinstein bit his lip. Then he bit her lip. "Harriet," he said, "I . . . I'm broke. Egg futures are down."

"I see. And can't you get help from your *shiksa?*"

"To you, any girl who's not Jewish is a *shiksa.*"

"Can we forget it?" Her voice was choked with recrimination. Weinstein had a sudden urge to kiss her, or if not her, somebody.

"Harriet, where did we go wrong?"

"We never faced reality."

"It wasn't my fault. You said it was north."

"Reality *is* north, Ike."

"No, Harriet. Empty dreams are north. Reality is west. False hopes are east, and I think Louisiana is south."

She still had the power to arouse him. He reached out for her, but she moved away and his hand came to rest in some sour cream.

"Is that why you slept with your analyst?" he finally blurted out. His face was knotted with rage. He felt like fainting but couldn't remember the proper way to fall.

"That was therapy," she said coldly. "According to Freud, sex is the royal road to the unconscious."

"Freud said *dreams* are the road to the unconscious."

"Sex, dreams—you're going to nit-pick?"

"Goodbye, Harriet."

It was no use. *Rien à dire, rien à faire.* Weinstein left and walked over to Union Square. Suddenly hot tears burst forth, as if from a broken dam. Hot, salty tears pent up for ages rushed out in an unabashed wave of emotion. The problem was, they were coming out of his ears. Look at this, he thought; I can't even cry properly. He dabbed his ear with Kleenex and went home.

Fine Times: An Oral Memoir

THE following are excerpts from the soon-to-be-published memoirs of Flo Guinness. Certainly the most colorful of all speakeasy owners during Prohibition, Big Flo, as her friends called her (many enemies called her that, too, mostly for convenience), emerges in these taped interviews as a woman with a lusty appetite for living, as well as a disappointed artist who had to give up her lifetime ambition to become a classical violinist, when she realized it would mean studying the violin. Here, for the first time, Big Flo speaks for herself.

Originally I danced at the Jewel Club in Chicago, for Ned Small. Ned was a shrewd businessman who made all his money by what we would now call "stealing." Of course, in those days it was quite different. Yes, sir, Ned had great charm—the kind you don't see today. He was famous for breaking both your legs if you disagreed with him. And he could do it, too, boys. He broke *more* legs! I'd say fifteen or sixteen a week was his average. But Ned was sweet on me, maybe 'cause I always told him straight to his face what I thought of him. "Ned," I told him over dinner once, "you're a mealymouth grifter with the morals of an alley cat." He laughed, but later that night I saw him looking up "mealymouth" in a dictionary. Anyhow, like I said, I danced at Ned Small's Jewel Club. I was his best dancer, boys—a dancer-*actress*. The other girls just hoofed, but I danced a little story. Like Venus emerging from her bath, only on Broadway and Forty-second Street, and she goes night-clubbing and dances till dawn and then has a massive coronary and loses control of the facial muscles on her left side. Sad stuff, boys. That's why I got respect.

One day, Ned Small calls me into his office and says, "Flo." (He always called me Flo, except when he got real mad at me. Then he'd call me Albert Schneiderman—I never knew why. Let's say the heart has strange ways.) So Ned says, "Flo, I want you to marry me." Well, you could've knocked me over with a feather. I started crying like a baby. "I mean it, Flo," he said. "I love you very deeply. It's not easy for me to say these things, but I want you to be the mother of my children. And if you don't I'll break both your legs." Two days later, to the minute, Ned Small and I tied the knot. Three days later, Ned was machine-gunned to death by the mob for spilling raisins on Al Capone's hat.

After that, of course, I was rich. First thing I did was buy my mother and father that farm they'd always talked about. They claimed they had never talked about a farm and actually wanted a car and some furs, but they gave it a try. Liked the rural life, too, although Dad got struck by lightning in the north forty and for six years afterward when asked his name could only say the word "Kleenex." As for me, three months later I was broke. Bad investments. I backed a whaling expedition in Cincinnati, on the advice of friends.

• • • • •

I danced for Big Ed Wheeler, who made bootleg hooch that was so strong it could only be sipped through a gas mask. Ed paid me three hundred dollars a week to do ten shows, which in those days was big money. Hell, with tips I made more than President Hoover. And he had to do twelve shows. I went on at nine and eleven, and Hoover went on at ten and two. Hoover was a good President, but he was always sitting in his dressing room humming. It drove me crazy. Then one day the owner of the Apex Club saw my act and offered me five hundred dollars a week to dance there. I put it squarely to Big Ed: "Ed, I got an offer of five hundred bucks from Bill Hallorhan's Apex Club."

"Flo," he said, "if you can get five hundred a week, I won't stand in your way." We shook hands and I went to tell Bill Hallorhan the good news, but several of Big Ed's friends had gotten there first and when I saw Bill Hallorhan his physical condition had undergone a change and he was now only a high-pitched voice that came from inside a cigar box. He said he had decided to get out of show business, leave Chicago, and settle down somewhere closer to the equator. I went on dancing for Big Ed Wheeler till the Capone mob bought him out. I say, "bought him out," boys, but the truth of it was Scarface Al offered him a tidy sum but Wheeler said no. Later that day, he was having lunch at the Rib and Chop House when his head burst into flames. No one knew why.

I bought the Three Deuces with money I'd saved, and in no time it was the hot spot in town. They all came—Babe Ruth, Jack Dempsey, Jolson, Man o' War. Man o' War was there every night. My God, how that horse could drink! I remember once Babe Ruth had this crush on a showgirl named Kelly Swain. He was so crazy about her he couldn't keep his mind on baseball and twice greased his body, thinking he was a famous channel swimmer.

"Flo," he said to me, "I'm nuts about this redhead, Kelly Swain. But she hates sports. I lied and told her I give a course on Wittgenstein, but I think she suspects something."

"Can you live without her, Babe," I asked him.

"No, Flo. And it's affecting my concentration. Yesterday, I got four hits and stole two bases, but this is January and there are no games scheduled. I did it in my hotel room. Can you help me?"

I promised him I'd speak to Kelly, and the next day I stopped by the Golden Abattoir, where she was dancing. I said, "Kelly, the Bambino is nuts about you. He knows you like culture and he says if you date him he'll give up baseball and join the Martha Graham troupe."

Kelly looked me squarely in the eye and said, "Tell that palooka I didn't come all the way from Chippewa Falls to wind up with some overstuffed right fielder. I got big plans." Two years later, she married Lord Osgood Wellington Tuttle and became Lady Tuttle. Her husband gave up an ambassadorship to play shortstop for the Tigers. Jumpin' Joe Tuttle. He holds the record for most times beaned in the first inning.

Gambling? Boys, I was present when Nick the Greek got his name. There was a small-time gambler named Jake the Greek, and Nick called me and said, "Flo, I'd like to be The Greek." And I said, "I'm sorry, Nick, you're not Greek. And under New York State gambling laws it's forbidden." And he said, "I know, Flo, but my parents always wanted me to be called The Greek. You think you could arrange a lunch meeting with Jake?" I said, "Sure, but if he knows what it's for he won't show." And Nick said, "Try, Flo. It would mean a lot to me."

So the two met at the Grill Room of Monty's Steak House, which did not allow women but I could go there because Monty was a great friend of mine and didn't regard me as either male or female but, in his own words, "undefined protoplasm." We ordered the specialty of the house, ribs, which Monty had a way of preparing so they tasted like human fingers. Finally, Nick said, "Jake, I'd like to be called The Greek." And Jake turned pale and said, "Look, Nick, if that's what you got me here for—" Well, boys, it got ugly. The two squared off. Then Nick said, "I'll tell you what I'll do. I'll cut you. High card gets to be called The Greek."

"But what if I win?" Jake said. "I'm *already* called The Greek."

"If you win, Jake, you can go through the phone book and pick any name you like. My compliments."

"No kidding?"

"Flo's the witness."

Well, you could feel the tension in that room. A deck of cards was brought out and they cut. Nick cut a queen, and Jake's hand was shaking. Then Jake cut an ace! Everybody let out a cheer, and Jake went through the phone book and selected the name Grover Lembeck. Everybody was happy, and from that day on women were allowed into Monty's, provided they could read hieroglyphics.

I remember once there was a big musical review at the Winter Garden, *Star-Spangled Vermin*. Jolson was the lead, but he quit because they wanted him to sing a song called "Kasha for Two," and he hated it. It had the line in it "Love is all, like a horse in a stall." Anyway, eventually it was sung by a young unknown named Felix Brompton, who was later arrested in a hotel room with a one-inch cardboard cutout of Helen Morgan. It was in all the papers. Well, Jolson come into the Three Deuces one night with Eddie Cantor, and he says to me, "Flo, I hear George Raft did his tap dance here last week." And I said, "George has never been here." And he said, "If you let him do his tap dance, I'd like to sing." And I said, "Al, he was never

128

here." And Al said, "Did he have any accompaniment on piano?" And I said, "Al, if you sing one note I'll personally throw you out." And with that Jolie got down on one knee and started on "Toot-Toot Tootsie." While he was singing, I sold the place, and by the time he was finished it was the Wing Ho Hand Laundry. Jolson never got over that or forgave me for it. On the way out, he tripped over a pile of shirts.

Slang Origins

How many of you have ever wondered where certain slang expressions come from? Like "She's the cat's pajamas," or to "take it on the lam." Neither have I. And yet for those who are interested in this sort of thing I have provided a brief guide to a few of the more interesting origins.

Unfortunately, time did not permit consulting any of the established works on the subject, and I was forced to either obtain the information from friends or fill in certain gaps by using my own common sense.

Take, for instance, the expression "to eat humble pie." During the reign of Louis the Fat, the culinary arts flourished in France to a degree unequaled anywhere. So obese was the French monarch that he had to be lowered onto the throne with a winch and packed into the seat itself with a large spatula. A typical dinner (according to DeRochet) consisted of a thin crêpe appetizer, some parsley, an ox, and custard. Food became the court obsession,

132

and no other subject could be discussed under penalty of death. Members of a decadent aristocracy consumed incredible meals and even dressed as foods. DeRochet tells us that M. Monsant showed up at the coronation as a weiner, and Étienne Tisserant received papal dispensation to wed his favorite codfish. Desserts grew more and more elaborate and pies grew larger and larger until the minister of justice suffocated trying to eat a seven-foot "Jumbo Pie." *Jumbo* pie soon became *jumble* pie and "to eat a jumble pie" referred to any kind of humiliating act. When the Spanish seamen heard the word *jumble,* they pronounced it "humble," although many preferred to say nothing and simply grin.

Now, while "humble pie" goes back to the French, "take it on the lam" is English in origin. Years ago, in England, "lamming" was a game played with dice and a large tube of ointment. Each player in turn threw dice and then skipped around the room until he hemorrhaged. If a person threw seven or under he would say the word "quintz" and proceed to twirl in a frenzy. If he threw over seven, he was forced to give every player a portion of his feathers and was given a good "lamming." Three "lammings" and a player was "kwirled" or declared a moral bankrupt. Gradually any game with feathers was called "lamming" and feathers became "lams." To "take it on the lam" meant to put on feathers and later, to escape, although the transition is unclear.

Incidentally, if two of the players disagreed on the rules, we might say they "got into a beef." This term goes back to the Renaissance when a man would court a woman by stroking the side of her head with a slab of meat. If she pulled away, it meant she was spoken for. If, however, she assisted by clamping the meat to her face and pushing it all over her head, it meant she would marry him. The meat was kept by the bride's parents and worn as a hat on special occasions. If, however, the husband took another lover, the wife could dissolve the marriage by running with the meat to the town square and yelling, "With thine own beef, I do reject thee. Aroo! Aroo!" If a couple "took to the beef" or "had a beef" it meant they were quarreling.

133

Another marital custom gives us that eloquent and colorful expression of disdain, "to look down one's nose." In Persia it was considered a mark of great beauty for a woman to have a long nose. In fact, the longer the nose, the more desirable the female, up to a certain point. Then it became funny. When a man proposed to a beautiful woman he awaited her decision on bended knee as she "looked down her nose at him." If her nostrils twitched, he was accepted, but if she sharpened her nose with pumice and began pecking him on the neck and shoulders, it meant she loved another.

Now, we all know when someone is very dressed up, we say he looks "spiffy." The term owes its origin to Sir Oswald Spiffy, perhaps the most renowned fop of Victorian England. Heir to treacle millions, Spiffy squandered his money on clothes. It was said that at one time he owned enough handkerchiefs for all the men, women and children in Asia to blow their noses for seven years without stopping. Spiffy's sartorial innovations were legend, and he was the first man ever to wear gloves on his head. Because of extra-sensitive skin, Spiffy's underwear had to be made of the finest Nova Scotia salmon, carefully sliced by one particular tailor. His libertine attitudes involved him in several notorious scandals, and he eventually sued the government over the right to wear earmuffs while fondling a dwarf. In the end, Spiffy died a broken man in Chichester, his total wardrobe reduced to kneepads and a sombrero.

Looking "spiffy," then, is quite a compliment, and one who does is liable to be dressed "to beat the band," a turn-of-the-century expression that originated from the custom of attacking with clubs any symphony orchestra whose conductor smiled during Berlioz. "Beating the band" soon became a popular evening out, and people dressed up in their finest clothes, carrying with them sticks and rocks. The practice was finally abandoned during a performance of the *Symphonie Fantastique* in New York when the entire string section suddenly stopped playing and exchanged gunfire with the first ten rows. Police ended the melee but not before a relative of J. P. Morgan's was wounded in the soft palate. After that, for a while at least, nobody dressed "to beat the band."

If you think some of the above derivations questionable, you might throw up your hands and say, "Fiddlesticks." This marvelous expression originated in Austria many years ago. Whenever a man in the banking profession announced his marriage to a circus pinhead, it was the custom for friends to present him with a bellows and a three-year supply of wax fruit. Legend has it that when Leo Rothschild made known his betrothal, a box of cello bows was delivered to him by mistake. When it was opened and found not to contain the traditional gift, he exclaimed, "What are these? Where are my bellows and fruit? Eh? All I rate is fiddlesticks!" The term "fiddlesticks" became a joke overnight in the taverns amongst the lower classes, who hated Leo Rothschild for never removing the comb from his hair after combing it. Eventually "fiddlesticks" meant any foolishness.

Well, I hope you've enjoyed some of these slang origins and that they stimulate you to investigate some on your own. And in case you were wondering about the term used to open this study, "the cat's pajamas," it goes back to an old burlesque routine of Chase and Rowe's, the two nutsy German professors. Dressed in oversized tails, Bill Rowe stole some poor victim's pajamas. Dave Chase, who got great mileage out of his "hard of hearing" specialty, would ask him:

CHASE: Ach, Herr Professor. Vot is dot bulge under your pocket?

ROWE: Dot? Dot's de chap's pajamas.

CHASE: The cat's pajamas? Ut mein Gott?

Audiences were convulsed by this sort of repartee and only a premature death of the team by strangulation kept them from stardom.

GETTING EVEN

CONTENTS

The Metterling Lists

Venal & Sons has at last published the long-awaited first volume of Metterling's laundry lists (*The Collected Laundry Lists of Hans Metterling*, Vol. I, 437 pp., plus XXXII-page introduction; indexed; $18.75), with an erudite commentary by the noted Metterling scholar Gunther Eisenbud. The decision to publish this work separately, before the completion of the immense four-volume *oeuvre*, is both welcome and intelligent, for this obdurate and sparkling book will instantly lay to rest the unpleasant rumors that Venal & Sons, having reaped rich rewards from the Metterling novels, play, and notebooks, diaries, and letters, was merely in search of continued profits from the same lode. How wrong the whisperers have been! Indeed, the very first Metterling laundry list

List No. 1
6 prs. shorts
4 undershirts

6 prs. blue socks
4 blue shirts
2 white shirts
6 handkerchiefs
  No Starch

serves as a perfect, near-total introduction to this troubled genius, known to his contemporaries as the "Prague Weirdo." The list was dashed off while Metterling was writing *Confessions of a Monstrous Cheese,* that work of stunning philosophical import in which he proved not only that Kant was wrong about the universe but that he never picked up a check. Metterling's dislike of starch is typical of the period, and when this particular bundle came back too stiff Metterling became moody and depressed. His landlady, Frau Weiser, reported to friends that "Herr Metterling keeps to his room for days, weeping over the fact that they have starched his shorts." Of course, Breuer has already pointed out the relation between stiff underwear and Metterling's constant feeling that he was being whispered about by men with jowls (*Metterling: Paranoid-Depressive Psychosis and the Early Lists*, Zeiss Press). This theme of a failure to follow instructions appears in Metterling's only play, *Asthma,* when Needleman brings the cursed tennis ball to Valhalla by mistake.

The obvious enigma of the second list

List No. 2
7 prs. shorts
5 undershirts
7 prs. black socks
6 blue shirts
6 handkerchiefs
  No Starch

is the seven pairs of black socks, since it has been long known that Metterling was deeply fond of blue. Indeed, for years the mention of any other color could send him into a rage, and he once pushed Rilke down into some honey because the poet said he preferred brown-eyed women. According to Anna Freud ("Metterling's Socks as an Expression of the Phallic Mother," *Journal of Psychoanalysis*, Nov., 1935), his sudden shift to the more sombre legwear is related to his unhappiness over the "Bayreuth Incident." It was there, during the first act of *Tristan*, that he sneezed, blowing the toupee off one of the opera's wealthiest patrons. The audience became convulsed, but Wagner defended him with his now classic remark "Everybody sneezes." At this, Cosima Wagner burst into tears and accused Metterling of sabotaging her husband's work.

That Metterling had designs on Cosima Wagner is undoubtedly true, and we know he took her hand once in Leipzig and again, four years later, in the Ruhr Valley. In Danzig, he referred to her tibia obliquely during a rainstorm, and she thought it best not to see him again. Returning to his home in a state of exhaustion, Metterling wrote *Thoughts of a Chicken*, and dedicated the original manuscript to the Wagners. When they used it to prop up the short leg of a kitchen table, Metterling became sullen and switched to dark socks. His housekeeper pleaded with him to retain his beloved blue or at least to try brown, but Metterling cursed her, saying, "Slut! And why not Argyles, eh?"

In the third list

List No. 3
6 handkerchiefs
5 undershirts
8 prs. socks
3 bedsheets
2 pillowcases

linens are mentioned for the first time: Metterling had a great fondness for linens, particularly pillow-cases, which

he and his sister, as children, used to put over their heads
while playing ghosts, until one day he fell into a rock
quarry. Metterling liked to sleep on fresh linen, and so do
his fictional creations. Horst Wasserman, the impotent
locksmith in *Filet of Herring*, kills for a change of sheets,
and Jenny, in *The Shepherd's Finger*, is willing to go to bed
with Klineman (whom she hates for rubbing butter on her
mother) "if it means lying between soft sheets." It is a
tragedy that the laundry never did the linens to Metterling's satisfaction, but to contend, as Pfaltz has done,
that his consternation over it prevented him from finishing
Whither Thou Goest, Cretin is absurd. Metterling enjoyed the
luxury of sending his sheets out, but he was not dependent
on it.

What prevented Metterling from finishing his long-
planned book of poetry was an abortive romance, which
figures in the "Famous Fourth" list:

LIST NO. 4
7 prs. shorts
6 handkerchiefs
6 undershirts
7 prs. black socks
 No Starch
Special One-Day Service

In 1884, Metterling met Lou Andreas-Salomé, and suddenly, we learn, he required that his laundry be done fresh
daily. Actually, the two were introduced by Nietzsche,
who told Lou that Metterling was either a genius or an
idiot and to see if she could guess which. At that time,
the special one-day service was becoming quite popular on
the Continent, particularly with intellectuals, and the
innovation was welcomed by Metterling. For one thing, it
was prompt, and Metterling loved promptness. He was

always showing up for appointments early —sometimes several days early, so that he would have to be put up in a guest room. Lou also loved fresh shipments of laundry every day. She was like a little child in her joy, often taking Metterling for walks in the woods and there unwrapping the latest bundle. She loved his undershirts and handkerchiefs, but most of all she worshipped his shorts. She wrote Nietzsche that Metterling's shorts were the most sublime thing she had ever encountered, including *Thus Spake Zarathustra*. Nietzsche acted like a gentleman about it, but he was always jealous of Metterling's underwear and told close friends he found it "Hegelian in the extreme." Lou Salomé and Metterling parted company after the Great Treacle Famine of 1886, and while Metterling forgave Lou, she always said of him that "his mind had hospital corners."

The fifth list

LIST NO. 5
6 undershirts
6 shorts
6 handkerchiefs

had always puzzled scholars, principally because of the total absence of socks. (Indeed, Thomas Mann, writing years later, became so engrossed with the problem he wrote an entire play about it, *The Hosiery of Moses*, which he accidentally dropped down a grating.) Why did this literary giant suddenly strike socks from his weekly list? Not, as some scholars say, as a sign of his oncoming madness, although Metterling had by now adopted certain odd behavior traits. For one thing, he believed that he was either being followed or was following somebody. He told close friends of a government plot to steal his chin, and once, on holiday in Jena, he could not say anything but the word "eggplant" for four straight days. Still, these seizures were sporadic and do not account for the missing socks. Nor does his emulation of Kafka, who for a brief period of his life stopped wearing socks, out of guilt. But Eisenbud assures us that Metterling continued to wear socks. He merely stopped sending them to the laundry! And why? Because at this time in his life he acquired a new house-keeper, Frau Milner, who consented to do his socks by hand—a gesture that so moved Metterling that he left the woman his entire fortune, which consisted of a black hat and some tobacco. She also appears as Hilda in his comic allegory, *Mother Brandt's Ichor*.

Obviously, Metterling's personality had begun to frag-ment by 1894, if we can deduce anything from the sixth list:

LIST NO. 6
25 handkerchiefs
1 undershirt
5 shorts
1 sock

and it is not surprising to learn that it was at this time he entered analysis with Freud. He had met Freud years be-fore in Vienna, when they both attended a production of *Oedipus*, from which Freud had to be carried out in a cold sweat. Their sessions were stormy, if we are to believe Freud's notes, and Metterling was hostile. He once threat-ened to starch Freud's beard and often said he reminded him of his laundryman. Gradually, Metterling's unusual relationship with his father came out. (Students of Met-terling are already familiar with his father, a petty official who would frequently ridicule Metterling by comparing him to a wurst.) Freud writes of a key dream Metterling described to him:

I am at a dinner party with some friends when suddenly a man walks in with a bowl of soup on a leash. He accuses my

*underwear of treason, and when a lady defends me her fore-
head falls off. I find this amusing in the dream, and laugh.
Soon everyone is laughing except my laundryman, who seems
stern and sits there putting porridge in his ears. My father
enters, grabs the lady's forehead, and runs away with it. He
races to a public square, yelling, "At last! At last! A forehead
of my own! Now I won't have to rely on that stupid son of
mine." This depresses me in the dream, and I am seized with
an urge to kiss the Burgomaster's laundry. (Here the patient
weeps and forgets the remainder of the dream.)*

With insights gained from this dream, Freud was able to
help Metterling, and the two became quite friendly outside
of analysis, although Freud would never let Metterling get
behind him.

In Volume II, it has been announced, Eisenbud will
take up Lists 7–25, including the years of Metterling's
"private laundress" and the pathetic misunderstanding
with the Chinese on the corner.

A Look at Organized Crime

I T IS no secret that organized crime in America takes in over forty billion dollars a year. This is quite a profitable sum, especially when one considers that the Mafia spends very little for office supplies. Reliable sources indicate that the Cosa Nostra laid out no more than six thousand dollars last year for personalized stationery, and even less for staples. Furthermore, they have one secretary who does all the typing, and only three small rooms for headquarters, which they share with the Fred Persky Dance Studio.

Last year, organized crime was directly responsible for more than one hundred murders, and *mafiosi* participated indirectly in several hundred more, either by lending the killers carfare or by holding their coats. Other illicit activities engaged in by Cosa Nostra members included gambling, narcotics, prostitution, hijacking, loansharking, and the transportation of a large whitefish across the state line for immoral purposes. The tentacles of this corrupt empire even reach into the government itself. Only a few months ago, two gang lords under federal indictment spent the night at the White House, and the President slept on the sofa.

History of Organized Crime in the United States

In 1921, Thomas (The Butcher) Covello and Ciro (The Tailor) Santucci attempted to organize disparate ethnic groups of the underworld and thus take over Chicago. This was foiled when Albert (The Logical Positivist) Corillo assassinated Kid Lipsky by locking him in a closet and sucking all the air out through a straw. Lipsky's brother Mendy (alias Mendy Lewis, alias Mendy Larsen, alias Mendy Alias) avenged Lipsky's murder by abducting Santucci's brother Gaetano (also known as Little Tony, or Rabbi Henry Sharpstein) and returning him several weeks later in twenty-seven separate mason jars. This signalled the beginning of a bloodbath.

Dominick (The Herpetologist) Mione shot Lucky Lorenzo (so nicknamed when a bomb that went off in his hat failed to kill him) outside a bar in Chicago. In return, Corillo and his men traced Mione to Newark and made his head into a wind instrument. At this point, the Vitale gang, run by Giuseppe Vitale (real name Quincy Baedeker), made their move to take over all bootlegging in Harlem from Irish Larry Doyle—a racketeer so suspicious that he refused to let anybody in New York ever get behind him, and walked down the street constantly pirouetting and spinning around. Doyle was killed when the Squillante Construction Company decided to erect their new offices on the bridge of his nose. Doyle's lieutenant, Little Petey (Big Petey) Ross, now took command; he resisted the Vitale takeover and lured Vitale to an empty midtown garage on the pretext that a costume party was being held there. Unsuspecting, Vitale walked into the garage dressed as a giant mouse, and was instantly riddled with machine-gun bullets. Out of loyalty to their slain chief, Vitale's men immediately defected to Ross. So did Vitale's fiancée, Bea Moretti, a showgirl and star of the hit Broadway musical *Say Kaddish*, who wound up marrying Ross, although she later sued him for divorce, charging that he once spread an unpleasant ointment on her.

Fearing federal intervention, Vincent Columbraro, the Buttered Toast King, called for a truce. (Columbraro had such tight control over all buttered toast moving in and out of New Jersey that one word from him could ruin break-fast for two-thirds of the nation.) All members of the underworld were summoned to a diner in Perth Amboy, where Columbraro told them that internal warfare must stop and that from then on they had to dress decently and stop slinking around. Letters formerly signed with a black hand would in the future be signed "Best Wishes," and all territory would be divided equally, with New Jersey going to Columbraro's mother. Thus the Mafia, or Costa Nostra (literally, "my toothpaste" or "our toothpaste"), was born. Two days later, Columbraro got into a nice hot tub to take a bath and has been missing for the past forty-six years.

Mob Structure

The Cosa Nostra is structured like any government or large corporation—or group of gangsters, for that matter. At the top is the *capo di tutti capi*, or boss of all bosses. Meetings are held at his house, and he is responsible for supplying cold cuts and ice cubes. Failure to do so means instant death. (Death, incidentally, is one of the worst things that can happen to a Cosa Nostra member, and many prefer simply to pay a fine.) Under the boss of bosses are his lieutenants, each of whom runs one section of town with his "family." Mafia families do not consist of a wife and children who always go to places like the circus or on picnics. They are actually groups of rather serious men, whose main joy in life comes from seeing how long certain people can stay under the East River before they start gurgling.

Initiation into the Mafia is quite complicated. A proposed member is blindfolded and led into a dark room. Pieces of Cranshaw melon are placed in his pockets, and he is required to hop around on one foot and cry out, "Toodles! Toodles!" Next, his lower lip is pulled out and snapped back by all the members of the board, or *commissione;* some may even wish to do it twice. Following this, some oats are put on his head. If he complains, he is disqualified. If, however, he says, "Good, I like oats on my head," he is welcomed into the brotherhood. This is done by kissing him on the cheek and shaking his hand. From that moment on, he is not permitted to eat chutney, to amuse his friends by imitating a hen, or to kill anybody named Vito.

Conclusions

Organized crime is a blight on our nation. While many young Americans are lured into a career of crime by its promise of an easy life, most criminals actually must work long hours, frequently in buildings without airconditioning. Identifying criminals is up to each of us. Usually they can be recognized by their large cufflinks and their failure to stop eating when the man sitting next to them is hit by a falling anvil. The best methods of combatting organized crime are:

1. Telling the criminals you are not at home.
2. Calling the police whenever an unusual number of men from the Sicilian Laundry Company begin singing in your foyer.
3. Wiretapping.

Wiretapping cannot be employed indiscriminately, but

its effectiveness is illustrated by this transcript of a conversation between two gang bosses in the New York area whose phones had been tapped by the F.B.I.

> ANTHONY: Hello? Rico?
> RICO: Hello?
> ANTHONY: Rico?
> RICO: Hello.
> ANTHONY: Rico?
> RICO: I can't hear you.
> ANTHONY: Is that you, Rico? I can't hear you.
> RICO: What?
> ANTHONY: Can you hear me?
> RICO: Hello?
> ANTHONY: Rico?
> RICO: We have a bad connection.
> ANTHONY: Can you hear me?
> RICO: Hello?
> ANTHONY: Rico?
> RICO: Hello?
> ANTHONY: Operator, we have a bad connection.
> OPERATOR: Hang up and dial again, sir.
> RICO: Hello?

Because of this evidence, Anthony (The Fish) Rotunno and Rico Panzini were convicted and are currently serving fifteen years in Sing Sing for illegal possession of Bensonhurst.

The Schmeed Memoirs

The Deformed Mistress

The seemingly inexhaustible spate of literature on the Third Reich continues unabated with the soon to be published memoirs of Friedrich Schmeed. Schmeed, the best-known barber in wartime Germany, provided tonsorial services for Hitler and many highly placed government and military officials. As was noted during the Nuremberg Trials, Schmeed not only seemed to be always at the right place at the right time but possessed "more than total recall," and was thus uniquely qualified to write this incisive guide to innermost Nazi Germany. Following are a few brief excerpts:

IN THE spring of 1940, a large Mercedes pulled up in front of my barbershop at 127 Koenigstrasse, and Hitler walked in. "I just want a light trim," he said, "and don't take too much off the top." I explained to him there would be a brief wait because von Ribbentrop was ahead of him. Hitler said he was in a rush and asked Ribbentrop if he could be taken next, but Ribbentrop insisted it would look bad for the Foreign Office if he were passed over. Hitler thereupon made a quick phone call, and Ribbentrop was immediately transferred to the Afrika Korps, and Hitler got his haircut. This sort of rivalry went on all the time. Once, Göring had Heydrich detained by the police on false pretenses, so that he could get the chair by the window. Göring was a dissolute and often wanted to sit on the hobbyhorse to get his haircuts. The Nazi high command was embarrassed by this but could do nothing. One day, Hess challenged him. "I want the hobbyhorse today, Herr Field Marshal," he said.

"Impossible. I have it reserved," Göring shot back.

"I have orders directly from the Führer. They state that
I am to be allowed to sit on the horse for my haircut." And
Hess produced a letter from Hitler to that effect. Göring
was livid. He never forgave Hess, and said that in the
future he would have his wife cut his hair at home with a
bowl. Hitler laughed when he heard this, but Göring was
serious and would have carried it out had not the Minister
of Arms turned down his requisition for a thinning shears.

I have been asked if I was aware of the moral implications of what I was doing. As I told the tribunal at Nuremberg, I did not know that Hitler was a Nazi. The truth was
that for years I thought he worked for the phone company.
When I finally did find out what a monster he was, it was
too late to do anything, as I had made a down payment on
some furniture. Once, toward the end of the war, I did
contemplate loosening the Führer's neck-napkin and
allowing some tiny hairs to get down his back, but at the
last minute my nerve failed me.

At Berchtesgaden one day, Hitler turned to me and
said, "How would I look in sideburns?" Speer laughed,
and Hitler became affronted. "I'm quite serious, Herr
Speer," he said. "I think I might look good in sideburns."
Göring, that obsequious clown, concurred instantly, saying, "The Führer in sideburns—what an excellent idea!"
Speer still disagreed. He was, in fact, the only one with
enough integrity to tell the Führer when he needed a haircut. "Too flashy," Speer said now. "Sideburns are the kind
of thing I'd associate with Churchill." Hitler became
incensed. Was Churchill contemplating sideburns, he
wanted to know, and if so, how many and when? Himmler, supposedly in charge of Intelligence, was summoned
immediately. Göring was annoyed by Speer's attitude and
whispered to him, "Why are you making waves, eh? If he
wants sideburns, let him have sideburns." Speer, usually
tactful to a fault, called Göring a hypocrite and "an order

of bean curd in a German uniform.'' Göring swore he would get even, and it was rumored later that he had special S.S. guards french Speer's bed.

Himmler arrived in a frenzy. He had been in the midst of a tap-dancing lesson when the phone rang, summoning him to Berchtesgaden. He was afraid it was about a misplaced carload of several thousand cone-shaped party hats that had been promised Rommel for his winter offensive. (Himmler was not accustomed to being invited to dinner at Berchtesgaden, because his eyesight was poor and Hitler could not bear to watch him bring the fork up to his face and then stick the food somewhere on his cheek.) Himmler knew something was wrong, because Hitler was calling him "Shorty," which he only did when annoyed. Suddenly the Führer turned on him, shouting, "Is Churchill going to grow sideburns?''

Himmler turned red.

"Well?''

Himmler said there had been word that Churchill contemplated sideburns but it was all unofficial. As to size and number, he explained, there would probably be two, of a medium length, but no one wanted to say before they could be sure. Hitler screamed and banged his fist on the table. (This was a triumph for Göring over Speer.) Hitler pulled out a map and showed us how he meant to cut off England's supply of hot towels. By blockading the Dardanelles, Doenitz could keep the towels from being brought ashore and laid across anxiously awaiting British faces. But the basic question remained: Could Hitler beat Churchill to sideburns? Himmler said Churchill had a head start and that it might be impossible to catch him. Göring, that vacuous optimist, said the Führer could probably grow sideburns quicker, particularly if we marshalled all of Germany's might in a concentrated effort. Von Rundstedt, at a meeting of the General Staff, said it was a mistake to try to grow sideburns on two fronts at once and advised

164

that it would be wiser to concentrate all efforts on one good sideburn. Hitler said he could do it on both cheeks simultaneously. Rommel agreed with von Rundstedt. "They will never come out even, *mein Führer*," he said. "Not if you rush them." Hitler became enraged and said that it was a matter for him and his barber. Speer promised he could triple our output of shaving cream by the fall, and Hitler was euphoric. Then, in the winter of 1942, the Russians launched a counter-offensive and the sideburns came to a halt. Hitler grew despondent, fearing that soon Churchill would look wonderful while he still remained "ordinary," but shortly thereafter we received news that Churchill had abandoned the idea of sideburns as too costly. Once again the Führer had been proved right.

After the Allied invasion, Hitler developed dry, unruly hair. This was due in part to the Allies' success and in part to the advice of Goebbels, who told him to wash it every day. When General Guderian heard this, he immediately returned home from the Russian front and told the Führer he must shampoo his hair no more than three times weekly. This was the procedure followed with great success by the General Staff in two previous wars. Hitler once again overruled his generals and continued washing daily. Bormann helped Hitler with the rinsing and always seemed to be there with a comb. Eventually, Hitler became dependent on Bormann, and before he looked in a mirror he would always have Bormann look in it first. As the Allied armies pushed east, Hitler's hair grew worse. Dry and unkempt, he often raged for hours about how he would get a nice haircut and a shave when Germany won the war, and maybe even a shine. I realize now he never had any intention of doing those things.

One day, Hess took the Führer's bottle of Vitalis and set out in a plane for England. The German high command was furious. They felt Hess planned to give it to the Allies in return for amnesty for himself. Hitler was particularly enraged when he heard the news, as he had just stepped out of the shower and was about to do his hair. (Hess later explained at Nuremberg that his plan was to give Churchill a scalp treatment in an effort to end the war. He had got as far as bending Churchill over a basin when he was apprehended.)

Late in 1944, Göring grew a mustache, causing talk that he was soon to replace Hitler. Hitler was furious and accused Göring of disloyalty. "There must be only one mustache among the leaders of the Reich, and it shall be mine!" he cried. Göring argued that two mustaches might give the German people a greater sense of hope about the war, which was going poorly, but Hitler thought not. Then, in January of 1945, a plot by several generals to shave Hitler's mustache in his sleep and proclaim Doenitz the new leader failed when von Stauffenberg, in the darkness of Hitler's bedroom, shaved off one of the Führer's eyebrows instead. A state of emergency was proclaimed, and suddenly Goebbels appeared at my shop. "An attempt was just made on the Führer's mustache; but it was unsuccessful," he said, trembling. Goebbels arranged for me to go on radio and address the German people, which I did, with a minimum of notes. "The Führer is all right," I assured them. "He still has his mustache. Repeat. The Führer still has his mustache. A plot to shave it has failed."

Near the end, I came to Hitler's bunker. The Allied armies were closing in on Berlin, and Hitler felt that if the Russians got there first he would need a full haircut but if the Americans did he could get by with a light trim. Everyone quarrelled. In the midst of all this, Bormann wanted a shave, and I promised him I would get to work on some blueprints. Hitler grew morose and remote. He talked of parting his hair from ear to ear and then claimed that the development of the electric razor would turn the war for

166

Germany. "We will be able to shave in seconds, eh, Schmeed?" he muttered. He mentioned other wild schemes and said that someday he would have his hair not just cut but shaped. Obsessed as usual by sheer size, he vowed he would eventually have a huge pompadour—"one that will make the world tremble and will require an honor guard to comb." Finally, we shook hands and I gave him a last trim. He tipped me one pfennig. "I wish it could be more," he said, "but ever since the Allies have overrun Europe I've been a little short."

My Philosophy

THE development of my philosophy came about as follows: My wife, inviting me to sample her very first soufflé, accidentally dropped a spoonful of it on my foot, fracturing several small bones. Doctors were called in, X-rays taken and examined, and I was ordered to bed for a month. During this convalescence, I turned to the works of some of Western society's most formidable thinkers—a stack of books I had laid aside for just such an eventuality. Scorning chronological order, I began with Kierkegaard and Sartre, then moved quickly to Spinoza, Hume, Kafka, and Camus. I was not bored, as I had feared I might be; rather, I found myself fascinated by the alacrity with which these great minds unflinchingly attacked morality, art, ethics, life, and death. I remember my reaction to a typically luminous observation of Kierkegaard's: "Such a relation which relates itself to its own self (that is to say, a self) must either have constituted itself or have been constituted by another." The concept brought tears to my

169

eyes. My word, I thought, to be that clever! (I'm a man who has trouble writing two meaningful sentences on "My Day at the Zoo.") True, the passage was totally incomprehensible to me, but what of it as long as Kierkegaard was having fun? Suddenly confident that metaphysics was the work I had always been meant to do, I took up my pen and began at once to jot down the first of my own musings. The work proceeded apace, and in a mere two afternoons —with time out for dozing and trying to get the two little BBs into the eyes of the bear—I had completed the philosophical work that I am hoping will not be uncovered until after my death, or until the year 3000 (whichever comes first), and which I modestly believe will assure me a place of reverence among history's weightiest thinkers. Here is but a small sample of the main body of intellectual treasure that I leave for posterity, or until the cleaning woman comes.

I. Critique of Pure Dread

In formulating any philosophy, the first consideration must always be: What can we know? That is, what can we be sure we know, or sure that we know we knew it, if indeed it is at all knowable. Or have we simply forgotten it and are too embarrassed to say anything? Descartes hinted at the problem when he wrote, "My mind can never know my body, although it has become quite friendly with my legs." By "knowable," incidentally, I do not mean that which can be known by perception of the senses, or that which can be grasped by the mind, but more that which can be said to be Known or to possess a Knownness or Knowability, or at least something you can mention to a friend.

Can we actually "know" the universe? My God, it's hard enough finding your way around in Chinatown. The point, however, is: Is there anything out there? And why?

And must they be so noisy? Finally, there can be no doubt that the one characteristic of "reality" is that it lacks essence. That is not to say it has no essence, but merely lacks it. (The reality I speak of here is the same one Hobbes described, but a little smaller.) Therefore the Cartesian dictum "I think, therefore I am" might be better expressed "Hey, there goes Edna with a saxophone!" So, then, to know a substance or an idea we must doubt it, and thus, doubting it, come to perceive the qualities it possesses in its finite state, which are truly "in the thing itself," or "of the thing itself," or of something or nothing. If this is clear, we can leave epistemology for the moment.

II. Eschatological Dialectics as a Means of Coping with Shingles

We can say that the universe consists of a substance, and this substance we will call "atoms," or else we will call it "monads." Democritus called it atoms. Leibnitz called it monads. Fortunately, the two men never met, or there would have been a very dull argument. These "particles" were set in motion by some cause or underlying principle, or perhaps something fell someplace. The point is that it's too late to do anything about it now, except possibly to eat plenty of raw fish. This, of course, does not explain why the soul is immortal. Nor does it say anything about an afterlife, or about the feeling my Uncle Sender has that he is being followed by Albanians. The causal relationship between the first principle (i.e., God, or a strong wind) and any teleological concept of being (Being) is, according to Pascal, "so ludicrous that it's not even funny (Funny)." Schopenhauer called this "will," but his physician diagnosed it as hay fever. In his later years, he became embittered by it, or more likely because of his increasing suspicion that he was not Mozart.

III. The Cosmos on Five Dollars a Day

What, then, is "beautiful"? The merging of harmony with the just, or the merging of harmony with something that just sounds like "the just"? Possibly harmony should have been merged with "the crust" and this is what's been giving us our trouble. Truth, to be sure, is beauty—or "the necessary." That is, what is good or possessing the qualities of "the good" results in "truth." If it doesn't, you can bet the thing is not beautiful, although it may still be waterproof. I am beginning to think I was right in the first place and that everything should be merged with the crust. Oh, well.

Two Parables

A man approaches a palace. Its only entrance is guarded by some fierce Huns who will only let men named Julius enter. The man tries to bribe the guards by offering them a year's supply of choice chicken parts. They neither scorn his offer nor accept it, but merely take his nose and twist it till it looks like a Molly screw. The man says it is imperative that he enter the palace because he is bringing the emperor a change of underwear. When the guards still refuse, the man begins to Charleston. They seem to enjoy his dancing but soon become morose over the treatment of the Navajos by the federal government. Out of breath, the man collapses. He dies, never having seen the emperor and owing the Steinway people sixty dollars on a piano he had rented from them in August.

· · · · ·

I am given a message to deliver to a general. I ride and ride, but the general's headquarters seem to get farther and farther away. Finally, a giant black panther leaps upon me and devours my mind and heart. This puts a terrific crimp in my evening. No matter how hard I try, I cannot catch the general, whom I see running in the distance in his shorts and whispering the word "nutmeg" to his enemies.

Aphorisms

It is impossible to experience one's own death objectively and still carry a tune.

· · · · ·

The universe is merely a fleeting idea in God's mind—a pretty uncomfortable thought, particularly if you've just made a down payment on a house.

· · · · ·

Eternal nothingness is O.K. if you're dressed for it.

· · · · ·

If only Dionysus were alive! Where would he eat?

· · · · ·

Not only is there no God, but try getting a plumber on weekends.

Yes, But Can the Steam Engine Do This?

I WAS leafing through a magazine while waiting for Joseph K., my beagle, to emerge from his regular Tuesday fifty-minute hour with a Park Avenue therapist—a Jungian veterinarian who, for fifty dollars per session, labors valiantly to convince him that jowls are not a social drawback—when I came across a sentence at the bottom of the page that caught my eye like an overdraft notice. It was just another item in one of those boilerplate specials with a title like "Historagrams" or "Betcha Didn't Know," but its magnitude shook me with the power of the opening strains of Beethoven's Ninth. "The sandwich," it read, "was invented by the Earl of Sandwich." Stunned by the news, I read it again and broke into an involuntary tremble. My mind whirled as it began to conjure with the immense dreams, the hopes and obstacles, that must have gone into the invention of the first sandwich. My eyes became moist as I looked out the window at the shimmering towers of the city, and I experienced a sense of eternity,

177

marvelling at man's ineradicable place in the universe. Man the inventor! Da Vinci's notebooks loomed before me —brave blueprints for the highest aspirations of the human race. I thought of Aristotle, Dante, Shakespeare. The First Folio. Newton. Handel's *Messiah.* Monet. Impressionism. Edison. Cubism. Stravinsky. $E = mc^2$ . . .

Holding firmly to a mental picture of the first sandwich lying encased at the British Museum, I spent the ensuing three months working up a brief biography of its great inventor, his nibs the Earl. Though my grasp of history is a bit shaky, and though my capacity for romanticizing easily dwarfs that of the average acidhead, I hope I have captured at least the essence of this unappreciated genius, and that these sparse notes will inspire a true historian to take it from here.

1718: Birth of the Earl of Sandwich to upper-class parents. Father is delighted at being appointed chief farrier to His Majesty the King—a position he will enjoy for several years, until he discovers he is a blacksmith and resigns embittered. Mother is a simple *Hausfrau* of German extraction, whose uneventful menu consists essentially of lard and gruel, although she does show some flair for the culinary imagination in her ability to concoct a passable sillabub.

1725–35: Attends school, where he is taught horseback riding and Latin. At school he comes in contact with cold cuts for the first time and displays an unusual interest in thinly sliced strips of roast beef and ham. By graduation this has become an obsession, and although his paper on "The Analysis and Attendant Phenomena of Snacks" arouses interest among the faculty, his classmates regard him as odd.

1736: Enters Cambridge University, at his parents' behest, to pursue studies in rhetoric and metaphysics, but displays little enthusiasm for either. In constant revolt against everything academic, he is charged with stealing loaves of bread and performing unnatural experiments with them. Accusations of heresy result in his expulsion.

1738: Disowned, he sets out for the Scandinavian countries, where he spends three years in intensive research on cheese. He is much taken with the many varieties of sardines he encounters and writes in his notebook, "I am convinced that there is an enduring reality, beyond anything man has yet attained, in the juxtaposition of foodstuffs. Simplify, simplify." Upon his return to England, he meets Nell Smallbore, a greengrocer's daughter, and they marry. She is to teach him all he will ever know about lettuce.

1741: Living in the country on a small inheritance, he works day and night, often skimping on meals to save money for food. His first completed work—a slice of bread, a slice of bread on top of that, and a slice of turkey on top of both—fails miserably. Bitterly disappointed, he returns to his studio and begins again.

1745: After four years of frenzied labor, he is convinced he is on the threshold of success. He exhibits before his peers two slices of turkey with a slice of bread in the middle. His work is rejected by all but David Hume, who senses the imminence of something great and encourages him. Heartened by the philosopher's friendship, he returns to work with renewed vigor.

1747: Destitute, he can no longer afford to work in roast beef or turkey and switches to ham, which is cheaper.

1750: In the spring, he exhibits and demonstrates three consecutive slices of ham stacked on one another; this arouses some interest, mostly in intellectual circles, but the general public remains unmoved. Three slices of bread on top of one another add to his reputation, and while a mature style is not yet evident, he is sent for by Voltaire.

1751: Journeys to France, where the dramatist-philosopher has achieved some interesting results with bread and mayonnaise. The two men become friendly and begin a correspondence that is to end abruptly when Voltaire runs out of stamps.

1758: His growing acceptance by opinion-makers wins him a commission by the Queen to fix "something special" for a luncheon with the Spanish ambassador. He works day and night, tearing up hundreds of blueprints, but finally—at 4:17 A.M., April 27, 1758—he creates a work consisting of several strips of ham enclosed, top and bottom, by two slices of rye bread. In a burst of inspiration, he garnishes the work with mustard. It is an immediate sensation, and he is commissioned to prepare all Saturday luncheons for the remainder of the year.

1760: He follows one success with another, creating "sandwiches," as they are called in his honor, out of roast beef, chicken, tongue, and nearly every conceivable cold cut. Not content to repeat tried formulas, he seeks out new ideas and devises the combination sandwich, for which he receives the Order of the Garter.

1769: Living on a country estate, he is visited by the greatest men of his century; Haydn, Kant, Rousseau, and Ben Franklin stop at his home, some enjoying his remarkable creations at table, others ordering to go.

1778: Though aging physically he still strives for new forms and writes in his diary, "I work long into the cold nights and am toasting everything now in an effort to keep warm." Later that year, his open hot roast-beef sandwich creates a scandal with its frankness.

1783: To celebrate his sixty-fifth birthday, he invents the hamburger and tours the great capitals of the world personally, making burgers at concert halls before large and appreciative audiences. In Germany, Goethe suggests serving them on buns—an idea that delights the Earl, and of the author of *Faust* he says, "This Goethe, he is some fellow." The remark delights Goethe, although the following year they break intellectually over the concept of rare, medium, and well done.

1790: At a retrospective exhibition of his works in London, he is suddenly taken ill with chest pains and is thought to be dying, but recovers sufficiently to supervise the construction of a hero sandwich by a group of talented followers. Its unveiling in Italy causes a riot, and it remains misunderstood by all but a few critics.

1792: He develops a genu varum, which he fails to treat in time, and succumbs in his sleep. He is laid to rest in Westminster Abbey, and thousands mourn his passing. At his funeral, the great German poet Hölderlin sums up his achievements with undisguised reverence: "He freed mankind from the hot lunch. We owe him so much."

Death Knocks

(The play takes place in the bedroom of the Nat Ackermans' two-story house, somewhere in Kew Gardens. The carpeting is wall-to-wall. There is a big double bed and a large vanity. The room is elaborately furnished and curtained, and on the walls there are several paintings and a not really attractive barometer. Soft theme music as the curtain rises. Nat Ackerman, a bald, paunchy fifty-seven-year-old dress manufacturer is lying on the bed finishing off tomorrow's Daily News. *He wears a bathrobe and slippers, and reads by a bed light clipped to the white headboard of the bed. The time is near midnight. Suddenly we hear a noise, and Nat sits up and looks at the window.)*

NAT: What the hell is that?

(Climbing awkwardly through the window is a sombre, caped figure. The intruder wears a black hood and skintight black clothes. The hood covers his head but not

185

his face, which is middle-aged and stark white. He is something like Nat in appearance. He huffs audibly and then trips over the windowsill and falls into the room.)

DEATH *(for it is no one else):* Jesus Christ. I nearly broke my neck.

NAT *(watching with bewilderment):* Who are you?

DEATH: Death.

NAT: Who?

DEATH: Death. Listen—can I sit down? I nearly broke my neck. I'm shaking like a leaf.

NAT: Who *are* you?

DEATH: *Death.* You got a glass of water?

NAT: Death? What do you mean, Death?

DEATH: What is wrong with you? You see the black costume and the whitened face?

NAT: Yeah.

DEATH: Is it Halloween?

NAT: No.

DEATH: Then I'm Death. Now can I get a glass of water—or a Fresca?

NAT: If this is some joke—

DEATH: What kind of joke? You're fifty-seven? Nat Ackerman? One-eighteen Pacific Street? Unless I blew it—where's that call sheet? *(He fumbles through pocket, finally producing a card with an address on it. It seems to check.)*

NAT: What do you want with me?

DEATH: What do I want? What do you think I want?

NAT: You must be kidding. I'm in perfect health.

DEATH *(unimpressed):* Uh-huh. *(Looking around)* This is a nice place. You do it yourself?

NAT: We had a decorator, but we worked with her.

DEATH *(looking at picture on the wall):* I love those kids with the big eyes.

NAT: I don't want to go yet.

DEATH: *You* don't want to go? Please don't start in. As it is, I'm nauseous from the climb.

NAT: What climb?

DEATH: I climbed up the drainpipe. I was trying to make a dramatic entrance. I see the big windows and you're awake reading. I figure it's worth a shot. I'll climb up and enter with a little—you know . . . *(Snaps fingers)* Meanwhile, I get my heel caught on some vines, the drainpipe breaks, and I'm hanging by a thread. Then my cape begins to tear. Look, let's just go. It's been a rough night.

NAT: You broke my drainpipe?

DEATH: Broke. It didn't break. It's a little bent. Didn't you hear anything? I slammed into the ground.

NAT: I was reading.

DEATH: You must have really been engrossed. *(Lifting newspaper Nat was reading)* "NAB COEDS IN POT ORGY." Can I borrow this?

NAT: I'm not finished.

DEATH: Er—I don't know how to put this to you, pal . . .

NAT: Why didn't you just ring downstairs?

DEATH: I'm telling you, I could have, but how does it look? This way I get a little drama going. Something. Did you read *Faust?*

NAT: What?

DEATH: And what if you had company? You're sitting there with important people. I'm Death—I should ring the bell and traipse right in the front? Where's your thinking?

NAT: Listen, Mister, it's very late.

DEATH: Yeah. Well, you want to go?

NAT: Go where?

DEATH: Death. It. The Thing. The Happy Hunting Grounds. *(Looking at his own knee)* Y'know, that's a pretty bad cut. My first job, I'm liable to get gangrene yet.

NAT: Now, wait a minute. I need time. I'm not ready to go.

DEATH: I'm sorry. I can't help you. I'd like to, but it's the moment.

NAT: How can it be the moment? I just merged with Modiste Originals.

DEATH: What's the difference, a couple of bucks more or less.

NAT: Sure, what do you care? You guys probably have all your expenses paid.

DEATH: You want to come along now?

NAT *(studying him):* I'm sorry, but I cannot believe you're Death.

DEATH: Why? What'd you expect—Rock Hudson?

NAT: No, it's not that.

DEATH: I'm sorry if I disappointed you.

NAT: Don't get upset. I don't know, I always thought you'd be . . . uh . . . taller.

DEATH: I'm five seven. It's average for my weight.

NAT: You look a little like me.

DEATH: Who should I look like? I'm your death.

NAT: Give me some time. Another day.

DEATH: I can't. What do you want me to say?

NAT: One more day. Twenty-four hours.

DEATH: What do you need it for? The radio said rain tomorrow.

NAT: Can't we work out something?

DEATH: Like what?

NAT: You play chess?

DEATH: No, I don't.

NAT: I once saw a picture of you playing chess.

DEATH: Couldn't be me, because I don't play chess. Gin rummy, maybe.

NAT: You play gin rummy?

DEATH: Do I play gin rummy? Is Paris a city?

NAT: You're good, huh?

DEATH: Very good.

NAT: I'll tell you what I'll do—

DEATH: Don't make any deals with me.

NAT: I'll play you gin rummy. If you win, I'll go immediately. If I win, give me some more time. A little bit—one more day.

DEATH: Who's got time to play gin rummy?

NAT: Come on. If you're so good.

DEATH: Although I feel like a game . . .

NAT: Come on. Be a sport. We'll shoot for a half hour.

DEATH: I really shouldn't.

NAT: I got the cards right here. Don't make a production.

DEATH: All right, come on. We'll play a little. It'll relax me.

NAT: (getting cards, pad, and pencil): You won't regret this.

DEATH: Don't give me a sales talk. Get the cards and give me a Fresca and put out something. For God's sake, a stranger drops in, you don't have potato chips or pretzels.

NAT: There's M&M's downstairs in a dish.

DEATH: M&M's. What if the President came? He'd get M&M's, too?

NAT: You're not the President.

DEATH: Deal.

(Nat deals, turns up a five.)

NAT: You want to play a tenth of a cent a point to make it interesting?

DEATH: It's not interesting enough for you?

NAT: I play better when money's at stake.

DEATH: Whatever you say, Newt.

NAT: Nat. Nat Ackerman. You don't know my name?

DEATH: Newt, Nat—I got such a headache.

NAT: You want that five?

DEATH: No.

NAT: So pick.

DEATH (*surveying his hand as he picks*): Jesus, I got nothing here.

NAT: What's it like?

DEATH: What's what like?

(*Throughout the following, they pick and discard.*)

NAT: Death.

DEATH: What should it be like? You lay there.

NAT: Is there anything after?

DEATH: Aha, you're saving twos.

NAT: I'm asking. Is there anything after?

DEATH (*absently*): You'll see.

NAT: Oh, then I will actually see something?

DEATH: Well, maybe I shouldn't have put it that way. Throw.

NAT: To get an answer from you is a big deal.

DEATH: I'm playing cards.

NAT: All right, play, play.

DEATH: Meanwhile, I'm giving you one card after another.

NAT: Don't look through the discards.

DEATH: I'm not looking. I'm straightening them up. What was the knock card?

NAT: Four. You ready to knock already?

DEATH: Who said I'm ready to knock? All I asked was what was the knock card?

NAT: And all I asked was is there anything for me to look forward to.

DEATH: Play.

NAT: Can't you tell me anything? Where do we go?

DEATH: We? To tell you the truth, *you* fall in a crumpled heap on the floor.

NAT: Oh, I can't wait for that! Is it going to hurt?

DEATH: Be over in a second.

NAT: Terrific. *(Sighs)* I needed this. A man merges with Modiste Originals . . .

DEATH: How's four points?

NAT: You're knocking?

DEATH: Four points is good?

NAT: No, I got two.

DEATH: You're kidding.

NAT: No, you lose.

DEATH: Holy Christ, and I thought you were saving sixes.

NAT: No. Your deal. Twenty points and two boxes. Shoot. *(Death deals.)* I must fall on the floor, eh? I can't be standing over the sofa when it happens?

DEATH: No. Play.

NAT: Why not?

DEATH: Because you fall on the floor! Leave me alone. I'm trying to concentrate.

NAT: Why must it be on the floor? That's all I'm saying! Why can't the whole thing happen and I'll stand next to the sofa?

DEATH: I'll try my best. Now can we play?

NAT: That's all I'm saying. You remind me of Moe Lefkowitz. He's also stubborn.

DEATH: I remind him of Moe Lefkowitz. I'm one of the most terrifying figures you could possibly imagine, and him I remind of Moe Lefkowitz. What is he, a furrier?

NAT: You should be such a furrier. He's good for eighty thousand a year. Passementeries. He's got his own factory. Two points.

DEATH: What?

NAT: Two points. I'm knocking. What have you got?

DEATH: My hand is like a basketball score.

NAT: And it's spades.

DEATH: If you didn't talk so much.

(They redeal and play on.)

NAT: What'd you mean before when you said this was your first job?

DEATH: What does it sound like?

NAT: What are you telling me—that nobody ever went before?

DEATH: Sure they went. But I didn't take them.

NAT: So who did?

DEATH: Others.

NAT: There's others?

DEATH: Sure. Each one has his own personal way of going.

NAT: I never knew that.

DEATH: Why should you know? Who are you?

NAT: What do you mean who am I? Why—I'm nothing?

DEATH: Not nothing. You're a dress manufacturer. Where do you come to knowledge of the eternal mysteries?

NAT: What are you talking about? I make a beautiful dollar. I sent two kids through college. One is in advertising, the other's married. I got my own home. I drive a Chrysler. My wife has whatever she wants. Maids, mink coat, vacations. Right now she's at the Eden Roc. Fifty dollars a day because she wants to be near her sister. I'm supposed to join her next week, so what do you think I am—some guy off the street?

DEATH: All right. Don't be so touchy.

NAT: Who's touchy?

DEATH: How would you like it if I got insulted quickly?

NAT: Did I insult you?

DEATH: You didn't say you were disappointed in me?

NAT: What do you expect? You want me to throw you a block party?

DEATH: I'm not talking about that. I mean me personally. I'm too short, I'm this, I'm that.

NAT: I said you looked like me. It's like a reflection.

DEATH: All right, deal, deal.

(They continue to play as music steals in and the lights dim until all is in total darkness. The lights slowly come up again, and now it is later and their game is over. Nat tallies.)

NAT: Sixty-eight . . . one-fifty . . . Well, you lose.

DEATH *(dejectedly looking through the deck):* I knew I shouldn't have thrown that nine. Damn it.

NAT: So I'll see you tomorrow.

DEATH: What do you mean you'll see me tomorrow?

NAT: I won the extra day. Leave me alone.

DEATH: You were serious?

NAT: We made a deal.

DEATH: Yeah, but—

NAT: Don't "but" me. I won twenty-four hours. Come back tomorrow.

DEATH: I didn't know we were actually playing for time.

NAT: That's too bad about you. You should pay attention.

DEATH: Where am I going to go for twenty-four hours?

NAT: What's the difference? The main thing is I won an extra day.

DEATH: What do you want me to do—walk the streets?

NAT: Check into a hotel and go to a movie. Take a *schvitz*. Don't make a federal case.

DEATH: Add the score again.

NAT: Plus you owe me twenty-eight dollars.

DEATH: *What?*

NAT: That's right, Buster. Here it is—read it.

DEATH *(going through pockets):* I have a few singles—not twenty-eight dollars.

NAT: I'll take a check.

DEATH: From what account?

NAT: Look who I'm dealing with.

DEATH: Sue me. Where do I keep my checking account?

NAT: All right, gimme what you got and we'll call it square.

DEATH: Listen, I need that money.

NAT: Why should you need money?

DEATH: What are you talking about? You're going to the Beyond.

NAT: So?

DEATH: So—you know how far that is?

NAT: So?

DEATH: So where's gas? Where's tolls?

NAT: We're going by car!

DEATH: You'll find out. *(Agitatedly)* Look—I'll be back tomorrow, and you'll give me a chance to win the money back. Otherwise I'm in definite trouble.

NAT: Anything you want. Double or nothing we'll play. I'm liable to win an extra week or a month. The way you play, maybe years.

DEATH: Meantime I'm stranded.

NAT: See you tomorrow.

DEATH *(being edged to the doorway):* Where's a good hotel? What am I talking about hotel, I got no money. I'll go sit in Bickford's. *(He picks up the* News.*)*

NAT: Out. Out. That's my paper. *(He takes it back.)*

DEATH *(exiting):* I couldn't just take him and go. I had to get involved in rummy.

NAT *(calling after him):* And be careful going downstairs. On one of the steps the rug is loose.

(And, on cue, we hear a terrific crash. Nat sighs, then crosses to the bedside table and makes a phone call.)

NAT: Hello, Moe? Me. Listen, I don't know if somebody's playing a joke, or what, but Death was just here. We played a little gin . . . No, *Death.* In person. Or somebody who claims to be Death. But, Moe, he's such a *schlep!*

CURTAIN

Spring Bulletin

THE number of college bulletins and adult-education come-ons that keep turning up in my mailbox convinces me that I must be on a special mailing list for dropouts. Not that I'm complaining; there is something about a list of extension courses that piques my interest with a fascination hitherto reserved for a catalogue of Hong Kong honeymoon accessories, sent to me once by mistake. Each time I read through the latest bulletin of extension courses, I make immediate plans to drop everything and return to school. (I was ejected from college many years ago, the victim of unproved accusations not unlike those once attached to Yellow Kid Weil.) So far, however, I am still an uneducated, unextended adult, and I have fallen into the habit of browsing through an imaginary, handsomely printed course bulletin that is more or less typical of them all:

Summer Session

ECONOMIC THEORY: A systematic application and critical evaluation of the basic analytic concepts of economic theory, with an emphasis on money and why it's good. Fixed coefficient production functions, cost and supply curves, and nonconvexity comprise the first semester, with the second semester concentrating on spending, making change, and keeping a neat wallet. The Federal Reserve System is analyzed, and advanced students are coached in the proper method of filling out a deposit slip. Other topics include: Inflation and Depression—how to dress for each. Loans, interest, welching.

HISTORY OF EUROPEAN CIVILIZATION: Ever since the discovery of a fossilized eohippus in the men's washroom at Siddon's Cafeteria in East Rutherford, New Jersey, it has been suspected that at one time Europe and America were connected by a strip of land that later sank or became East Rutherford, New Jersey, or both. This throws a new perspective on the formation of European society and enables historians to conjecture about why it sprang up in an area that would have made a much better Asia. Also studied in the course is the decision to hold the Renaissance in Italy.

INTRODUCTION TO PSYCHOLOGY: The theory of human behavior. Why some men are called "lovely individuals" and why there are others you just want to pinch. Is there a split between mind and body, and, if so, which is better to have? Aggression and rebellion are discussed. (Students particularly interested in these aspects of psychology are advised to take one of these Winter Term courses: Introduction to Hostility; Intermediate Hostility; Advanced

Hatred; Theoretical Foundations of Loathing.) Special consideration is given to a study of consciousness as opposed to unconsciousness, with many helpful hints on how to remain conscious.

PSYCHOPATHOLOGY: Aimed at understanding obsessions and phobias, including the fear of being suddenly captured and stuffed with crabmeat, reluctance to return a volleyball serve, and the inability to say the word "mackinaw" in the presence of women. The compulsion to seek out the company of beavers is analyzed.

PHILOSOPHY I: Everyone from Plato to Camus is read, and the following topics are covered:

Ethics: The categorical imperative, and six ways to make it work for you.

Aesthetics: Is art the mirror of life, or what?

Metaphysics: What happens to the soul after death? How does it manage?

Epistemology: Is knowledge knowable? If not, how do we know this?

The Absurd: Why existence is often considered silly, particularly for men who wear brown-and-white shoes. Manyness and oneness are studied as they relate to otherness. (Students achieving oneness will move ahead to twoness.)

PHILOSOPHY XXIX-B: Introduction to God. Confrontation with the Creator of the universe through informal lectures and field trips.

THE NEW MATHEMATICS: Standard mathematics has recently been rendered obsolete by the discovery that for years we have been writing the numeral five backward. This has led to a reevaluation of counting as a method of getting from one to ten. Students are taught advanced concepts of Boolean Algebra, and formerly unsolvable equations are dealt with by threats of reprisals.

FUNDAMENTAL ASTRONOMY: A detailed study of the universe and its care and cleaning. The sun, which is made of gas, can explode at any moment, sending our entire planetary system hurtling to destruction; students are advised what the average citizen can do in such a case. They are also taught to identify various constellations, such as the Big Dipper, Cygnus the Swan, Sagittarius the Archer, and the twelve stars that form Lumides the Pants Salesman.

MODERN BIOLOGY: How the body functions, and where it can usually be found. Blood is analyzed, and it is learned why it is the best possible thing to have coursing through one's veins. A frog is dissected by students and its digestive tract is compared with man's, with the frog giving a good account of itself except on curries.

RAPID READING: This course will increase reading speed a little each day until the end of the term, by which time the student will be required to read *The Brothers Karamazov* in fifteen minutes. The method is to scan the page and eliminate everything except pronouns from one's field of vision. Soon the pronouns are eliminated. Gradually the student is encouraged to nap. A frog is dissected. Spring comes. People marry and die. Pinkerton does not return.

MUSICOLOGY III: The Recorder. The student is taught how to play "Yankee Doodle" on this end-blown wooden flute, and progresses rapidly to the Brandenburg Concertos. Then slowly back to "Yankee Doodle."

MUSIC APPRECIATION: In order to "hear" a great piece of music correctly, one must: (1) know the birthplace of the composer, (2) be able to tell a rondo from a scherzo, and back it up with action. Attitude is important. Smiling is bad form unless the composer has intended the music to be funny, as in *Till Eulenspiegel*, which abounds in musical jokes (although the trombone has the best lines.) The ear, too, must be trained, for it is our most easily deceived organ and can be made to think it is a nose by bad placement of stereo speakers. Other topics include: The four-bar rest and its potential as a political weapon. The Gregorian Chant: Which monks kept the beat.

WRITING FOR THE STAGE: All drama is conflict. Character development is also very important. Also what they say. Students learn that long, dull speeches are not so effective, while short, "funny" ones seem to go over well. Simplified audience psychology is explored: Why is a play about a lovable old character named Gramps often not as interesting in the theatre as staring at the back of someone's head and trying to make him turn around? Interesting aspects of stage history are also examined. For example, before the invention of italics, stage directions were often mistaken for dialogue, and great actors frequently found themselves saying, "John rises, crosses left." This naturally led to embarrassment and, on some occasions, dreadful notices. The phenomenon is analyzed in detail, and students are guided in avoiding mistakes. Required text: A. F. Shulte's *Shakespeare: Was He Four Women?*

INTRODUCTION TO SOCIAL WORK: A course designed to instruct the social worker who is interested in going out "in the field." Topics covered include: how to organize street gangs into basketball teams, and vice versa; playgrounds as a means of preventing juvenile crime, and how to get potentially homicidal cases to try the sliding pond; discrimination; the broken home; what to do if you are hit with a bicycle chain.

YEATS AND HYGIENE, A COMPARATIVE STUDY: The poetry of William Butler Yeats is analyzed against a background of proper dental care. (Course open to a limited number of students.)

Hassidic Tales, with a Guide to Their Interpretation by the Noted Scholar

A MAN journeyed to Chelm in order to seek the advice of Rabbi Ben Kaddish, the holiest of all ninth-century rabbis and perhaps the greatest *noodge* of the medieval era.

"Rabbi," the man asked, "where can I find peace?"

The Hassid surveyed him and said, "Quick, look behind you!"

The man turned around, and Rabbi Ben Kaddish smashed him in the back of the head with a candlestick. "Is that peaceful enough for you?" he chuckled, adjusting his *yarmulke*.

In this tale, a meaningless question is asked. Not only is the question meaningless but so is the man who journeys to Chelm to ask it. Not that he was so far away from Chelm to begin with, but why shouldn't he stay where he is? Why is he bothering Rabbi Ben Kaddish—the Rabbi doesn't have enough trouble? The truth is, the Rabbi's in over his head with gamblers, and he has also been named in a paternity case by a Mrs. Hecht. No, the point of this tale is that this man has nothing better to do with his time than journey around and get on people's nerves. For this, the Rabbi bashes his head in, which, according to the Torah, is one of the most subtle methods of showing concern. In a similar version of this tale, the Rabbi leaps on top of the man in a frenzy and carves the story of Ruth on his nose with a stylus.

• • • • •

Rabbi Raditz of Poland was a very short rabbi with a long beard, who was said to have inspired many pogroms with his sense of humor. One of his disciples asked, "Who did God like better—Moses or Abraham?"

"Abraham," the Zaddik said.

"But Moses led the Israelites to the Promised Land," said the disciple.

"All right, so Moses," the Zaddik answered.

"I understand, Rabbi. It was a stupid question."

"Not only that, but you're stupid, your wife's a *meeskeit,* and if you don't get off my foot you're excommunicated."

Here the Rabbi is asked to make a value judgment between Moses and Abraham. This is not an easy matter, particularly for a man who has never read the Bible and has been faking it. And what is meant by the hopelessly relative term "better"? What is "better" to the Rabbi is not necessarily "better" to his disciple. For instance, the Rabbi likes to sleep on his stomach. The disciple also likes to sleep on the Rabbi's stomach. The problem here is obvious. It should also be noted that to step on a rabbi's foot (as the disciple does in the tale) is a sin, according to the Torah, comparable to the fondling of matzos with any intent other than eating them.

• • • • •

A man who could not marry off his ugly daughter visited Rabbi Shimmel of Cracow. "My heart is heavy," he told the Rev, "because God has given me an ugly daughter."

"How ugly?" the Seer asked.

"If she were lying on a plate with a herring, you wouldn't be able to tell the difference."

The Seer of Cracow thought for a long time and finally asked, "What kind of herring?"

The man, taken aback by the query, thought quickly and said, "Er—Bismarck."

"Too bad," the Rabbi said. "If it was Maatjes, she'd have a better chance."

Here is a tale that illustrates the tragedy of transient qualities such as beauty. Does the girl actually resemble a herring? Why not? Have you seen some of the things walking around these days, particularly at resort areas? And even if she does, are not all creatures beautiful in God's eyes? Perhaps, but if a girl looks more at home in a jar of wine sauce than in an evening gown she's got big problems. Oddly enough, Rabbi Shimmel's own wife was said to resemble a squid, but this was only in the face, and she more than made up for it by her hacking cough—the point of which escapes me.

• • • • •

Rabbi Zwi Chaim Yisroel, an Orthodox scholar of the Torah and a man who developed whining to an art unheard of in the West, was unanimously hailed as the wisest man of the Renaissance by his fellow-Hebrews, who totalled a sixteenth of one per cent of the population. Once, while he was on his way to synagogue to celebrate the sacred Jewish holiday commemorating God's reneging on every promise, a woman stopped him and asking the following question: "Rabbi, why are we not allowed to eat

pork?"

"We're *not?*" the Rev said incredulously. "Uh-oh."

This is one of the few stories in all Hassidic literature that deals with Hebrew law. The Rabbi knows he shouldn't eat pork; he doesn't care, though, because he *likes* pork. Not only does he like pork; he gets a kick out of rolling Easter eggs. In short, he cares very little about traditional Orthodoxy and regards God's covenant with Abraham as "just so much chin music." Why pork was proscribed by Hebraic law is still unclear, and some scholars believe that the Torah merely suggested not eating pork at certain restaurants.

•••••

Rabbi Baumel, the scholar of Vitebsk, decided to embark on a fast to protest the unfair law prohibiting Russian Jews from wearing loafers outside the ghetto. For sixteen weeks, the holy man lay on a crude pallet, staring at the ceiling and refusing nourishment of any kind. His pupils feared for his life, and then one day a woman came to his bedside and, leaning down to the learned scholar, asked, "Rabbi, what color hair did Esther have?" The Rev turned weakly on his side and faced her. "Look what she picks to ask me!" he said. "You know what kind of a headache I got from sixteen weeks without a bite!" With that, the Rabbi's disciples escorted her personally into the *sukkah*, where she ate bounteously from the horn of plenty until she got the tab.

This is a subtle treatment of the problem of pride and vanity, and seems to imply that fasting is a big mistake. Particularly on an empty stomach. Man does not bring on his own unhappiness, and suffering is really God's will, although why He gets such a kick out of it is beyond me. Certain Orthodox tribes believe suffering is the only way to redeem oneself, and scholars write of a cult called the Essenes, who deliberately went around bumping into walls. God, according to the later books of Moses, is benevolent, although there are still a great many subjects he'd rather not go into.

• • • • •

Rabbi Yekel of Zans, who had the best diction in the world until a Gentile stole his resonant underwear, dreamed three nights running that if he would only journey to Vorki he would find a great treasure there. Bidding his wife and children goodbye, he set out on a trip, saying he would return in ten days. Two years later, he was found wandering the Urals and emotionally involved with a panda. Cold and starving, the Rev was taken back to his home, where he was revived with steaming soup and flanken. Following that, he was given something to eat. After dinner, he told this story: Three days out of Zans, he was set upon by wild nomads. When they learned he was a Jew, they forced him to alter all their sports jackets and take in their trousers. As if this were not humiliation enough, they put sour cream in his ears and sealed them with wax. Finally, the Rabbi escaped and headed for the nearest town, winding up in the Urals instead, because he was ashamed to ask directions.

After telling the story, the Rabbi rose and went into his bedroom to sleep, and, behold, under his pillow was the treasure that he originally sought. Ecstatic, he got down and thanked God. Three days later, he was back wandering in the Urals again, this time in a rabbit suit.

The above small masterpiece amply illustrates the absurdity of mysticism. The Rabbi dreams *three* straight nights. The Five Books of Moses subtracted from the Ten Commandments leaves five. Minus the brothers Jacob and

Esau leaves *three*. It was reasoning like this that led Rabbi Yitzhok Ben Levi, the great Jewish mystic, to hit the double at Aqueduct fifty-two days running and still wind up on relief.

The Gossage—Vardebedian Papers

My Dear Vardebedian:

I was more than a bit chagrined today, on going through the morning's mail, to find that my letter of September 16, containing my twenty-second move (knight to the king's fourth square), was returned unopened due to a small error in addressing—precisely, the omission of your name and residence (how Freudian can one get?), coupled with a failure to append postage. That I have been disconcerted of late due to equivocation in the stock market is no secret, and though on the above-mentioned September 16 the culmination of a long-standing downward spiral dropped Amalgamated Anti-Matter off the Big Board once and for all, reducing my broker suddenly to the legume family, I do not offer this as an excuse for my negligence and monumental ineptitude. I goofed. Forgive me. That you failed to notice the missing letter indicates a certain disconcertion on your part, which I put down to zeal, but

215

heaven knows we all make mistakes. That's life—and chess.

Well, then, the error laid bare, simple rectification follows. If you would be so good as to transfer my knight to your king's fourth square I think we may proceed with our little game more accurately. The announcement of checkmate which you made in this morning's mail is, I fear, in all fairness, a false alarm, and if you will reexamine the positions in light of today's discovery, you will find that it is *your* king that lies close to mate, exposed and undefended, an immobile target for my predatory bishops. Ironic, the vicissitudes of miniature war! Fate, in the guise of the dead-letter office, waxes omnipotent and—*voilà!*—the worm turns. Once again, I beg you accept sincerest apologies for the unfortunate carelessness, and I await anxiously your next move.

Enclosed is my forty-fifth move: My knight captures your queen.

Sincerely,
Gossage

Gossage:

Received the letter this morning containing your forty-fifth move (your knight captures my queen?), and also your lengthy explanation regarding the mid-September ellipsis in our correspondence. Let me see if I understand you correctly. Your knight, which I removed from the board weeks ago, you now claim should be resting on the king's fourth square, owing to a letter lost in the mail twenty-three moves ago. I was not aware that any such mishap had occurred, and remember distinctly your making a twenty-second move, which I think was your rook to the queen's sixth square, where it was subsequently butchered in a gambit of yours that misfired tragically.

Currently, the king's fourth square is occupied by *my* rook, and as you are knightless, the dead-letter office notwithstanding, I cannot quite understand what piece you are using to capture my queen with. What I think you mean, as most of your pieces are blockaded, is that you request your king be moved to my bishop's fourth square (your only possibility)—an adjustment I have taken the liberty of making and then countering with today's move, my forty-sixth, wherein I capture your queen and put your king in check. Now your letter becomes clearer.

I think now the last remaining moves of the game can be played out with smoothness and alacrity.

Faithfully,
Vardebedian

Vardebedian:

I have just finished perusing your latest note, the one containing a bizarre forty-sixth move dealing with the removal of my queen from a square on which it has not rested for eleven days. Through patient calculation, I think I have hit upon the cause of your confusion and misunderstanding of the existing facts. That your rook rests on the king's fourth square is an impossibility commensurate with two like snowflakes; if you will refer back to the ninth move of the game, you will see clearly that your rook has long been captured. Indeed, it was that same daring sacrificial combination that ripped your center and cost you *both* your rooks. What are they doing on the board now?

I offer for your consideration that what happened is as follows: The intensity of foray and whirlwind exchanges on and about the twenty-second move left you in a state of slight dissociation, and in your anxiety to hold your own at that point you failed to notice that my usual letter was not forthcoming but instead moved your own pieces twice, giving you a somewhat unfair advantage, wouldn't you say? This is over and done with, and to retrace our steps tediously would be difficult, if not impossible. Therefore, I feel the best way to rectify this entire matter is to allow me the opportunity of two consecutive moves at this time. Fair is fair.

First, then, I take your bishop with my pawn. Then, as this leaves your queen unprotected, I capture her also. I think we can now proceed with the last stages unhampered.

Sincerely,
Gossage

P.S.: I am enclosing a diagram showing exactly how the board looks, for your edification in your closing play. As you can see, your king is trapped, unguarded and alone in the center. Best to you.

G.

Gossage:

Received your latest letter today, and while it was just shy of coherence, I think I can see where your bewilderment lies. From your enclosed diagram, it has become apparent to me that for the past six weeks we have been playing two completely different chess games—myself according to our correspondence, you more in keeping with the world as you would have it, rather than with any rational system of order. The knight move which allegedly got lost in the mail would have been impossible on the twenty-second move, as the piece was then standing on the edge of the last file, and the move you describe would have brought it to rest on the coffee table, next to the board.

As for granting you two consecutive moves to make up for one allegedly lost in the mail—surely you jest, Pops. I will honor your first move (you may take my bishop), but I cannot allow the second, and as it is now my turn, I retaliate by removing your queen with my rook. The fact that you tell me I have no rooks means little in actuality, as I

need only glance downward at the board to see them darting about with cunning and vigor.

Finally, that diagram of what you fantasize the board
to look like indicates a freewheeling, Marx Brothers approach to the game, and, while amusing, this hardly
speaks well for your assimilation of *Nimzowitsch on Chess*,
which you hustled from the library under your alpaca
sweater last winter, because I saw you. I suggest you study
the diagram I enclose and rearrange your board accord-
ingly, that we might finish up with some degree of preci-
sion.

Hopefully,
Vardebedian

Vardebedian:

Not wanting to protract an already disoriented business (I know your recent illness has left your usually hardy
constitution somewhat fragmented and disorganized,
causing a mild breach with the real world as we know it), I
must take this opportunity to undo our sordid tangle of
circumstances before it progresses irrevocably to a
Kafkaesque conclusion.

Had I realized you were not gentleman enough to
allow me an equalizing second move, I would not, on my
forty-sixth move, have permitted my pawn to capture your
bishop. According to your own diagram, in fact, these two
pieces were so placed as to render that impossible, bound
as we are to rules established by the World Chess Federa-
tion and not the New York State Boxing Commission.
Without doubting that your intent was constructive in
removing my queen, I interject that only disaster can ensue
when you arrogate to yourself this arbitrary power of decision and begin to play dictator, masking tactical blunders
with duplicity and aggression—a habit you decried in our
world leaders several months ago in your paper on "De
Sade and Non-Violence."

Unfortunately, the game having gone on non-stop, I have not been able to calculate exactly on which square you ought to replace the purloined knight, and I suggest we leave it to the gods by having me close my eyes and toss it back on the board, agreeing to accept whatever spot it may land on. It should add an element of spice to our little encounter. My forty-seventh move: My rook captures your knight.

> Sincerely,
> Gossage

Gossage:

How curious your last letter was! Well-intended, concise, containing all the elements that would appear to make up what passes among certain reference groups as a communicative effect, yet tinged throughout by what Jean-Paul Sartre is so fond of referring to as "nothingness." One is immediately struck by a profound sense of despair, and reminded vividly of the diaries sometimes left by doomed explorers lost at the Pole, or the letters of German soldiers at Stalingrad. Fascinating how the senses disintegrate when faced with an occasional black truth, and scamper amuck, substantiating mirage and constructing a precarious buffer against the onslaught of all too terrifying existence!

Be that as it may, my friend, I have just spent the better part of a week sorting out the miasma of lunatic alibis known as your correspondence in an effort to adjust matters, that our game may be finished simply once and for all. Your queen is gone. Kiss it off. So are both your rooks. Forget about one bishop altogether, because I took it. The other is so impotently placed away from the main action of the game that don't count on it or it'll break your heart.

As regards the knight you lost squarely but refuse to give up, I have replaced it at the only conceivable position it could appear, thus granting you the most incredible brace of unorthodoxies since the Persians whipped up this little diversion way back when. It lies at my bishop's seventh square, and if you can pull your ebbing faculties together long enough to appraise the board you will notice this same coveted piece now blocks your king's only means of escape from my suffocating pincer. How fitting that your greedy plot be turned to my advantage! The knight, grovelling its way back into play, torpedoes your end game!

My move is queen to knight five, and I predict mate in one move.

Cordially,
Vardebedian

Vardebedian:

Obviously the constant tension incurred defending a series of numbingly hopeless chess positions has rendered the delicate machinery of your psychic apparatus sluggish, leaving its grasp of external phenomena a jot flimsy. You give me no alternative but to end the contest swiftly and mercifully, removing the pressure before it leaves you permanently damaged.

Knight—yes, knight!—to queen six. Check.

Gossage

Gossage:

Bishop to queen five. Checkmate.

Sorry the competition proved too much for you, but if it's any consolation, several local chess masters have, upon observing my technique, flipped out. Should you want a rematch, I suggest we try Scrabble, a relatively new interest of mine, and one that I might conceivably not run away with so easily.

Vardebedian

Vardebedian:

Rook to knight eight. Checkmate.

Rather than torment you with the further details of my mate, as I believe you are basically a decent man (one day, some form of therapy will bear me out), I accept your invitation to Scrabble in good spirits. Get out your set. Since you played white in chess and thereby enjoyed the advantage of the first move (had I known your limitations, I would have spotted you more), I shall make the first play. The seven letters I have just turned up are O, A, E, J, N, R, and Z—an unpromising jumble that should guarantee, even to the most suspicious, the integrity of my draw. Fortunately, however, an extensive vocabulary, coupled with a penchant for esoterica, has enabled me to bring etymological order out of what, to one less literate, might seem a mishmash. My first word is "ZANJERO." Look it up. Now lay it out, horizontally, the E resting on the center square. Count carefully, not overlooking the double word score for an opening move and the fifty-point bonus for my use of all seven letters. The score is now 116–0.

Your move.

Gossage

Notes from the Overfed

(After reading Dostoevski and the new "Weight Watchers" magazine on the same plane trip)

I AM FAT. I am disgustingly fat. I am the fattest human I know. I have nothing but excess poundage all over my body. My fingers are fat. My wrists are fat. My eyes are fat. (Can you imagine fat eyes?) I am hundreds of pounds overweight. Flesh drips from me like hot fudge off a sundae. My girth has been an object of disbelief to everyone who's seen me. There is no question about it, I'm a regular fatty. Now, the reader may ask, are there advantages or disadvantages to being built like a planet? I do not mean to be facetious or speak in paradoxes, but I must answer that fat in itself is above bourgeois morality. It is simply fat. That fat could have a value of its own, that fat could be, say, evil or pitying, is, of course, a joke. Absurd! For what is fat after all but an accumulation of pounds? And what are pounds? Simply an aggregate composite of cells. Can a cell be moral? Is a cell beyond good or evil? Who knows—they're so small. No, my friend, we must never attempt to distinguish between good fat and bad fat.

We must train ourselves to confront the obese without judging, without thinking this man's fat is first-rate fat and this poor wretch's is grubby fat.

Take the case of K. This fellow was porcine to such a degree that he could not fit through the average doorframe without the aid of a crowbar. Indeed, K. would not think to pass from room to room in a conventional dwelling without first stripping completely and then buttering himself. I am no stranger to the insults K. must have borne from passing gangs of young rowdies. How frequently he must have been stung by cries of "Tubby!" and "Blimp!" How it must have hurt when the governor of the province turned to him on the Eve of Michaelmas and said, before many dignitaries, "You hulking pot of *kasha!*"

Then one day, when K. could stand it no longer, he dieted. Yes, dieted! First sweets went. Then bread, alcohol, starches, sauces. In short, K. gave up the very stuff that makes a man unable to tie his shoelaces without help from the Santini Brothers. Gradually he began to slim down. Rolls of flesh fell from his arms and legs. Where once he looked roly-poly, he suddenly appeared in public with a normal build. Yes, even an attractive build. He seemed the happiest of men. I say "seemed," for eighteen years later, when he was near death and fever raged throughout his slender frame, he was heard to cry out, "My fat! Bring me my fat! Oh, please! I must have my fat! Oh, somebody lay some avoirdupois on me! What a fool I've been. To part with one's fat! I must have been in league with the Devil!" I think that the point of the story is obvious.

Now the reader is probably thinking, Why, then, if you are Lard City, have you not joined a circus? Because—and I confess this with no small embarrassment—I cannot leave the house. I cannot go out because I cannot get my pants on. My legs are too thick to dress. They are the living result of more corned beef than there is on Second Avenue —I would say about twelve thousand sandwiches per leg.

And not all lean, even though I specified. One thing is certain: If my fat could speak, it would probably speak of man's intense loneliness—with, oh, perhaps a few additional pointers on how to make a sailboat out of paper. Every pound on my body wants to be heard from, as do Chins Four through Twelve inclusive. My fat is strange fat. It has seen much. My calves alone have lived a lifetime. Mine is not happy fat, but it is real fat. It is not fake fat. Fake fat is the worst fat you can have, although I don't know if the stores still carry it.

But let me tell you how it was that I became fat. For I was not always fat. It is the Church that has made me thus. At one time I was thin—quite thin. So thin, in fact, that to call me fat would have been an error in perception. I remained thin until one day—I think it was my twentieth birthday—when I was having tea and cracknels with my uncle at a fine restaurant. Suddenly my uncle put a question to me. "Do you believe in God?" he asked. "And if so, what do you think He weighs?" So saying, he took a long and luxurious draw on his cigar and, in that confident, assured manner he has cultivated, lapsed into a coughing fit so violent I thought he would hemorrhage.

"I do not believe in God," I told him. "For if there is a God, then tell me, Uncle, why is there poverty and baldness? Why do some men go through life immune to a thousand mortal enemies of the race, while others get a migraine that lasts for weeks? Why are our days numbered and not, say, lettered? Answer me, Uncle. Or have I shocked you?"

I knew I was safe in saying this, because nothing ever shocked the man. Indeed, he had seen his chess tutor's mother raped by Turks and would have found the whole incident amusing had it not taken so much time.

"Good nephew," he said, "there is a God, despite what you think, and He is everywhere. Yes! Everywhere!"

"Everywhere, Uncle? How can you say that when you

don't even know for sure if we exist? True, I am touching your wart at this moment, but could that not be an illusion? Could not all life be an illusion? Indeed, are there not certain sects of holy men in the East who are convinced that *nothing* exists outside their minds except for the Oyster Bar at Grand Central Station? Could it not be simply that we are alone and aimless, doomed to wander in an indifferent universe, with no hope of salvation, nor any prospect except misery, death, and the empty reality of eternal nothing?''

I could see that I made a deep impression on my uncle with this, for he said to me, "You wonder why you're not invited to more parties! Jesus, you're morbid!" He accused me of being nihilistic and then said, in that cryptic way the senile have, "God is not always where one seeks Him, but I assure you, dear nephew, He is everywhere. In these cracknels, for instance." With that, he departed, leaving me his blessing and a check that read like the tab for an aircraft carrier.

I returned home wondering what it was he meant by that one simple statement "He is everywhere. In these cracknels, for instance." Drowsy by then, and out of sorts, I lay down on my bed and took a brief nap. In that time, I had a dream that was to change my life forever. In the dream, I am strolling in the country, when I suddenly notice I am hungry. Starved, if you will. I come upon a restaurant and I enter. I order the open-hot-roast-beef sandwich and a side of French. The waitress, who resembles my landlady (a thoroughly insipid woman who reminds one instantly of some of the hairier lichens), tries to tempt me into ordering the chicken salad, which doesn't look fresh. As I am conversing with this woman, she turns into a twenty-four-piece starter set of silverware. I become hysterical with laughter, which suddenly turns to tears and then into a serious ear infection. The room is suffused with a radiant glow, and I see a shimmering figure ap-

proach on a white steed. It is my podiatrist, and I fall to the
ground with guilt.

Such was my dream. I awoke with a tremendous sense
of well-being. Suddenly I was optimistic. Everything was
clear. My uncle's statement reverberated to the core of my
very existence. I went to the kitchen and started to eat. I ate
everything in sight. Cakes, breads, cereals, meat, fruits.
Succulent chocolates, vegetables in sauce, wines, fish,
creams and noodles, éclairs, and wursts totalling in excess
of sixty thousand dollars. If God is everywhere, I had con-
cluded, then He is in food. Therefore, the more I ate the
godlier I would become. Impelled by this new religious
fervor, I glutted myself like a fanatic. In six months, I was
the holiest of holies, with a heart entirely devoted to my
prayers and a stomach that crossed the state line by itself. I
last saw my feet one Thursday morning in Vitebsk,
although for all I know they are still down there. I ate and
ate and grew and grew. To reduce would have been the
greatest folly. Even a sin! For when we lose twenty
pounds, dear reader (and I am assuming you are not as
large as I), we may be losing the twenty best pounds we
have! We may be losing the pounds that contain our
genius, our humanity, our love and honesty or, in the case
of one inspector general I knew, put some unsightly flab
around the hips.

Now, I know what you are saying. You are saying this
is in direct contradiction to everything—yes, everything—I
put forth before. Suddenly I am attributing to neuter flesh,
values! Yes, and what of it? Because isn't life that very
same kind of contradiction? One's opinion of fat can
change in the same manner that the seasons change, that
our hair changes, that life itself changes. For life is change
and fat is life, and fat is also death. Don't you see? Fat is
everything! Unless, of course, you're overweight.

A Twenties Memory

I FIRST came to Chicago in the twenties, and that was to see a fight. Ernest Hemingway was with me and we both stayed at Jack Dempsey's training camp. Hemingway had just finished two short stories about prize fighting, and while Gertrude Stein and I both thought they were decent, we agreed they still needed much work. I kidded Hemingway about his forthcoming novel and we laughed a lot and had fun and then we put on some boxing gloves and he broke my nose.

That winter, Alice Toklas, Picasso, and myself took a villa in the south of France. I was then working on what I felt was a major American novel but the print was too small and I couldn't get through it.

In the afternoons, Gertrude Stein and I used to go antique hunting in the local shops, and I remember once asking her if she thought I should become a writer. In the typically cryptic way we were all so enchanted with, she said, "No." I took that to mean yes and sailed for Italy the next day. Italy reminded me a great deal of Chicago, particularly Venice, because both cities have canals and the streets abound with statues and cathedrals by the greatest sculptors of the Renaissance.

That month we went to Picasso's studio in Arles, which was then called Rouen or Zurich, until the French renamed it in 1589 under Louis the Vague. (Louis was a sixteenth-century bastard king who was just mean to everybody.) Picasso was then beginning on what was later to be known as his "blue period," but Gertrude Stein and I had coffee with him, and so he began it ten minutes later. It lasted four years, so the ten minutes did not really mean much.

Picasso was a short man who had a funny way of walking by putting one foot in front of the other until he would take what he called "steps." We laughed at his delightful notions, but toward the late 1930s, with fascism on the rise, there was very little to laugh about. Both Gertrude Stein and I examined Picasso's newest works very carefully, and Gertrude Stein was of the opinion that "art, all art, is merely an expression of something." Picasso disagreed and said, "Leave me alone. I was eating." My own feelings were that Picasso was right. He had been eating.

Picasso's studio was so unlike Matisse's, in that, while Picasso's was sloppy, Matisse kept everything in perfect order. Oddly enough, just the reverse was true. In September of that year, Matisse was commissioned to paint an allegory, but with his wife's illness, it remained unpainted and was finally wallpapered instead. I recall these events so perfectly because it was just before the winter that we all lived in that cheap flat in the north of Switzerland where it will occasionally rain and then just as suddenly stop. Juan Gris, the Spanish cubist, had convinced Alice Toklas to pose for a still life and, with his typical abstract conception of objects, began to break her face and body down to its basic geometrical forms until the police came and pulled him off. Gris was provincially Spanish, and Gertrude Stein used to say that only a true Spaniard could behave as he did; that is, he would speak Spanish and sometimes return to his family in Spain. It was really quite marvellous to see.

I remember one afternoon we were sitting at a gay bar in the south of France with our feet comfortably up on stools in the north of France, when Gertrude Stein said, "I'm nauseous." Picasso thought this to be very funny and Matisse and I took it as a cue to leave for Africa. Seven weeks later, in Kenya, we came upon Hemingway. Bronzed and bearded now, he was already beginning to develop that familiar flat prose style about the eyes and mouth. Here, in the unexplored dark continent, Hemingway had braved chapped lips a thousand times.

"What's doing, Ernest?" I asked him. He waxed eloquent on death and adventure as only he could, and when I awoke he had pitched camp and sat around a great fire fixing us all fine derma appetizers. I kidded him about his new beard and we laughed and sipped cognac and then we put on some boxing gloves and he broke my nose.

That year I went to Paris a second time to talk with a thin, nervous European composer with aquiline profile and remarkably quick eyes who would someday be Igor Stravinsky and then, later, his best friend. I stayed at the home of Man and Sting Ray and Salvador Dali joined us for dinner several times and Dali decided to have a one-man show which he did and it was a huge success, as one man showed up and it was a gay and fine French winter.

I remember one night Scott Fitzgerald and his wife returned home from their New Year's Eve party. It was April. They had consumed nothing but champagne for the past three months, and one previous week, in full evening dress, had driven their limousine off a ninety-foot cliff into the ocean on a dare. There was something real about the Fitzgeralds; their values were basic. They were such modest people, and when Grant Wood later convinced them to pose for his "American Gothic" I remember how flattered they were. All through their sittings, Zelda told me, Scott kept dropping the pitchfork.

I became increasingly friendly with Scott in the next few years, and most of our friends believed that he based the protagonist of his latest novel on me and that I had based my life on his previous novel and I finally wound up getting sued by a fictional character.

Scott was having a big discipline problem and, while we all adored Zelda, we agreed that she had an adverse affect on his work, reducing his output from one novel a year to an occasional seafood recipe and a series of commas.

Finally, in 1929, we all went to Spain together, where Hemingway introduced us to Manolete who was sensitive almost to the point of being effeminate. He wore tight toreador pants or sometimes pedal pushers. Manolete was a great, great artist. Had he not become a bullfighter, his grace was such that he could have been a world-famous accountant.

We had great fun in Spain that year and we travelled and wrote and Hemingway took me tuna fishing and I caught four cans and we laughed and Alice Toklas asked me if I was in love with Gertrude Stein because I had dedicated a book of poems to her even though they were T. S. Eliot's and I said, yes, I loved her, but it could never work because she was far too intelligent for me and Alice Toklas agreed and then we put on some boxing gloves and Gertrude Stein broke my nose.

Count Dracula

SOMEWHERE in Transylvania, Dracula the monster lies sleeping in his coffin, waiting for night to fall. As exposure to the sun's rays would surely cause him to perish, he stays protected in the satin-lined chamber bearing his family name in silver. Then the moment of darkness comes, and through some miraculous instinct the fiend emerges from the safety of his hiding place and, assuming the hideous forms of the bat or the wolf, he prowls the countryside, drinking the blood of his victims. Finally, before the first rays of his archenemy, the sun, announce a new day, he hurries back to the safety of his hidden coffin and sleeps, as the cycle begins anew.

Now he starts to stir. The fluttering of his eyelids are a response to some age-old, unexplainable instinct that the sun is nearly down and his time is near. Tonight, he is particularly hungry and as he lies there, fully awake now, in red-lined Inverness cape and tails, waiting to feel with uncanny perception the precise moment of darkness before opening the lid and emerging, he decides who this evening's victims will be. The baker and his wife, he thinks to himself. Succulent, available, and unsuspecting. The thought of the unwary couple whose trust he has carefully cultivated excites his blood lust to a fever pitch, and he can barely hold back these last seconds before climbing out of the coffin to seek his prey.

Suddenly he knows the sun is down. Like an angel of hell, he rises swiftly, and changing into a bat, flies pell-mell to the cottage of his tantalizing victims.

"Why, Count Dracula, what a nice surprise," the baker's wife says, opening the door to admit him. (He has once again assumed human form, as he enters their home, charmingly concealing his rapacious goal.)

"What brings you here so early?" the baker asks.

"Our dinner date," the Count answers. "I hope I haven't made an error. You did invite me for tonight, didn't you?"

"Yes, tonight, but that's not for seven hours."

"Pardon me?" Dracula queries, looking around the room puzzled.

"Or did you come by to watch the eclipse with us?"

"Eclipse?"

"Yes. Today's the total eclipse."

"What?"

"A few moments of darkness from noon until two minutes after. Look out the window."

"Uh-oh—I'm in big trouble."

"Eh?"

"And now if you'll excuse me . . ."

"What, Count Dracula?"

"Must be going—aha—oh, god . . ." Frantically he fumbles for the door knob.

"Going? You just came."

"Yes—but—I think I blew it very badly . . ."

"Count Dracula, you're pale."

"Am I? I need a little fresh air. It was nice seeing you . . ."

"Come. Sit down. We'll have a drink."

"Drink? No, I must run. Er—you're stepping on my cape."

"Sure. Relax. Some wine."

"Wine? Oh no, gave it up—liver and all that, you know. And now I really must buzz off. I just remembered, I left the lights on at my castle—bills'll be enormous . . ."

"Please," the baker says, his arm around the Count in firm friendship. "You're not intruding. Don't be so polite. So you're early."

"Really, I'd like to stay but there's a meeting of old Roumanian Counts across town and I'm responsible for the cold cuts."

"Rush, rush, rush. It's a wonder you don't get a heart attack."

"Yes, right—and now—"

"I'm making Chicken Pilaf tonight," the baker's wife chimes in. "I hope you like it."

"Wonderful, wonderful," the Count says, with a smile, as he pushes her aside into some laundry. Then, opening a closet door by mistake, he walks in. "Christ, where's the goddamn front door?"

"Ach," laughs the baker's wife, "such a funny man, the Count."

"I knew you'd like that," Dracula says, forcing a chuckle, "now get out of my way." At last he opens the front door but time has run out on him.

"Oh, look, Mama," says the baker, "the eclipse must be over. The sun is coming out again."

"Right," says Dracula, slamming the front door. "I've decided to stay. Pull down the window shades quickly— *quickly!* Let's move it!"

"What window shades?" asks the baker.

"There are none, right? Figures. You got a basement in this joint?"

"No," says the wife affably, "I'm always telling Jarslov to build one but he never listens. That's some Jarslov, my husband."

"I'm all choked up. Where's the closet?"

"You did that one already, Count Dracula. Unt Mama and I laughed at it."

"Ach—such a funny man, the Count."

"Look, I'll be in the closet. Knock at seven-thirty." And with that, the Count steps inside the closet and slams the door.

"Hee-hee—he is so funny, Jarslov."

"Oh, Count. Come out of the closet. Stop being a big silly." From inside the closet comes the muffled voice of Dracula.

"Can't—please—take my word for it. Just let me stay here. I'm fine. Really."

"Count Dracula, stop the fooling. We're already helpless with laughter."

"Can I tell you, I love this closet."

"Yes, but . . ."

"I know, I know . . . it seems strange, and yet here I am, having a ball. I was just saying to Mrs. Hess the other day, give me a good closet and I can stand in it for hours. Sweet woman, Mrs. Hess. Fat but sweet . . . Now, why don't you run along and check back with me at sunset. Oh, Ramona, la da da de da da de, Ramona . . ."

Now the Mayor and his wife, Katia, arrive. They are passing by and have decided to pay a call on their good friends, the baker and his wife.

"Hello, Jarslov. I hope Katia and I are not intruding?"

"Of course not, Mr. Mayor. Come out, Count Dracula! We have company!"

"Is the Count here?" asks the Mayor surprised.

"Yes, and you'll never guess where," says the baker's wife.

"It's so rare to see him around this early. In fact I can't ever remember seeing him around in the daytime."

"Well, he's here. Come out, Count Dracula!"

"Where is he?" Katia asks, not knowing whether to laugh or not.

"Come on out now! Let's go!" The baker's wife is getting impatient.

"He's in the closet," says the baker, apologetically.

"Really?" asks the Mayor.

"Let's go," says the baker with mock good humor as he knocks on the closet door. "Enough is enough. The Mayor's here."

"Come on out, Dracula," His Honor shouts, "let's have a drink."

"No, go ahead. I've got some business in here."

"In the closet?"

"Yes, don't let me spoil your day. I can hear what you're saying. I'll join in if I have anything to add."

Everyone looks at one another and shrugs. Wine is poured and they all drink.

"Some eclipse today," the Mayor says, sipping from his glass.

"Yes," the baker agrees. "Incredible."

"Yeah. Thrilling," says a voice from the closet.

"What, Dracula?"

"Nothing, nothing. Let it go."

And so the time passes, until the Mayor can stand it no longer and forcing open the door to the closet, he shouts, "Come on, Dracula. I always thought you were a mature man. Stop this craziness."

The daylight streams in, causing the evil monster to shriek and slowly dissolve to a skeleton and then to dust before the eyes of the four people present. Leaning down to the pile of white ash on the closet floor, the baker's wife shouts, "Does this mean dinner's off tonight?"

A Little Louder, Please

U NDERSTAND you are dealing with a man who knocked off *Finegans Wake* on the roller coaster at Coney Island, penetrating the abstruse Joycean arcana with ease, despite enough violent lurching to shake loose my silver fillings. Understand also that I am among the select few who spotted instantly in the Museum of Modern Art's impacted Buick that precise interplay of nuance and shading that Odilon Redon could have achieved had he forsaken the delicate ambiguity of pastels and worked with a car press. Also, laddies, as one whose spate of insights first placed *Godot* in proper perspective for the many confused playgoers who milled sluggishly in the lobby during intermission, miffed at ponying up scalper's money for arglebargle bereft of one up-tune or a single spangled bimbo, I would have to say my rapport with the seven livelies is pretty solid. Add to this the fact that eight radios conducted simultaneously at Town Hall killed me, and that I still occasionally sit in with my own Philco, after hours, in a Harlem basement where we blow some late weather and news, and where once a laconic field hand named Jess, who had never studied in his life, played the closing Dow-Jones averages with great feeling. Real soul stuff. Finally, to lock my case up tight, note that mine is a stock visage at happenings and underground-movie premières, and that I am a frequent contributor to *Sight and Stream*, a cerebral quarterly dedicated to advanced concepts in cinema and fresh-water fishing. If these are not credentials enough to tag me Joe Sensitive, then, brother, I give up. And yet, with this much perception dripping from me, like maple syrup off waffles, I was reminded recently that I possess an Achilles' heel culturewise that runs up my leg to the back of my neck.

It began one day last January when I was standing in McGinnis' Bar on Broadway, engulfing a slab of the world's richest cheesecake and suffering the guilty, cholesterolish hallucination that I could hear my aorta congealing into a hockey puck. Standing next to me was a nerve-shattering blonde, who waxed and waned under a black chemise with enough provocation to induce lycanthropy in a Boy Scout. For the previous fifteen minutes, my "pass the relish" had been the central theme of our relationship, despite several attempts on my part to generate a little action. As it was, she *had* passed the relish, and I was forced to ladle a small amount on my cheesecake as witness to the integrity of my request.

"I understand egg futures are up," I ventured finally, feigning the insouciance of a man who merged corporations as a sideline. Unaware that her stevedore boy friend had entered, with Laurel and Hardy timing, and was standing right behind me, I gave her a lean, hungry look and can remember cracking wise about Krafft-Ebing just before losing consciousness. The next thing I recall was running down the street to avoid the ire of what appeared to be a Sicilian cousin's club bent on avenging the girl's

honor. I sought refuge in the cool dark of a newsreel theatre, where a tour de force by Bugs Bunny and three
Librium restored my nervous system to its usual timbre.
The main feature came on and turned out to be a travel-
ogue on the New Guinea bush—a topic rivalling "Moss
Formations" and "How Penguins Live" for my attention
span. "Throwbacks," droned the narrator, "living today
not a whit differently from man millions of years ago, slay
the wild boar [whose standard of living didn't appear to be
up perceptibly, either] and sit around the fire at night acting out the day's kill in pantomime." Pantomime. It hit me
with sinus-clearing clarity. Here was a chink in my cultural
armor—the only chink, to be sure, but one that has
plagued me ever since childhood, when a dumb-show production of Gogol's *The Overcoat* eluded my grasp entirely
and had me convinced I was simply watching fourteen
Russians doing calisthenics. Always, pantomime was a
mystery to me—one that I chose to forget about because of
the embarrassment it caused me. But here was that failing
again and, to my chagrin, just as bad as ever. I did not
understand the frenetic gesticulations of the leading New
Guinea aborigine any more than I have ever understood
Marcel Marceau in any of those little skits that fill multitudes with such unbounded adulation. I writhed in my
seat as the amateur jungle thespian mutely titillated his
fellow-primitives, finally garnering hefty mitt with money
notices from the tribal elders, and then I slunk, dejected,
from the theatre.

At home that evening, I became obsessed with my
shortcoming. It was cruelly true: despite my canine celerity
in other areas of artistic endeavor, all that was needed was
one evening of mine to limn me clearly as Markham's hoe
man—stolid, stunned, and a brother to the ox in spades. I
began to rage impotently, but the back of my thigh tight-
ened and I was forced to sit. After all, I reasoned, what
more elemental form of communication is there? Why was

this universal art form patent in meaning to all but me? I tried raging impotently again, and this time brought it off, but mine is a quiet neighborhood, and several minutes later two rednecked spokesmen for the Nineteenth Precinct dropped by to inform me that raging impotently could mean a five-hundred-dollar fine, six months' imprisonment, or both. I thanked them and made a beeline for the sheets, where my struggle to sleep off my monstrous imperfection resulted in eight hours of nocturnal anxiety I wouldn't wish on Macbeth.

A further bone-chilling example of my mimetic shortcomings materialized only a few weeks later, when two free tickets to the theatre turned up at my door—the result of my correctly identifying the singing voice of Mama Yancey on a radio program a fortnight prior. First prize was a Bentley, and in my excitement to get my call in to the disc jockey promptly I had bolted naked from the tub. Seizing the telephone with one wet hand while attempting to turn off the radio with the other, I ricocheted off the ceiling, while lights dimmed for miles around, as they did when Lepke got the chair. My second orbit around the chandelier was interrupted by the open drawer of a Louis Quinze desk, which I met head on, catching an ormolu mount across the mouth. A florid insignia on my face, which now looked as if it had been stamped by a rococo cookie cutter, plus a knot on my head the size of an auk egg, affected my lucidity, causing me to place second to Mrs. Sleet Mazursky, and, scotching my dreams of the Bentley, I settled for a pair of freebees to an evening of Off Broadway theatrics. That a famed international pantomimist was on the bill cooled my ardor to the temperature of a polar cap, but, hoping to break the jinx, I decided to attend. I was unable to get a date on only six weeks' notice, so I used the extra ticket to tip my window-washer, Lars, a lethargic menial with all the sensitivity of the Berlin Wall. At first, he thought the little orange pasteboard was edible, but when I explained that it was good for an evening of pantomime— one of the only spectator events outside of a fire that he could hope to understand—he thanked me profusely.

On the night of the performance, the two of us—I in my opera cape and Lars with his pail—split with aplomb from the confines of a Checker cab and, entering the theatre, strode imperiously to our seats, where I studied the program and learned, with some nervousness, that the curtain-raiser was a little silent entertainment entitled *Going to a Picnic*. It began when a wisp of a man walked onstage in kitchen-white makeup and a tight black leotard. Standard picnic dress—I wore it myself to a picnic in Central Park last year, and, with the exception of a few adolescent malcontents who took it as a signal to re-edit my salients, it went unnoticed. The mime now proceeded to spread a picnic blanket, and, instantly, my old confusion set in. He was either spreading a picnic blanket or milking a small goat. Next, he elaborately removed his shoes, except that I'm not positive they were his shoes, because he drank one of them and mailed the other to Pittsburgh. I say "Pittsburgh," but actually it is hard to mime the concept of Pittsburgh, and as I look back on it, I now think what he was miming was not Pittsburgh at all but a man driving a golf cart through a revolving door—or possibly two men dismantling a printing press. How this pertains to a picnic escapes me. The pantomimist then began sorting an invisible collection of rectangular objects, undoubtedly heavy, like a complete set of the *Encyclopaedia Britannica*, which I suspect he was removing from his picnic basket, although from the way he held them they could also have been the Budapest String Quartet, bound and gagged.

By this time, to the surprise of those sitting next to me, I found myself trying, as usual, to help the mime clarify the details of his scene by guessing aloud exactly what he was doing. "Pillow . . . big pillow. Cushion? *Looks* like cushion . . ." This well-meaning participation often upsets the true lover of silent theatre, and I have noticed a tendency on such occasions for those sitting next to me to express uneasiness in various forms, ranging from significant throat-clearings to a lion's-paw swipe on the back of the head, which I once received from a member of a Manhasset housewives' theatre party. On this occasion, a dowager resembling Ichabod Crane snapped her lorgnette quirtlike across my knuckles, with the admonition "Cool it, stud." Then, warming to me, she explained, with the patiently slow enunciation of one addressing a shell-shocked infantryman, that the mime was now dealing humorously with the various elements that traditionally confound the picnic-goer—ants, rain, and the always-good-for-a-laugh forgotten bottle opener. Temporarily enlightened, I rocked with laughter at the notion of a man harassed by the absence of a bottle opener, and marvelled at its limitless possibilities.

Finally, the mime began blowing glass. Either blowing glass or tattooing the student body of Northwestern University. It seemed like the student body of Northwestern University, but it could have been the men's choir—or a diathermy machine—or any large, extinct quadruped, often amphibious and usually herbivorous, the fossilized remains of which have been found as far north as the Arctic. By now, the audience was doubled up with laughter over the hijinks on the stage. Even the obtuse Lars was wiping tears of joy from his face with his squeegee. But for me it was hopeless; the more I tried, the less I understood. A defeated weariness stole over me, and I slipped off my loafers and called it a day. The next thing I knew, a couple of charwomen at work in the balcony were batting around the pros and cons of bursitis. Gathering my senses by the dim glow of the theatre work light, I straightened my tie and departed for Riker's, where a hamburger and a chocolate malted gave me no trouble whatever as to their meaning, and, for the first time that evening, I threw off my guilty burden. To this day, I remain incomplete culturally, but I'm working on it. If you ever see an aesthete at a pantomime squinting, writhing, and muttering to himself, come up and say hello—but catch me early in the performance; I don't like to be bothered once I'm asleep.

Conversations with Helmholtz

THE following are a few samples of conversations taken from the soon-to-be-published book *Conversations with Helmholtz*.

Dr. Helmholtz, now nearing ninety, was a contemporary of Freud's, a pioneer in psychoanalysis, and founder of the school of psychology that bears his name. He is perhaps best known for his experiments in behavior, in which he proved that death is an acquired trait.

Helmholtz resides on a country estate in Lausanne, Switzerland, with his manservant, Hrolf, and his Great Dane, Hrolf. He spends most of his time writing, and is currently revising his autobiography to include himself. The "conversations" were held over a period of several months between Helmholtz and his student and disciple, Fears Hoffnung, whom Helmholtz loathes beyond description but tolerates because he brings him nougat. Their talks covered a variety of subjects, from psychopathology and religion to why Helmholtz can't seem to get a credit card.

258

"The Master," as Hoffnung calls him, emerges as a warm and perceptive human being who maintains he would gladly trade the accomplishments of a lifetime if he could only get rid of his rash.

April 1: Arrived at the Helmholtz house at precisely 10:00 A.M. and was told by the maid that the doctor was in his room sorting some mail. In my anxiety, I thought she said the doctor was in his room sorting some meal. As it turned out, I had heard correctly and Helmholtz was sorting some meal. He had large fistfuls of grain in each hand and was arranging it in random piles. When queried about this he said, "Ach—if only more people sorted meal." His answer puzzled me, but I thought it best not to pursue the matter. As he reclined in his leather chair, I asked him about the early days of psychoanalysis.

"When I first met Freud, I was already at work on my theories. Freud was in a bakery. He was attempting to buy some *Schnecken*, but could not bear to ask for them by name. Freud was too embarrassed to say the word '*Schnecken*,' as you probably know. 'Let me have some of those little cakes,' he would say, pointing to them. The baker said, 'You mean these *Schnecken*, Herr Professor?' At that, Freud flushed crimson and fled out the door muttering, 'Er, no—nothing—never mind.' I purchased the pastries effortlessly and brought them to Freud as a gift. We became good friends. I have thought ever since, certain people are ashamed to say certain words. Are there any words that embarrass you?"

I explained to Dr. Helmholtz that I could not order the Lobstermato (a tomato stuffed with lobster) in a certain restaurant. Helmholtz found that a particularly asinine word and wished he could scratch the face of the man who conceived it.

Talk turned back to Freud, who seems to dominate Helmholtz's every thought, although the two men hated each other after an argument over some parsley.

"I remember one case of Freud's. Edna S. Hysterical paralysis of the nose. Could not imitate a bunny when called upon to do so. This caused her great anxiety amongst her friends, who were often cruel. 'Come, Liebchen, show us how you make like a bunny.' Then they'd wiggle their nostrils freely, much to the amusement of each other.

"Freud had her to his office for a series of analytic sessions, but something went amiss and instead of achieving transference to Freud, she achieved transference to his coat tree, a tall wooden piece of furniture across the room. Freud became panicky, as in those days psychoanalysis was regarded skeptically, and when the girl ran off on a cruise with the coat tree Freud swore he'd never practice again. Indeed, for a while, he toyed seriously with the idea of becoming an acrobat, until Ferenczi convinced him he'd never learn to tumble really well."

I could see Helmholtz was getting drowsy now, as he had slid from his chair to the floor under the table, where he lay asleep. Not wishing to press his kindness, I tiptoed out.

April 5: Arrived to find Helmholtz practicing his violin. (He is a marvellous amateur violinist, although he cannot read music and can play only one note.) Again, Helmholtz discussed some of the problems of early psychoanalysis.

"Everyone curried favor with Freud. Rank was jealous of Jones. Jones envied Brill. Brill was annoyed by Adler's presence so much he hid Adler's porkpie hat. Once Freud had some toffee in his pocket and gave a piece to Jung. Rank was infuriated. He complained to me that Freud was favoring Jung. Particularly in the distribution of sweets. I ignored it, as I did not particularly care for Rank since he had recently referred to my paper on 'Euphoria in Snails' as 'the zenith of mongoloid reasoning.'

"Years later, Rank brought the incident up to me while

we were motoring in the Alps. I reminded him how fool-
ishly he had acted at the time and he admitted he had been
under unusual strain because his first name, Otto, was
spelled the same forwards or backwards and this
depressed him."

Helmholtz invited me to dinner. We sat at a large oak
table which he claims was a gift from Greta Garbo, although she denies any knowledge of it or of Helmholtz. A
typical Helmholtz dinner consisted of: a large raisin, generous portions of fatback, and an individual can of salmon.
After dinner there were mints and Helmholtz brought out
his collection of lacquered butterflies, which caused him to
become petulant when he realized they would not fly.

Later, in the sitting room, Helmholtz and I relaxed over
some cigars. (Helmholtz forgot to light his cigar, but was
drawing so hard it was actually getting smaller.) We discussed some of the Master's most celebrated cases.

"There was Joachim B. A man in his mid-forties who
could not enter a room that had a cello in it. What was
worse, once he was in a room with a cello he could not
leave unless asked to do so by a Rothschild. In addition to
that, Joachim B. stuttered. But not when he spoke. Only
when he wrote. If he wrote the word 'but,' for instance, it
would appear in his letter 'b-b-b-b-b-but.' He was much
teased about this impediment, and attempted suicide by
trying to suffocate himself inside a large crepe. I cured him
with hypnosis, and he was able to achieve a normal
healthy life, although in later years he constantly fanta-
sized meeting a horse who advised him to take up
architecture."

Helmholtz talked about the notorious rapist, V., who at
one time held all London in terror.

"A most unusual case of perversion. He had a recur-
ring sexual fantasy in which he is humiliated by a group of
anthropologists and forced to walk around bowlegged,
which he confessed gave him great sexual pleasure. He

recalled as a child surprising his parents' housekeeper, a woman of loose morals, in the act of kissing some water-cress, which he found erotic. As a teen-ager he was pun-ished for varnishing his brother's head, although his father, a house painter by trade, was more upset over the fact he gave the boy only one coat.

"V. attacked his first woman at eighteen, and thereafter raped half a dozen per week for years. The best I was able to do with him in therapy was to substitute a more socially acceptable habit to replace his aggressive tendencies; and thereafter when he chanced upon an unsuspecting female, instead of assaulting her, he would produce a large halibut from his jacket and show it to her. While the sight of it caused consternation in some, the women were spared any violence and some even confessed their lives were immea-surably enriched by the experience."

April 12: This time Helmholtz was not feeling too well. He had gotten lost in a meadow the previous day and fallen down on some pears. He was confined to bed, but sat upright and even laughed when I told him I had an abscess.

We discussed his theory of reverse-psychology, which came to him shortly after Freud's death. (Freud's death, according to Ernest Jones, was the event that caused the final break between Helmholtz and Freud, and the two rarely spoke afterwards.)

At the time, Helmholtz had developed an experiment where he would ring a bell and a team of white mice would escort Mrs. Helmholtz out the door and deposit her on the curb. He did many such behavioristic experiments and only stopped when a dog trained to salivate on cue refused to let him in the house for the holidays. He is, incidentally, still credited with the classic paper on "Unmotivated Giggling in Caribou."

"Yes, I founded the school of reverse psychology. Quite

by accident, in fact. My wife and I were both comfortably tucked in bed when I suddenly desired a drink of water. Too lazy to get it myself, I asked Mrs. Helmholtz to get it for me. She refused, saying she was exhausted from lifting chick peas. We argued over who should get it. Finally, I said, 'I don't really want a glass of water anyhow. In fact, a glass of water is the last thing in the world I want.' At that, the woman sprang up and said, 'Oh, you don't want any water, eh? That's too bad.' And she quickly left bed and got me some. I tried to discuss the incident with Freud at the analysts' outing in Berlin, but he and Jung were partners in the three-legged race and were too wrapped up in the festivities to listen.

"Only years later did I find a way to utilize this principle in the treatment of depression, and was able to cure the great opera singer, J., of the morbid apprehension he would one day wind up in a hamper."

April 18: Arrived to find Helmholtz trimming some rose bushes. He was quite eloquent on the beauty of flowers, which he loves because "they're not always borrowing money."

We talked about contemporary psychoanalysis, which Helmholtz regards as a myth kept alive by the couch industry.

"These modern analysts! They charge so much. In my day, for five marks Freud himself would treat you. For ten marks, he would treat you and press your pants. For fifteen marks, Freud would let *you* treat *him*, and that included a choice of any two vegetables. Thirty dollars an hour! Fifty dollars an hour! The Kaiser only got twelve and a quarter for being Kaiser! And he had to walk to work! And the length of treatment! Two years! Five years! If one of us couldn't cure a patient in six months we would refund his money, take him to any musical revue and he would receive either a mahogany fruit bowl or a set of stainless steel carving knives. I remember you could always tell the patients Jung failed with, as he would give them large stuffed pandas."

We strolled along the garden path and Helmholtz turned to other subjects of interest. He was a veritable spate of insights and I managed to preserve some by jotting them down.

On the human condition: "If man were immortal, do you realize what his meat bills would be?"

On religion: "I don't believe in an afterlife, although I am bringing a change of underwear."

On literature: "All literature is a footnote to Faust. I have no idea what I mean by that."

I am convinced Helmholtz is a very great man.

Viva Vargas!

Excerpts from the Diary of a
Revolutionary

JUNE 3: Viva Vargas! Today we took to the hills. Outraged and disgusted at the exploitation of our little country by the corrupt Arroyo régime, we sent Julio to the place with a list of our grievances and demands, none hastily arrived at nor, in my opinion, excessive. As it turned out, Arroyo's busy schedule did not include taking time away from being fanned to meet with our beloved rebel emissary, and instead he referred the entire matter to his minister, who said he would give our petitions his full consideration, but first he just wanted to see how long Julio could smile with his head under molten lava.

Because of many indignations such as this one, we have at last, behind the inspired leadership of Emilio Molina Vargas, decided to take matters into our own hands. If this be treason, we yelled on street corners, let us make the most of it.

I was, unfortunately, lolling in a hot tub when word

arrived that the police would be by shortly to hang me. Bounding from my bath with understandable alacrity, I stepped on a wet bar of soap and cascaded off the front patio, luckily breaking the fall with my teeth, which skidded around the ground like loose Chiclets. Though naked and bruised, survival dictated I act quickly, and mounting El Diablo, my stallion, I gave the rebel yell! The horse reared and I slid down his back to the ground, fracturing certain small bones.

Were all this not devastating enough, I scarcely got twenty feet by foot when I remembered my printing press, and not wanting to leave behind such a potent political weapon or piece of evidence, I doubled back to retrieve it. As luck would have it, the thing weighed more than it looked, and lifting it was a job more suited to a derrick than a hundred-and-ten-pound college student. When the police arrived, my hand was caught in the machinery as it roared uncontrollably, reprinting large passages of Marx down my bare back. Don't ask me how I managed to tear loose and vault out a back window. Luckily I eluded the police and made my way to safety in Vargas' camp.

June 4: How peaceful it is here in the hills. Living out under the stars. A group of dedicated men all working toward a common goal. Although I had anticipated a say in the actual planning of the campaigns, Vargas felt my services might better be employed as company cook. This is not an easy job with foodstuffs scarce, but somebody has to do it and, all things considered, my first meal was a big hit. True, not all the men are terribly partial to Gila monster but we can't be choosy, and apart from some picayune eaters who are prejudiced against any reptile, dinner came off without incident.

I overheard Vargas today and he is quite sanguine about our prospects. He feels we will gain control of the capital sometime in December. His brother, Luis, on the other hand, an introspective man by nature, feels it is only a question of time before we starve to death. The Vargas brothers constantly bicker over military strategy and political philosophy, and it is hard to imagine that these two great rebel chieftains were only last week a couple of men's room attendants at the local Hilton. Meanwhile, we wait.

June 10: Spent the day drilling. How miraculously we are being changed from a scruffy band of guerrillas to a hard-core army. This morning Hernandez and I practiced using machetes, our razor-sharp sugar-cane knives, and due to a burst of overzealousness by my partner, I found out I had type-O blood. The worst thing is the waiting. Arturo has a guitar but can only play "Cielito Lindo," and while the men rather liked to hear it at first, he seldom gets any more requests for it. I tried preparing the Gila monster a new way and I think the men enjoyed it, although I noticed some had to chew hard and snap their heads back to get it down.

I overheard Vargas again today. He and his brother were discussing their plans after we take the capital. I wonder what post he is saving for me when the revolution is completed. I am quite confident my fierce loyalty, which can only be described as canine, will pay off.

July 1: A party of our best men raided a village for food today, and got a chance to employ many of the tactics we have been working on. Most of the rebels acquitted themselves nicely, and even though the group was slaughtered, Vargas considers it a moral victory. Those of us who were not in on the raid sat around camp while Arturo favored us with some "Cielito Lindo." Morale remains high, even though food and arms are virtually nonexistent and time passes slowly. Luckily we are distracted by the hundred-degree heat, which I think accounts for much of the funny gurgling noise the men make. Our time will come.

July 10: Today was generally a good day, despite the fact that we were ambushed by Arroyo's men and badly decimated. This was partially my fault as I gave away our position by inadvertently shrieking the names of the Christian triumvirate when a tarantula crawled over my leg. For several moments I could not dislodge the tenacious little spider as it made its way into the inner recesses of my garments, causing me to gyrate spastically toward the stream and thrash about in it for what seemed like forty-five minutes. Shortly after, Arroyo's soldiers opened fire on us. We fought gamely, although the shock of being surprised created a mild disorganization, and for the first ten minutes our men were shooting at each other. Vargas narrowly escaped catastrophe as a live hand grenade landed at his feet. He commanded me to fall on it, aware that he alone is indispensable to our cause, and I did so. As providence would have it, the grenade did not explode and I walked away unharmed except for a slight twitch and the inability to fall asleep unless someone holds my hand.

July 15: The morale of the men seems to be holding up, despite certain minor setbacks. First, Miguel stole some ground-to-ground missiles but mistook them for ground-to-air missiles and, attempting to down several of Arroyo's planes, blew all our trucks up. When he tried to laugh it off, José became furious and they fought. Later, they patched things up and deserted. Desertion, incidentally, could become a major problem, although at this moment optimism and team spirit have held it down to three out of every four men. I, of course, remain loyal and do the cooking, but the men still do not seem to appreciate the difficulty of that assignment. The fact is, my life has been threatened if I don't come up with an alternative to Gila

Getting Even

monster. Sometimes soldiers can be so unreasonable. Still, perhaps one of these days I will surprise them with something new. Meanwhile we sit around the camp and wait. Vargas is pacing in his tent and Arturo sits playing "Cielito Lindo."

271

August 1: Despite all we have to be thankful for, there is no doubt that a certain tension has set in here at rebel headquarters. Little things, apparent only to the observant eye, indicate an undercurrent of uneasiness. For one thing, there are quite a few stabbings among the men, as quarrels become more frequent. Also an attempt to raid an ammunitions depot and rearm ourselves ended in a rout when Jorge's signal flare went off prematurely in his pocket. All the men were chased except for Jorge, who was captured after banging off two dozen buildings like a pinball. Back at camp in the evening, when I brought out the Gila monster the men rioted. Several of them held me down while Ramon struck me with my ladle. I was mercifully saved by an electrical storm that claimed three lives. Finally, with frustrations at a peak, Arturo struck up "Cielito Lindo" and some of the less musically inclined ones in the group took him behind a rock and forced-fed him his guitar.

On the plus side of the ledger, Vargas' diplomatic envoy, after many unsuccessful attempts, managed to conclude an interesting deal with the CIA where, in return for our unswerving fealty toward their policies forever, they are obligated to supply us with no less than fifty barbecued chickens.

Vargas now feels that perhaps he was premature in predicting a December success and indicates that total victory might require additional time. Strangely enough, he has turned from his field maps and charts and relies more heavily now on astrological readings and the entrails of birds.

August 12: The situation has taken a turn for the worse. As luck would have it, the mushrooms I so carefully picked to vary the menu with, turned out to be poisonous, and while the only really disconcerting side effect was some minor convulsions most of the men suffered, they seemed unduly embittered. On top of that, the CIA has reconsidered our chances of bringing off the revolution and as a result threw Arroyo and his cabinet a conciliatory brunch at Wolfie's in Miami Beach. This, coupled with a gift of 24 jet bombers, Vargas interprets as a subtle shift in their sympathies.

Morale still seems reasonably high and, while the desertion rate has risen, it is still limited to those who can walk. Vargas himself appears to be a bit morose and has taken to saving string. It is now his feeling that life under the Arroyo régime might not be all that uncomfortable, and he wonders if we should not reorient the men that are left, abandon the ideals of the revolution, and form a rhumba band. Meanwhile the heavy rains have caused the mountain to landslide, and the Juarez brothers were carried off into the gorge as they slept. We have dispatched an emissary to Arroyo, with a modified list of our demands, taking care to strike out the portions concerning his unconditional surrender and substituting in its place an award-winning recipe for guacamole. I wonder how it will all turn out.

August 15: We have taken the capital! The incredible details follow:

After much deliberation, the men took a vote and decided to pin our last hopes on a suicide mission, guessing that the element of surprise might be just the thing to offset Arroyo's superior forces. As we marched through the jungle, towards the palace, hunger and fatigue slowly sapped a portion of our resolve and, approaching our destination, we decided to switch tactics and see if grovelling would work. We turned ourselves over to the palace guards, who brought us at gunpoint before Arroyo. The dictator took into consideration the mitigating fact that we had given up voluntarily, and while he still planned to disembowel Vargas, the rest of us were going to get off with being skinned alive. Reevaluating our situation in light of this fresh concept, we succumbed to panic and bolted in all directions while the guards opened fire. Vargas and I raced upstairs and, seeking a place to hide, burst into Madame Arroyo's boudoir, surprising her in a moment of illicit passion with Arroyo's brother. Both became flustered. Arroyo's brother then drew his revolver and let fly a shot. Unbeknownst to him, this acted as a signal to a group of mercenaries who had been hired by the CIA to help clean us out of the hills in return for Arroyo's granting the United States rights to open Orange Julius stands here. The mercenaries, who were themselves confused regarding their loyalties due to weeks of American foreign policy equivocating, attacked the palace by mistake. Arroyo and his staff suddenly suspected a CIA double cross and turned their guns on the invaders. Concurrently a long-smoldering plot to assassinate Arroyo by several Maoists misfired when a bomb they planted in a taco went off prematurely, exorcising the left wing of the palace and projecting Arroyo's wife and brother through some wood beams.

Grabbing a valise of Swiss bankbooks, Arroyo made for the rear door and his ever-ready Lear jet. His pilot took off amidst a volley of gunfire but, confused by the hectic events of the moment, threw the wrong switch, sending the plane into a nose dive. Moments later, it crashed into the mercenary army camp, laying their ranks waste and causing them to give up.

Throughout this, Vargas, our beloved leader, brilliantly adopted a policy of watchful waiting, which he executed by crouching motionless at the fireplace and assuming the

274

disguise of a decorative blackamoor. As the coast became clear he advanced on tiptoe to the central office and assumed power, pausing only to open the royal refrigerator and slap together a deviled ham sandwich.

We celebrated all through the night and everyone got very drunk. I spoke with Vargas afterwards about the serious business of running a country. While he believes free elections are essential to any democracy, he prefers to wait until the people become a bit more educated before there is any voting. Until then, he has improvised a workable system of government based on divine monarchy and has rewarded my loyalty by allowing me to sit by his right hand at mealtime. Plus I also am responsible for seeing the latrine is spotless.

The Discovery and Use of the Fake Ink Blot

THERE is no evidence of a fake ink blot appearing any-where in the West before the year 1921, although Napoleon was known to have had great fun with the joy buzzer, a device concealed in the palm of the hand causing an electric-like vibration upon contact. Napoleon would offer the regal hand in friendship to a foreign digni-tary, buzz the unsuspecting victim's palm and roar with imperial laughter as the redfaced dupe did an improvised jig to the delight of the court.

The joy buzzer underwent many modifications, the most celebrated of which occurred after the introduction of chewing gum by Santa Anna (I believe chewing gum was originally a dish of his wife's that simply would not go down) and took the form of a spearmint-gum pack equipped with a subtle mousetrap mechanism. The sucker, offered a fresh stick, experienced a piercing sting as the iron bar came springing down on his naive fingertips. The first reaction was generally one of pain, then contagious laughter, and finally a kind of folk wisdom. It is no secret that the snappy-chewing-gum gag lightened matters at the Alamo considerably; and although there were no survivors, most observers feel things could have gone substantially worse without this cunning little gimmick.

With the advent of the Civil War, Americans turned more and more to escaping the horrors of a disintegrating nation; and while the Northern generals preferred amusing themselves with the dribble glass, Robert E. Lee passed many a crucial moment with his brilliant use of the squirt flower. In the early part of the War, no one ever came away from smelling the apparent "lovely carnation" in Lee's lapel without getting a generous eyeful of Suwanee River water. As things went badly for the South, however, Lee abandoned the once-fashionable artifice and relied simply on placing a carpet tack on the chair seats of people whom he did not like.

After the War and right up to the early 1900s and the so-called era of the robber barons, sneezing powder and a little tin can marked ALMONDS, wherefrom several huge spring serpents would leap into the victim's face, provided all that was worthy in the area of tomfoolery. It is said J. P. Morgan preferred the former, while the elder Rockefeller felt more at home with the latter.

Then, in 1921, a group of biologists meeting in Hong Kong to buy suits discovered the fake ink blot. It had long been a staple of the Oriental repertoire of diversions, and several of the later dynasties retained power by their brilliant manipulation of what appeared to be a spilled bottle and an ugly inkstain, but was in reality a tin blot.

The first ink blots, it was learned, were crude, constructed to eleven feet in diameter and fooled nobody.

However, with the discovery of the concept of smaller sizes by a Swiss physicist, who proved that an object of a particular size could be reduced in size simply by "making it smaller," the fake ink blot came into its own.

It remained in its own until 1934, when Franklin Delano Roosevelt removed it from its own and placed it in someone else's. Roosevelt utilized it cleverly to settle a strike in Pennsylvania, the details of which are amusing. Embarrassed leaders of both labor and management were convinced that a bottle of ink had been spilled, ruining someone's priceless Empire sofa. Imagine how relieved they were to learn it was all in fun. Three days later the steel mills were reopened.

Mr. Big

I WAS sitting in my office, cleaning the debris out of my thirty-eight and wondering where my next case was coming from. I like being a private eye, and even though once in a while I've had my gums massaged with an automobile jack, the sweet smell of greenbacks makes it all worth it. Not to mention the dames, which are a minor preoccupation of mine that I rank just ahead of breathing. That's why, when the door to my office swung open and a long-haired blonde named Heather Butkiss came striding in and told me she was a nudie model and needed my help, my salivary glands shifted into third. She wore a short skirt and a tight sweater and her figure described a set of parabolas that could cause cardiac arrest in a yak.

"What can I do for you, sugar?"

"I want you to find someone for me."

"Missing person? Have you tried the police?"

"Not exactly, Mr. Lupowitz."

"Call me Kaiser, sugar. All right, so what's the scam?"

"God."

"God?"

"That's right, God. The Creator, the Underlying Principle, the First Cause of Things, the All Encompassing. I
want you to find Him for me."

I've had some fruit cakes up in the office before, but
when they're built like she was, you listened.

"Why?"

"That's my business, Kaiser. You just find Him."

"I'm sorry, sugar. You got the wrong boy."

"But why?"

"Unless I know all the facts," I said, rising.

"O.K., O.K.," she said, biting her lower lip. She
straightened the seam of her stocking, which was strictly
for my benefit, but I wasn't buying any at the moment.

"Let's have it on the line, sugar."

"Well, the truth is—I'm not really a nudie model."

"No?"

"No. My name is not Heather Butkiss, either. It's Claire
Rosensweig and I'm a student at Vassar. Philosophy major.
History of Western Thought and all that. I have a paper
due January. On Western religion. All the other kids in the
course will hand in speculative papers. But I want to *know*.
Professor Grebanier said if anyone finds out for sure,
they're a cinch to pass the course. And my dad's promised
me a Mercedes if I get straight A's."

I opened a deck of Luckies and a pack of gum and had
one of each. Her story was beginning to interest me.
Spoiled coed. High IQ and a body I wanted to know better.

"What does God look like?"

"I've never seen him."

"Well, how do you know He exists?"

"That's for you to find out."

"Oh, great. Then you don't know what he looks like?
Or where to begin looking?"

"No. Not really. Although I suspect he's everywhere. In the air, in every flower, in you and I—and in this chair."

"Uh huh." So she was a pantheist. I made a mental note of it and said I'd give her case a try—for a hundred bucks a day, expenses, and a dinner date. She smiled and okayed the deal. We rode down in the elevator together. Outside it was getting dark. Maybe God did exist and maybe He didn't, but somewhere in that city there were sure a lot of guys who were going to try and keep me from finding out.

My first lead was Rabbi Itzhak Wiseman, a local cleric who owed me a favor for finding out who was rubbing pork on his hat. I knew something was wrong when I spoke to him because he was scared. Real scared.

"Of course there's a you-know-what, but I'm not even allowed to say His name or He'll strike me dead, which I could never understand why someone is so touchy about having his name said."

"You ever see Him?"

"Me? Are you kidding? I'm lucky I get to see my grandchildren."

"Then how do you know He exists?"

"How do I know? What kind of question is that? Could I get a suit like this for fourteen dollars if there was no one up there? Here, feel a gabardine—how can you doubt?"

"You got nothing more to go on?"

"Hey—what's the Old Testament? Chopped liver? How do you think Moses got the Israelites out of Egypt? With a smile and a tap dance? Believe me, you don't part the Red Sea with some gismo from Korvette's. It takes power."

"So he's tough, eh?"

"Yes. Very tough. You'd think with all that success he'd be a lot sweeter."

"How come you know so much?"

"Because we're the chosen people. He takes best care of

us of all His children, which I'd also like to someday discuss with Him."

"What do you pay Him for being chosen?"

"Don't ask."

So that's how it was. The Jews were into God for a lot. It was the old protection racket. Take care of them in return for a price. And from the way Rabbi Wiseman was talking, He soaked them plenty. I got into a cab and made it over to Danny's Billiards on Tenth Avenue. The manager was a slimy little guy I didn't like.

"Chicago Phil here?"

"Who wants to know?"

I grabbed him by the lapels and took some skin at the same time.

"What, punk?"

"In the back," he said, with a change of attitude.

Chicago Phil. Forger, bank robber, strong-arm man, and avowed atheist.

"The guy never existed, Kaiser. This is the straight dope. It's a big hype. There's no Mr. Big. It's a syndicate. Mostly Sicilian. It's international. But there is no actual head. Except maybe the Pope."

"I want to meet the Pope."

"It can be arranged," he said, winking.

"Does the name Claire Rosensweig mean anything to you?"

"No."

"Heather Butkiss?"

"Oh, wait a minute. Sure. She's that peroxide job with the bazooms from Radcliffe."

"Radcliffe? She told me Vassar."

"Well, she's lying. She's a teacher at Radcliffe. She was mixed up with a philosopher for a while."

"Pantheist?"

"No. Empiricist, as I remember. Bad guy. Completely rejected Hegel or any dialectical methodology."

"One of those."

"Yeah. He used to be a drummer with a jazz trio. Then he got hooked on Logical Positivism. When that didn't work, he tried Pragmatism. Last I heard he stole a lot of money to take a course in Schopenhauer at Columbia. The mob would like to find him—or get their hands on his textbooks so they can resell them."

"Thanks, Phil."

"Take it from me, Kaiser. There's no one out there. It's a void. I couldn't pass all those bad checks or screw society the way I do if for one second I was able to recognize any authentic sense of Being. The universe is strictly phenomenological. Nothing's eternal. It's all meaningless."

"Who won the fifth at Aqueduct?"

"Santa Baby."

I had a beer at O'Rourke's and tried to add it all up, but it made no sense at all. Socrates was a suicide—or so they said. Christ was murdered. Neitzsche went nuts. If there was someone out there, He sure as hell didn't want anybody to know it. And why was Claire Rosensweig lying about Vassar? Could Descartes have been right? Was the universe dualistic? Or did Kant hit it on the head when he postulated the existence of God on moral grounds?

That night I had dinner with Claire. Ten minutes after the check came, we were in the sack and, brother, you can have your Western thought. She went through the kind of gymnastics that would have won first prize in the Tia Juana Olympics. After, she lay on the pillow next to me, her long blond hair sprawling. Our naked bodies still intertwined. I was smoking and staring at the ceiling.

"Claire, what if Kierkegaard's right?"

"You mean?"

"If you can never really *know*. Only have faith."

"That's absurd."

"Don't be so rational."

"Nobody's being rational, Kaiser." She lit a cigarette.

"Just don't get ontological. Not now. I couldn't bear it if you were ontological with me."

She was upset. I leaned over and kissed her, and the phone rang. She got it.

"It's for you."

The voice on the other end was Sergeant Reed of Homicide.

"You still looking for God?"

"Yeah."

"An all-power Being? Great Oneness, Creator of the Universe? First Cause of All Things?"

"That's right."

"Somebody with that description just showed up at the morgue. You better get down here right away."

It was Him all right, and from the looks of Him it was a professional job.

"He was dead when they brought Him in."

"Where'd you find Him?"

"A warehouse on Delancey Street."

"Any clues?"

"It's the work of an existentialist. We're sure of that."

"How can you tell?"

"Haphazard way how it was done. Doesn't seem to be any system followed. Impulse."

"A crime of passion?"

"You got it. Which means you're a suspect, Kaiser."

"Why me?"

"Everybody down at headquarters knows how you feel about Jaspers."

"That doesn't make me a killer."

"Not yet, but you're a suspect."

Outside on the street I sucked air into my lungs and tried to clear my head. I took a cab over to Newark and got out and walked a block to Giordino's Italian Restaurant. There, at a back table, was His Holiness. It was the Pope, all right. Sitting with two guys I had seen in half a dozen police line-ups.

"Sit down," he said, looking up from his fettucine. He held out a ring. I gave him my toothiest smile, but didn't kiss it. It bothered him and I was glad. Point for me.

"Would you like some fettucine?"

"No thanks, Holiness. But you go ahead."

"Nothing? Not even a salad?"

"I just ate."

"Suit yourself, but they make a great Roquefort dressing here. Not like the Vatican, where you can't get a decent meal."

"I'll come right to the point, Pontiff. I'm looking for God."

"You came to the right person."

"Then He does exist?" They all found this very amusing and laughed. The hood next to me said, "Oh, that's funny. Bright boy wants to know if He exists."

I shifted my chair to get comfortable and brought the leg down on his little toe. "Sorry." But he was steaming.

"Sure He exists, Lupowitz, but I'm the only one that communicates with Him. He speaks only through me."

"Why you, pal?"

"Because I got the red suit."

"This get-up?"

"Don't knock it. Every morning I rise, put on this red suit, and suddenly I'm a big cheese. It's all in the suit. I mean, face it, if I went around in slacks and a sports jacket, I couldn't get arrested religion-wise."

"Then it's a hype. There's no God."

"I don't know. But what's the difference? The money's good."

"You ever worry the laundry won't get your red suit back on time and you'll be like the rest of us?"

"I use the special one-day service. I figure it's worth the extra few cents to be safe."

"Name Claire Rosensweig mean anything to you?"

"Sure. She's in the science department at Bryn Mawr."

"Science, you say? Thanks."

"For what?"

"The answer, Pontiff." I grabbed a cab and shot over the George Washington Bridge. On the way I stopped at my office and did some fast checking. Driving to Claire's apartment, I put the pieces together, and for the first time they fit. When I got there she was in a diaphanous peignoir and something seemed to be troubling her.

"God is dead. The police were here. They're looking for you. They think an existentialist did it."

"No, sugar. It was you."

"What? Don't make jokes, Kaiser."

"It was you that did it."

"What are you saying?"

"You, baby. Not Heather Butkiss or Claire Rosensweig, but Doctor Ellen Shepherd."

"How did you know my name?"

"Professor of physics at Bryn Mawr. The youngest one ever to head a department there. At the mid-winter Hop you get stuck on a jazz musician who's heavily into philosophy. He's married, but that doesn't stop you. A couple of nights in the hay and it feels like love. But it doesn't work out because something comes between you. God. Y'see, sugar, he believed, or wanted to, but you, with your pretty little scientific mind, had to have absolute certainty."

"No, Kaiser, I swear."

"So you pretend to study philosophy because that gives you a chance to eliminate certain obstacles. You get rid of Socrates easy enough, but Descartes takes over, so you use Spinoza to get rid of Descartes, but when Kant doesn't come through you have to get rid of him too."

"You don't know what you're saying."

"You made mincemeat out of Leibnitz, but that wasn't good enough for you because you knew if anybody believed Pascal you were dead, so he had to be gotten rid of too, but that's where you made your mistake because you trusted Martin Buber. Except, sugar, he was soft. He believed in God, so you had to get rid of God yourself."

"Kaiser, you're mad!"

"No, baby. You posed as a pantheist and that gave you access to Him—*if* He existed, which he did. He went with you to Shelby's party and when Jason wasn't looking, you killed Him."

"Who the hell are Shelby and Jason?"

"What's the difference? Life's absurd now anyway."

"Kaiser," she said, suddenly trembling. "You wouldn't turn me in?"

"Oh yes, baby. When the Supreme Being gets knocked off, *somebody's* got to take the rap."

"Oh, Kaiser, we could go away together. Just the two of us. We could forget about philosophy. Settle down and maybe get into semantics."

"Sorry, sugar. It's no dice."

She was all tears now as she started lowering the shoulder straps of her peignoir and I was standing there suddenly with a naked Venus whose whole body seemed to be saying, Take me—I'm yours. A Venus whose right hand tousled my hair while her left hand had picked up a forty-five and was holding it behind my back. I let go with a slug from my thirty-eight before she could pull the trigger, and she dropped her gun and doubled over in disbelief.

"How could you, Kaiser?"

She was fading fast, but I managed to get it in, in time.

"The manifestation of the universe as a complex idea unto itself as opposed to being in or outside the true Being of itself is inherently a conceptual nothingness or Nothingness in relation to any abstract form of existing or to exist or having existed in perpetuity and not subject to laws of physicality or motion or ideas relating to non-matter or the lack of objective Being or subjective otherness."

It was a subtle concept but I think she understood before she died.

SIDE EFFECTS

CONTENTS

Remembering Needleman

It has been four weeks and it is still hard for me to believe Sandor Needleman is dead. I was present at the cremation and at his son's request, brought the marshmallows, but few of us could think of anything but our pain.

Needleman was constantly obsessing over his funeral plans and once told me, "I much prefer cremation to burial in the earth, and both to a weekend with Mrs. Needleman." In the end, he chose to have himself cremated and donated his ashes to the University of Heidelberg, which scattered them to the four winds and got a deposit on the urn.

I can still see him with his crumpled suit and grey sweater. Preoccupied with weighty matters, he frequently would forget to remove the coat hanger from his jacket while he wore it. I reminded him of it one time at a Princeton Commencement and he smiled calmly and said, "Good, let those who have taken issue with my theories

299

think at least that I have broad shoulders." Two days later he was committed to Bellevue for doing a sudden back somersault in the midst of a conversation with Stravinsky.

Needleman was not an easily understood man. His reticence was mistaken for coldness, but he was capable of great compassion, and after witnessing a particularly horrible mine disaster once, he could not finish a second helping of waffles. His silence, too, put people off, but he felt speech was a flawed method of communication and he preferred to hold even his most intimate conversations with signal flags.

When he was dismissed from the faculty of Columbia University for his controversy with the then head of the school, Dwight Eisenhower, he waited for the renowned ex-general with a carpet beater and pelted him until Eisenhower ran for cover into a toy store. (The two men had a bitter public disagreement over whether the class bell signaled the end of a period or the beginning of another.)

Needleman had always hoped to die a quiet death. "Amidst my books and papers like my brother Johann." (Needleman's brother had suffocated under a rolltop desk while searching for his rhyming dictionary.)

Who would have thought that while Needleman would be watching the demolition of a building on his lunch hour, he would be tapped in the head by a wrecking ball? The blow caused massive shock and Needleman expired with a broad smile. His last, enigmatic words were, "No thanks, I already own a penguin."

As always, at the time of Needleman's death he was at work on several things. He was creating an Ethics, based on his theory that "good and just behavior is not only more moral but could be done by phone." Also, he was halfway through a new study of semantics, proving (as he so violently insisted) that sentence structure is innate but that whining is acquired. Finally, yet another book on the

Holocaust. This one with cutouts. Needleman had always been obsessed by the problem of evil and argued quite eloquently that true evil was only possible if its perpetrator was named Blackie or Pete. His own flirtation with National Socialism caused a scandal in academic circles, though despite everything from gymnastics to dance lessons, he could not master the goose step.

Nazism was for him merely a reaction against academic philosophy, a position he always attempted to impress on friends and then would grab at their faces with feigned excitement and say, "Aha! Got your nose." It is easy to criticize his position on Hitler at first, but one must take into account his own philosophical writings. He had rejected contemporary ontology and insisted that man existed prior to infinity though not with too many options. He differentiated between existence and Existence, and knew one was preferable, but could never remember which. Human freedom for Needleman consisted of being aware of the absurdity of life. "God is silent," he was fond of saying, "now if we can only get Man to shut up."

Authentic Being, reasoned Needleman, could only be achieved on weekends and even then it required the borrowing of a car. Man, according to Needleman, was not a "thing" apart from nature, but was involved "in nature," and could not observe his own existence without first pretending to be indifferent and then running around to the opposite end of the room quickly in the hopes of glimpsing himself.

His term for the life process was *Angst Zeit*, loosely meaning Anxiety-Time and suggested man was a creature doomed to exist in "time" even though that was not where the action was. After much reflection, Needleman's intellectual integrity convinced him that he didn't exist, his friends didn't exist, and the only thing that was real was his IOU to the bank for six million marks. Hence, he was charmed by the National Socialist's philosophy of power,

302

or as Needleman put it, "I have the kind of eyes that are set off by a brown shirt." After it became apparent that National Socialism was just the type of menace that Needleman stood against, he fled Berlin. Disguised as a bush and moving sideways only, three quick paces at a time, he crossed the border without being noticed.

Everywhere in Europe Needleman went, students and intellectuals were eager to help him, awed by his reputation. On the run, he found time to publish *Time, Essence, and Reality: A Systematic Reevaluation of Nothingness* and his delightful lighter treatise, *The Best Places to Eat While in Hiding*. Chaim Weizmann and Martin Buber took up a collection and obtained signed petitions to permit Needleman to emigrate to the United States, but at the time the hotel of his choice was full. With German soldiers minutes from his hideout in Prague, Needleman decided to come to America after all, but a scene occurred at the airport when he was overweight with his luggage. Albert Einstein, who was on that same flight, explained to him that if he would just remove the shoe trees from his shoes he could take everything. The two frequently corresponded after that. Einstein once wrote him, "Your work and my work are very similar although I'm still not exactly sure what your work is."

Once in America, Needleman was rarely out of public controversy. He published his famous, *Non-Existence: What To Do If It Suddenly Strikes You*. Also the classic work on linguistic philosophy, *Semantic Modes of Non-Essential Functioning*, which was made into the hit movie, *They Flew By Night*.

Typically, he was asked to resign from Harvard because of his affiliation with the Communist party. He felt only in a system with no economic inequality could there be real freedom and cited as the model society an ant farm. He could observe ants for hours and used to muse wistfully, "They're truly harmonious. If only their women were prettier they'd have it made." Interestingly, when Needleman was called by the House Un-American Activities Committee, he named names and justified it to his friends by citing his philosophy: "Political actions have no moral consequences but exist outside of the realm of true Being." For once the academic community stood chastened and it was not until weeks later that the faculty at Princeton decided to tar and feather Needleman. Needleman, incidentally, used this same reasoning to justify his concept of free love, but neither of two young coeds would buy it and the sixteen-year-old blew the whistle on him.

Needleman was passionate about the halting of nuclear testing and flew to Los Alamos, where he and several students refused to remove themselves from the site of a scheduled atomic detonation. As minutes ticked off and it became apparent the test would proceed as planned, Needleman was heard to mutter, "Uh-oh," and made a run for it. What the newspapers did not print was that he had not eaten all day.

It is easy to remember the public Needleman. Brilliant, committed, the author of *Styles of Modes*. But it is the private Needleman I will always fondly recall, the Sandor Needleman who was never without some favorite hat. Indeed, he was cremated with a hat on. A first, I believe. Or the Needleman who loved Walt Disney movies so passionately and who, despite lucid explanations of animation by Max Planck, could not be dissuaded from putting in a person-to-person call to Minnie Mouse.

When Needleman was staying at my house as a guest, I knew he liked a particular brand of tuna fish. I stocked the guest kitchen with it. He was too shy to admit his fondness for it to me, but once, thinking he was alone, opened every can and mused, "You are all my children."

At the opera in Milan with my daughter and me, Needleman leaned out of his box and fell into the orchestra pit. Too proud to admit it was a mistake, he attended the opera every night for a month and repeated it each time. Soon he developed a mild brain concussion. I pointed out that he could stop falling as his point had been made. He said, "No. A few more times. It's really not so bad."

I remember Needleman's seventieth birthday. His wife bought him pajamas. Needleman was obviously disappointed as he had hinted for a new Mercedes. Still, it is the mark of the man that he retired to the study and had his tantrum privately. He reentered the party smiling and wore the pajamas to the opening night of two short plays by Arabel.

The Condemned

BRISSEAU was asleep in the moonlight. Lying on his back in bed, with his fat stomach jutting into the air and his mouth forming an inane smile, he appeared to be some kind of inanimate object, like a large football or two tickets to the opera. A moment later, when he rolled over and the moonlight seemed to strike him from a different angle, he looked exactly like a twenty-seven-piece starter set of silverware, complete with salad bowl and soup tureen.

He's dreaming, Cloquet thought, as he stood over him, revolver in hand. *He's* dreaming, and I exist in reality. Cloquet hated reality but realized it was still the only place to get a good steak. He had never taken a human life before. True, he had once shot a mad dog, but only after it had been certified as mad by a team of psychiatrists. (The dog was diagnosed as manic-depressive after it had tried to bite off Cloquet's nose and then could not stop laughing.)

In his dream, Brisseau was on a sunlit beach and

running joyously toward his mother's outstretched arms, but just as he began to embrace the weeping grey-haired woman, she turned into two scoops of vanilla ice cream. Brisseau moaned and Cloquet lowered the revolver. He had entered through the window and stood poised over Brisseau for more than two hours, unable to pull the trigger. Once, he had even cocked the hammer and placed the muzzle of the gun right in Brisseau's left ear. Then there was a sound at the door, and Cloquet leaped behind the bureau, leaving the pistol sticking out of Brisseau's ear.

Madame Brisseau, who was wearing a flowered bathrobe, entered the room, turned on a small lamp, and noticed the weapon protruding straight up out of the side of her husband's head. Almost maternally, she sighed and removed it, placing it beside the pillow. She tucked in a loose corner of the quilt, snapped off the lamp, and left.

Cloquet, who had fainted, awoke an hour later. For one panicky moment, he imagined he was a child again, back on the Riviera, but after fifteen minutes went by and he saw no tourists it came to him that he was still behind Brisseau's chest of drawers. He returned to the bed, seized the pistol, and again pointed it at Brisseau's head, but he was still unable to squeeze off the shot that would end the life of the infamous Fascist informer.

Gaston Brisseau came from a wealthy, right-wing family, and decided early in life to become a professional informer. As a young man, he took speech lessons so that he could inform more clearly. Once, he had confessed to Cloquet, "God, I enjoy tattling on people."

"But why?" Cloquet said.

"I don't know. Getting them in Dutch, squealing."

Brisseau ratted on his friends for the pure sake of it, Cloquet thought. Unredeemable evil! Cloquet had once known an Algerian who loved smacking people on the back of the head and then smiling and denying it. It seemed the world was divided into good and bad people.

The good ones slept better, Cloquet thought, while the bad ones seemed to enjoy the waking hours much more.

Cloquet and Brisseau had met years before, under dramatic circumstances. Brisseau had gotten drunk at the Deux Magots one night and staggered toward the river. Thinking he was already home in his apartment, he removed his clothes, but instead of getting into bed he got into the Seine. When he tried to pull the blankets over himself and got a handful of water, he began screaming. Cloquet, who at that moment happened to be chasing his toupee across the Pont-Neuf, heard a cry from the icy water. The night was windy and dark, and Cloquet had a split second to decide if he would risk his life to save a stranger. Unwilling to make such a momentous decision on an empty stomach, he went to a restaurant and dined. Then, stricken with remorse, he purchased some fishing tackle and returned to fish Brisseau out of the river. At first he tried a dry fly, but Brisseau was too clever to bite, and in the end Cloquet was forced to coax Brisseau to shore with an offer of free dance lessons and then land him with a net. While Brisseau was being measured and weighed, the two became friends.

Now Cloquet stepped closer to Brisseau's sleeping hulk and again cocked the pistol. A feeling of nausea swept over him as he contemplated the implications of his action. This was an existential nausea, caused by his intense awareness of the contingency of life, and could not be relieved with an ordinary Alka-Seltzer. What was required was an Existential Alka-Seltzer—a product sold in many Left Bank drugstores. It was an enormous pill, the size of an automobile hubcap, that, dissolved in water, took away the queasy feeling induced by too much awareness of life. Cloquet had also found it helpful after eating Mexican food.

If I choose to kill Brisseau, Cloquet thought now, I am defining myself as a murderer. I will become Cloquet who kills, rather than simply what I am: Cloquet who teaches Psychology of Fowl at the Sorbonne. By choosing my action, I choose it for all mankind. But what if everyone in the world behaved like me and came here and shot Brisseau through the ear? What a mess! Not to mention the commotion from the doorbell ringing all night. And of course we'd need valet parking. Ah, God, how the mind boggles when it turns to moral or ethical considerations! Better not to think too much. Rely more on the body—the body is more dependable. It shows up for meetings, it looks good in a sports jacket, and where it really comes in handy is when you want to get a rubdown.

Cloquet felt a sudden need to reaffirm his own existence, and looked into the mirror over Brisseau's bureau. (He could never pass a mirror without sneaking a peek, and once at a health club he had stared at his reflection in a swimming pool for so long that the management was forced to drain it.) It was no use. He couldn't shoot a man. He dropped the pistol and fled.

Out on the street, he decided to go to La Coupole for a brandy. He liked La Coupole because it was always bright and crowded, and he could usually get a table—quite a difference from his own apartment, where it was dark and gloomy and where his mother, who lived there, too, always refused to seat him. But tonight La Coupole was filled. Who are all these faces, Cloquet wondered. They seem to blur into an abstraction: "The People." But there are no people, he thought—only individuals. Cloquet felt this was a brilliant perception, one that he could use impressively at some chic dinner party. Because of observations such as this, he had not been invited to a social gathering of any sort since 1931.

He decided to go to Juliet's house.

"Did you kill him?" she asked as he entered her flat.

"Yes," Cloquet said.

"Are you sure he is dead?"

"He seemed dead. I did my imitation of Maurice Chevalier, and it usually gets a big hand. This time, nothing."

"Good. Then he'll never betray the Party again."

Juliet was a Marxist, Cloquet reminded himself. And the most interesting type of Marxist—the kind with long, tanned legs. She was one of the few women he knew who could hold two disparate concepts in her mind at once, such as Hegel's dialectic and why if you stick your tongue in a man's ear while he is making a speech he will start to sound like Jerry Lewis. She stood before him now in a tight skirt and blouse, and he wanted to possess her—to own her the way he owned any other object, such as his radio or the rubber pig mask he had worn to harass the Nazis during the Occupation.

Suddenly he and Juliet were making love—or was it merely sex? He knew there was a difference between sex and love, but felt that either act was wonderful unless one of the partners happened to be wearing a lobster bib. Women, he reflected, were a soft, enveloping presence. Existence was a soft, enveloping presence, too. Sometimes it enveloped you totally. Then you could never get out again except for something really important, like your mother's birthday or jury duty. Cloquet often thought there was a great difference between Being and Being-in-the-World, and figured that no matter which group he belonged to the other was definitely having more fun.

He slept well after the lovemaking, as usual, but the next morning, to his great surprise, he was arrested for the murder of Gaston Brisseau.

At police headquarters, Cloquet protested his innocence, but he was informed that his fingerprints had been found all over Brisseau's room and on the recovered pistol. When he broke into Brisseau's house, Cloquet had also made the mistake of signing the guestbook. It was hopeless. The case was open-and-shut.

312

The trial, which took place over the following weeks, was like a circus, although there was some difficulty getting the elephants into the courtroom. At last, the jury found Cloquet guilty, and he was sentenced to the guillotine. An appeal for clemency was turned down on a technicality when it was learned Cloquet's lawyer had filed it while wearing a cardboard mustache.

Six weeks later, on the eve of his execution, Cloquet sat alone in his cell, still unable to believe the events of the past months—particularly the part about the elephants in the courtroom. By this time the next day, he would be dead. Cloquet had always thought of death as something that happened to other people. "I notice it happens to fat people a lot," he told his lawyer. To Cloquet himself, death seemed to be only another abstraction. Men die, he thought, but does Cloquet die? This question puzzled him, but a few simple line drawings on a pad done by one of the guards set the whole thing clear. There was no evading it. Soon he would no longer exist.

I will be gone, he thought wistfully, but Madame Plotnick, whose face looks like something on the menu in a seafood restaurant, will still be around. Cloquet began to panic. He wanted to run and hide, or, even better, to become something solid and durable—a heavy chair, for instance. A chair has no problems, he thought. It's there; nobody bothers it. It doesn't have to pay rent or get involved politically. A chair can never stub its toe or misplace its earmuffs. It doesn't have to smile or get a haircut, and you never have to worry that if you take it to a party it will suddenly start coughing or make a scene. People just sit in a chair, and then when those people die other people sit in it. Cloquet's logic comforted him, and when the jailers came at dawn to shave his neck, he pretended to be a chair. When they asked him what he wanted for his last meal, he said, "You're asking furniture what it wants to eat? Why not just upholster me?" When they stared at him, he weakened and said, "Just some Russian dressing."

Cloquet had always been an atheist, but when the priest, Father Bernard, arrived, he asked if there was still time for him to convert.

Father Bernard shook his head. "This time of year, I think most of your major faiths are filled," he said. "Probably the best I could do on such short notice is maybe make a call and get you into something Hindu. I'll need a passport-sized photograph, though."

No use, Cloquet reflected. I will have to meet my fate alone. There is no God. There is no purpose to life. Nothing lasts. Even the works of the great Shakespeare will disappear when the universe burns out—not such a terrible thought, of course, when it comes to a play like *Titus Andronicus*, but what about the others? No wonder some people commit suicide! Why not end this absurdity? Why go through with this hollow charade called life? Why, except that somewhere within us a voice says, "Live." Always, from some inner region, we hear the command, "Keep living!" Cloquet recognized the voice; it was his insurance salesman. Naturally, he thought—Fishbein doesn't want to pay off.

Cloquet longed to be free—to be out of jail, skipping through an open meadow. (Cloquet always skipped when he was happy. Indeed, the habit had kept him out of the Army.) The thought of freedom made him feel simultaneously exhilarated and terrified. If I were truly free, he thought, I could exercise my possibilities to the fullest. Perhaps I could become a ventriloquist, as I have always wanted. Or show up at the Louvre in bikini underwear, with a fake nose and glasses.

He grew dizzy as he contemplated his choices and was about to faint, when a jailer opened his cell door and told him that the real murderer of Brisseau had just confessed. Cloquet was free to go. Cloquet sank to his knees and kissed the floor of his cell. He sang the "Marseillaise." He wept! He danced! Three days later, he was back in jail for showing up at the Louvre in bikini underwear, with a fake nose and glasses.

By Destiny Denied

(Notes for an eight-hundred-page novel—the big book they're all waiting for)

BACKGROUND—SCOTLAND, 1823:

A man has been arrested for stealing a crust of bread. "I only like the crust," he explains, and he is identified as the thief who has recently terrorized several chophouses by stealing just the end cut of roast beef. The culprit, Solomon Entwhistle, is hauled into court, and a stern judge sentences him to from five to ten years (whichever comes first) at hard labor. Entwhistle is locked in a dungeon, and in an early act of enlightened penology the key is thrown away. Despondent but determined, Entwhistle begins the arduous task of tunnelling to freedom. Meticulously digging with a spoon, he tunnels beneath the prison walls, then continues, spoonful by spoonful, under Glasgow to London. He pauses to emerge at Liverpool, but finds that he prefers the tunnel. Once in London, he stows away aboard a freighter bound for the New World, where he dreams of starting life over, this time as a frog.

Arriving at Boston, Entwhistle meets Margaret Figg, a

comely New England schoolteacher whose specialty is
baking bread and then placing it on her head. Enticed,
Entwhistle marries her, and the two open a small store,
trading pelts and whale blubber for scrimshaw in an ever-
increasing cycle of meaningless activity. The store is an
instant success, and by 1850 Entwhistle is wealthy, educated, respected, and cheating on his wife with a large pos-
sum. He has two sons by Margaret Figg—one normal, the
other simple-minded, though it is hard to tell the difference unless someone hands them each a yo-yo. His small
trading post will go on to become a giant modern department store, and when he dies at eighty-five, from a combination of smallpox and a tomahawk in the skull, he is
happy.

(Note: Remember to make Entwhistle likable.)

Locale and observations, 1976:

Walking east on Alton Avenue, one passes the Costello
Brothers Warehouse, Adelman's Tallis Repair Shop, the
Chones Funeral Parlor, and Higby's Poolroom. John
Higby, the owner, is a stubby man with bushy hair who
fell off a ladder at the age of nine and requires two days'
advance notice to stop grinning. Turning north, or "uptown," from Higby's (actually, it is downtown, and the
real uptown is now located crosstown), one comes to a
small green park. Here citizens stroll and chat, and though
the place is free of muggings and rapes, one is frequently
accosted by panhandlers or men claiming to know Julius
Caesar. Now the cool autumn breeze (known here as the
santana, since it comes every year at the same time and
blows most of the older population out of their shoes)
causes the last leaves of summer to fall and drift into dead
heaps. One is struck by an almost existential feeling of
purposelessness—particularly since the massage parlors
closed. There is a definite sense of metaphysical "otherness," which cannot be explained except to say it's nothing

like what usually goes on in Pittsburgh. The town in its way is a metaphor, but for what? Not only is it a metaphor, it's a simile. It's "where it's at." It's "now." It's also "later." It's every town in America and it's no town. This causes great confusion among the mailmen. And the big department store is Entwhistle's.

Blanche (Base her on Cousin Tina):
Blanche Mandelstam, sweet but beefy, with nervous, pudgy fingers and thick-lensed glasses ("I wanted to be an Olympic swimmer," she told her doctor, "but I had some problems with buoyancy"), awakens to her clock radio.

Years ago, Blanche would have been considered pretty, though not later than the Pleistocene epoch. To her husband, Leon, however, she is "the most beautiful creature in the world, except for Ernest Borgnine." Blanche and Leon met long ago, at a high-school dance. (She is an excellent dancer, although during the tango she constantly consults a diagram she carries of some feet.) They talked freely and found they enjoyed many things in common. For example, both enjoyed sleeping on bacon bits. Blanche was impressed with the way Leon dressed, for she had never seen anyone wear three hats simultaneously. The couple were married, and it was not long before they had their first and only sexual experience. "It was totally sublime," Blanche recalls, "although I do remember Leon attempting to slash his wrists."

Blanche told her new husband that although he made a reasonable living as a human guinea pig, she wanted to keep her job in the shoe department of Entwhistle's. Too proud to be supported, Leon reluctantly agreed, but insisted that when she reached the age of ninety-five she must retire. Now the couple sat down to breakfast. For him, it was juice, toast, and coffee. For Blanche, the usual—a glass of hot water, a chicken wing, sweet-and-pungent pork, and cannelloni. Then she left for Entwhistle's.

(Note: Blanche should go around singing, the way Cousin Tina does, though not always the Japanese national anthem.)

Carmen (A study in psychopathology based on traits observed in Fred Simdong, his brother Lee, and their cat Sparky):

Carmen Pinchuck, squat and bald, emerged from a steaming shower and removed his shower cap. Although totally without hair, he detested getting his scalp wet. "Why should I?" he told friends. "Then my enemies would have the advantage over me." Someone suggested that this attitude might be considered strange, but he laughed, and then, his eyes tensely darting around the room to see if he was being watched, he kissed some throw pillows. Pinchuck is a nervous man who fishes in his spare time but has not caught anything since 1923. "I guess it's not in the cards," he chortles. But when an acquaintance pointed out that he was casting his line into a jar of sweet cream he grew uneasy.

Pinchuck has done many things. He was expelled from high school for moaning in class, and has since worked as a shepherd, psychotherapist, and mime. He is currently employed by the Fish and Wildlife Service, where he is paid to teach Spanish to squirrels. Pinchuck has been described by those who love him as "a punk, a loner, a psychopath, and apple-cheeked." "He likes to sit in his room and talk back to the radio," one neighbor said. "He can be very loyal," another remarked. "Once when Mrs. Monroe slipped on the ice, he slipped on some ice out of sympathy." Politically, Pinchuck is, by his own admission, an independent, and in the last Presidential election his write-in vote was for Cesar Romero.

Now, donning his tweed hackie's cap and lifting a box wrapped in brown paper, Pinchuck left his rooming house for the street. Then, realizing he was naked except for his tweed hackie's cap, he returned, dressed, and set out for Entwhistle's.

(Note: Remember to go into greater detail about Pinchuck's hostility toward his cap.)

The Meeting (rough):

The doors to the department store opened at ten sharp, and although Monday was generally a slow day, a sale on radioactive tuna fish quickly jammed the basement. An air of imminent apocalypse hung over the shoe department like a wet tarpaulin as Carmen Pinchuck handed his box to Blanche Mandelstam and said, "I'd like to return these loafers. They're too small."

"Do you have a sales slip?" Blanche countered, trying to remain poised, although she confessed later that her world had suddenly begun falling apart. ("I can't deal with people since the accident," she has told friends. Six months ago, while playing tennis, she swallowed one of the balls. Since then her breathing has become irregular.)

"Er, no," Pinchuck replied nervously. "I lost it." (The central problem of his life is that he is always misplacing things. Once he went to sleep and when he awoke his bed was missing.) Now, as customers lined up behind him impatiently, he broke into a cold sweat.

"You'll have to have it O.K.'d by the floor manager," Blanche said, referring Pinchuck to Mr. Dubinsky, whom she had been having an affair with since Halloween. (Lou Dubinsky, a graduate of the best typing school in Europe, was a genius until alcohol reduced his speed to one word per day and he was forced to go to work in a department store.)

"Have you worn them?" Blanche continued, fighting back tears. The notion of Pinchuck in his loafers was unbearable to her. "My father used to wear loafers," she confessed. "Both on the same foot."

Pinchuck was writhing now. "No," he said. "Er—I

mean yes. I had them on briefly, but only while I took a bath."

"Why did you buy them if they're too small?" Blanche asked, unaware that she was articulating a quintessential human paradox.

The truth was that Pinchuck had not felt comfortable in the shoes but he could never bring himself to say no to a salesman. "I want to be *liked*," he admitted to Blanche. "Once I bought a live wildebeest because I couldn't say no." (Note: O. F. Krumgold has written a brilliant paper about certain tribes in Borneo that do not have a word for "no" in their language and consequently turn down requests by nodding their heads and saying, "I'll get back to you." This corroborates his earlier theories that the urge to be liked at any cost is not socially adaptive but genetic, much the same as the ability to sit through operetta.)

By eleven-ten, the floor manager, Dubinsky, had O.K.'d the exchange, and Pinchuck was given a larger pair of shoes. Pinchuck confessed later that the incident had caused him to experience severe depression and wooziness, which he also attributed to the news of his parrot's wedding.

Shortly after the Entwhistle affair, Carmen Pinchuck quit his job and became a Chinese waiter at the Sung Ching Cantonese Palace. Blanche Mandelstam then suffered a major nervous breakdown and tried to elope with a photograph of Dizzy Dean. (Note: Upon reflection, perhaps it would be best to make Dubinsky a hand puppet.) Late in January, Entwhistle's closed its doors for the last time, and Julie Entwhistle, the owner, took his family, whom he loved very dearly, and moved them into the Bronx Zoo.

(This last sentence should remain intact. It seems very very great. End of Chapter 1 notes.)

The UFO Menace

UFOS ARE back in the news, and it is high time we took a serious look at this phenomenon. (Actually, the time is ten past eight, so not only are we a few minutes late but I'm hungry.) Up until now, the entire subject of flying saucers has been mostly associated with kooks or oddballs. Frequently, in fact, observers will admit to being a member of both groups. Still, persistent sightings by responsible individuals have caused the Air Force and the scientific community to reexamine a once skeptical attitude, and the sum of two hundred dollars has now been allocated for a comprehensive study of the phenomenon. The question is: Is anything out there? And if so, do they have ray guns?

All UFOs may not prove to be of extraterrestrial origin, but experts do agree that any glowing cigar-shaped aircraft capable of rising straight up at twelve thousand miles per second would require the kind of maintenance and spark-plugs available only on Pluto. If these objects are indeed from another planet, then the civilization that designed them must be millions of years more advanced than our own. Either that or they are very lucky. Professor Leon Speciman postulates a civilization in outer space that is more advanced than ours by approximately fifteen minutes. This, he feels, gives them a great advantage over us, since they needn't rush to get to appointments.

Dr. Brackish Menzies, who works at the Mount Wilson Observatory, or else is under observation at the Mount Wilson Mental Hospital (the letter is not clear), claims that travellers moving at close to the speed of light would require many millions of years to get here, even from the nearest solar system, and, judging from the shows on Broadway, the trip would hardly be worth it. (It is impossible to travel faster than light, and certainly not desirable, as one's hat keeps blowing off.)

Interestingly, according to modern astronomers, space is finite. This is a very comforting thought—particularly for people who can never remember where they have left things. The key factor in thinking about the universe, however, is that it is expanding and will one day break apart and disappear. That is why if the girl in the office down the hall has some good points but perhaps not all the qualities you require it's best to compromise.

The most frequently asked question about the UFOs is: If saucers come from outer space, why have their pilots not attempted to make contact with us, instead of hovering mysteriously over deserted areas? My own theory is that for creatures from another solar system "hovering" may be a socially acceptable mode of relating. It may, indeed, be pleasurable. I myself once hovered over an eighteen-year-old actress for six months and had the best time of my life. It should also be recalled that when we talk of "life" on other planets we are frequently referring to amino acids, which are never very gregarious, even at parties.

Most people tend to think of UFOs as a modern

problem, but could they be a phenomenon that man has been aware of for centuries? (To us a century seems quite long, particularly if you are holding an I.O.U., but by astronomical standards it is over in a second. For that reason, it is always best to carry a toothbrush and be ready to leave on a moment's notice.) Scholars now tell us that the sighting of unidentified flying objects dates as far back as Biblical times. For instance, there is a passage in the Book of Leviticus that reads, "And a great and silver ball appeared over the Assyrian Armies, and in all of Babylonia there was wailing and gnashing of teeth, till the Prophets bade the multitudes get a grip on themselves and shape up."

Was this phenomenon related to one described years later by Parmenides: "Three orange objects did appear suddenly in the heavens and did circle midtown Athens, hovering over the baths and causing several of our wisest philosophers to grab for towels"? And, again, were those "orange objects" similar to what is described in a recently discovered twelfth-century Saxon-church manuscript: "A lauch launched he; wer richt laith to weet a cork-heild schonne; whilst a red balle lang owre swam aboone. I thank you, ladies and gentlemen"?

This last account was taken by medieval clergy to signify that the world was coming to an end, and there was great disappointment when Monday came and everyone had to go back to work.

Finally, and most convincingly, in 1822 Goethe himself notes a strange celestial phenomenon. "En route home from the Leipzig Anxiety Festival," he wrote, "I was crossing a meadow, when I chanced to look up and saw several fiery red balls suddenly appear in the southern sky. They descended at a great rate of speed and began chasing me. I screamed that I was a genius and consequently could not run very fast, but my words were wasted. I became enraged and shouted imprecations at them, whereupon they flew away frightened. I related this story to Beethoven, not realizing he had already gone deaf, and he smiled and nodded and said, 'Right.' "

As a general rule, careful on-the-scene investigations disclose that most "unidentified" flying objects are quite ordinary phenomena, such as weather balloons, meteorites, satellites, and even once a man named Lewis Mandelbaum, who blew off the roof of the World Trade Center. A typical "explained" incident is the one reported by Sir Chester Ramsbottom, on June 5, 1961, in Shropshire: "I was driving along the road at 2 A.M. and saw a cigar-shaped object that seemed to be tracking my car. No matter which way I drove, it stayed with me, turning sharply at right angles. It was a fierce, glowing red, and in spite of twisting and turning the car at high speed I could not lose it. I became alarmed and began sweating. I let out a shriek of terror and apparently fainted, but awoke in a hospital, miraculously unharmed." Upon investigation, experts determined that the "cigar-shaped object" was Sir Chester's nose. Naturally, all his evasive actions could not lose it, since it was attached to his face.

Another explained incident began in late April of 1972, with a report from Major General Curtis Memling, of Andrews Air Force Base: "I was walking across a field one night and suddenly I saw a large silver disc in the sky. It flew over me, not fifty feet above my head, and repeatedly described aerodynamic patterns impossible for any normal aircraft. Suddenly it accelerated and shot away at terrific speed."

Investigators became suspicious when they noticed that General Memling could not describe this incident without giggling. He later admitted he had just come from a showing of the film "War of the Worlds," at the post movie theatre, and "got a very big kick out of it." Ironically, General Memling reported another UFO sighting in 1976, but it was soon discovered that he, too, had become

fixated on Sir Chester Ramsbottom's nose—an occurrence
that caused consternation in the Air Force and eventually
led to General Memling's court-martial.

If most UFO sightings can be satisfactorily explained,
what of those few which cannot? Following are some of
the most mystifying examples of "unsolved" encounters,
the first reported by a Boston man in May, 1969: "I was
walking by the beach with my wife. She's not a very attractive woman. Rather overweight. In fact, I was pulling her
on a dolly at the time. Suddenly I looked up and saw a
huge white saucer that seemed to be descending at great
speed. I guess I panicked, because I dropped the rope on
my wife's dolly and began running. The saucer passed
directly over my head and I heard an eerie, metallic voice
say, 'Call your service.' When I got home, I phoned my
answering service and received a message that my brother
Ralph had moved and to forward all his mail to Neptune. I
never saw him again. My wife suffered a severe breakdown over the incident and now cannot converse without
using a hand puppet."

From I. M. Axelbank, of Athens, Georgia, February,
1971: "I am an experienced pilot and was flying my private
Cessna from New Mexico to Amarillo, Texas, to bomb
some people whose religious persuasion I do not wholly
agree with, when I noticed an object flying alongside me.
At first I thought it was another plane, until it emitted a
green beam of light, forcing my plane to drop eleven thousand feet in four seconds and causing my toupee to snap
off my head and tear a two-foot hole in the roof. I repeatedly called for help on my radio, but for some reason could
only get the old 'Mr. Anthony' program. The UFO came
very close to my plane again and then shot away at blinding speed. By this time I had lost my bearings and was
forced to make an emergency landing on the turnpike. I
continued the trip in the plane on the ground and only got

into trouble when I tried to run a toll booth and broke off my wings."

One of the eeriest accounts occurred in August, 1975, to a man on Montauk Point, in Long Island: "I was in bed at my beach house, but could not sleep because of some fried chicken in the icebox that I felt entitled to. I waited till my wife dropped off, and tiptoed into the kitchen. I remember looking at the clock. It was precisely four-fifteen. I'm quite certain of this, because our kitchen clock has not worked in twenty-one years and is always at that time. I also noticed that our dog, Judas, was acting funny. He was standing up on his hind legs and singing, 'I Enjoy Being a Girl.' Suddenly the room turned bright orange. At first, I thought my wife had caught me eating between meals and set fire to the house. Then I looked out the window, where to my amazement I saw a gigantic cigar-shaped aircraft hovering just over the treetops in the yard and emitting an orange glow. I stood transfixed for what must have been several hours, though our clock still read four-fifteen, so it was difficult to tell. Finally, a large, mechanical claw extended from the aircraft and snatched the two pieces of chicken from my hand and quickly retreated. The machine then rose and, accelerating at great speed, vanished into the sky. When I reported the incident to the Air Force, they told me that what I had seen was a flock of birds. When I protested, Colonel Quincy Bascomb personally promised that the Air Force would return the two pieces of chicken. To this day, I have only received one piece."

Finally, an account in January, 1977, by two Louisiana factory workers: "Roy and I was catfishing in the bog. I enjoy the bog, as does Roy. We was not drinking, although we had brought with us a gallon of methyl chloride, which we both favor with either a twist of lemon or a small onion. Anyways, at about midnight we looked up and saw a bright-yellow sphere descend into the bog. At first Roy mistook it for a whooping crane and took a shot at it, but I said, 'Roy, that ain't no crane, 'cause it's got no beak.' That's how you can tell a crane. Roy's son Gus has a beak, you know, and thinks he's a crane. Anyways, all of a sudden this door slides open and several creatures emerge. These creatures looked like little portable radios with teeth and short hair. They also had legs, although where the toes usually are they had wheels. The creatures motioned to me to come forward, which I did, and they injected me with a fluid that caused me to smile and act like Bopeep. They spoke with one another in a strange tongue, which sounded like when you back your car over a fat person. They took me aboard the aircraft and gave me what seemed to be a complete physical examination. I went along with it, as I had not had a checkup in two years. By now they had mastered my own language, but they still made simple mistakes like using 'hermeneutics,' when they meant 'heuristic.' They told me they were from another galaxy and were here to tell the earth that we must learn to live in peace or they will return with special weapons and laminate every first-born male. They said they would get the results of my blood test back in a couple of days and if I didn't hear from them I could go ahead and marry Clair."

My Apology

O F ALL the famous men who ever lived, the one I would most like to have been was Socrates. Not just because he was a great thinker, because I have been known to have some reasonably profound insights myself, although mine invariably revolve around a Swedish airline stewardess and some handcuffs. No, the great appeal for me of this wisest of all Greeks was his courage in the face of death. His decision was not to abandon his principles, but rather to give his life to prove a point. I personally am not quite as fearless about dying and will, after any untoward noise such as a car backfiring, leap directly into the arms of the person I am conversing with. In the end, Socrates' brave death gave his life authentic meaning; something my existence lacks totally, although it does possess a minimal relevance to the Internal Revenue Department. I must confess I have tried putting myself in this great philosopher's sandals many times and no matter how often I do, I immediately wind up dozing off and having the following dream.

(The scene is my prison cell. I am usually sitting alone, working out some deep problem of rational thought like: Can an object be called a work of art if it can also be used to clean the stove? Presently I am visited by Agathon and Simmias.)

AGATHON: Ah, my good friend and wise old sage. How go your days of confinement?

ALLEN: What can one say of confinement, Agathon? Only the body may be circumscribed. My mind roams freely, unfettered by the four walls and therefore in truth I ask, does confinement exist?

AGATHON: Well, what if you want to take a walk?

ALLEN: Good question. I can't.

(The three of us sit in classical poses, not unlike a frieze. Finally Agathon speaks.)

AGATHON: I'm afraid the word is bad. You have been condemned to death.

ALLEN: Ah, it saddens me that I should cause debate in the senate.

AGATHON: No debate. Unanimous.

ALLEN: Really?

AGATHON: First ballot.

ALLEN: Hmmm. I had counted on a little more support.

SIMMIAS: The senate is furious over your ideas for a Utopian state.

ALLEN: I guess I should never have suggested having a philosopher-king.

SIMMIAS: Especially when you kept pointing to yourself and clearing your throat.

ALLEN: And yet I do not regard my executioners as evil.

AGATHON: Nor do I.

ALLEN: Er, yeah, well . . . for what is evil but merely good in excess?

AGATHON: How so?

ALLEN: Look at it this way. If a man sings a lovely song it is beautiful. If he keeps singing, one begins to get a headache.

AGATHON: True.

ALLEN: And if he definitely won't stop singing, eventually you want to stuff socks down his throat.

AGATHON: Yes. Very true.

ALLEN: When is the sentence to be carried out?

AGATHON: What time is it now?

ALLEN: Today!?

AGATHON: They need the jail cell.

ALLEN: Then let it be! Let them take my life. Let it be recorded that I died rather than abandon the principles of truth and free inquiry. Weep not, Agathon.

AGATHON: I'm not weeping. This is an allergy.

ALLEN: For to the man of the mind, death is not an end but a beginning.

SIMMIAS: How so?

ALLEN: Well, now give me a minute.

SIMMIAS: Take your time.

ALLEN: It is true, Simmias, that man does not exist before he is born, is it not?

SIMMIAS: Very true.

ALLEN: Nor does he exist after his death.

SIMMIAS: Yes. I agree.

ALLEN: Hmmm.

SIMMIAS: So?

ALLEN: Now, wait a minute. I'm a little confused. You know they only feed me lamb and it's never well-cooked.

SIMMIAS: Most men regard death as the final end. Consequently they fear it.

ALLEN: Death is a state of non-being. That which is not, does not exist. Therefore death does not exist. Only truth exists. Truth and beauty. Each is interchangeable, but are aspects of themselves. Er, what specifically did they say they had in mind for me?

AGATHON: Hemlock.

ALLEN: *(Puzzled)* Hemlock?

AGATHON: You remember that black liquid that ate through your marble table?

ALLEN: Really?

AGATHON: Just one cupful. Though they do have a back-up chalice should you spill anything.

ALLEN: I wonder if it's painful?

AGATHON: They asked if you would try not to make a scene. It disturbs the other prisoners.

ALLEN: Hmmm . . .

AGATHON: I told everyone you would die bravely rather than renounce your principles.

ALLEN: Right, right . . . er, did the concept of "exile" ever come up?

AGATHON: They stopped exiling last year. Too much red tape.

ALLEN: Right . . . yeah . . . *(Troubled and distracted but trying to remain self-possessed)* I er . . . so er . . . so—what else is new?

AGATHON: Oh, I ran into Isosceles. He has a great idea for a new triangle.

ALLEN: Right . . . right . . . *(Suddenly dropping all pretense of courage)* Look, I'm going to level with you—I don't want to go! I'm too young!

AGATHON: But this is your chance to die for truth!

ALLEN: Don't misunderstand me. I'm all for truth. On the other hand I have a lunch date in Sparta next week and I'd hate to miss it. It's my turn to buy. You know those Spartans, they fight so easily.

SIMMIAS: Is our wisest philosopher a coward?

ALLEN: I'm not a coward, and I'm not a hero. I'm somewhere in the middle.

SIMMIAS: A cringing vermin.

ALLEN: That's approximately the spot.

AGATHON: But it was you who proved that death doesn't exist.

ALLEN: Hey, listen—I've proved a lot of things. That's how I pay my rent. Theories and little observations. A puckish remark now and then. Occasional maxims. It beats picking olives, but let's not get carried away.

AGATHON: But you have proved many times that the soul is immortal.

ALLEN: And it is! On paper. See, that's the thing about philosophy—it's not all that functional once you get out of class.

SIMMIAS: And the eternal "forms"? You said each thing always did exist and always will exist.

ALLEN: I was talking mostly about heavy objects. A statue or something. With people it's a lot different.

AGATHON: But all that talk about death being the same as sleep.

ALLEN: Yes, but the difference is that when you're dead and somebody yells, "Everybody up, it's morning," it's very hard to find your slippers.

(The executioner arrives with a cup of hemlock. He bears a close facial resemblance to the Irish comedian Spike Milligan.)

EXECUTIONER: Ah—here we are. Who gets the poison?

AGATHON: *(Pointing to me)* He does.

ALLEN: Gee, it's a big cup. Should it be smoking like that?

EXECUTIONER: Yes. And drink it all because a lot of times the poison's at the bottom.

ALLEN: *(Usually here my behavior is totally different from Socrates' and I am told I scream in my sleep.)* No —I won't! I don't want to die! Help! No! Please!

(He hands me the bubbling brew amidst my disgusting pleading and all seems lost. Then because of some innate survival instinct the dream always takes an upturn and a messenger arrives.)

MESSENGER: Hold everything! The senate has revoted! The charges are dropped. Your value has been reassessed and it is decided you should be honored instead.

ALLEN: At last! At last! They came to their senses! I'm a free man! Free! And to be honored yet! Quick, Agathon and Simmias, get my bags. I must be going. Praxiteles will want to get an early start on my bust. But before I leave, I give a little parable.

SIMMIAS: Gee, that really was a sharp reversal. I wonder if they know what they're doing?

ALLEN: A group of men live in a dark cave. They are unaware that outside the sun shines. The only light they know is the flickering flame of a few small candles which they use to move around.

AGATHON: Where'd they get the candles?

ALLEN: Well, let's just say they have them.

AGATHON: They live in a cave and have candles? It doesn't ring true.

ALLEN: Can't you just buy it for now?

AGATHON: O.K., O.K., but get to the point.

ALLEN: And then one day, one of the cave dwellers wanders out of the cave and sees the outside world.

SIMMIAS: In all its clarity.

ALLEN: Precisely. In all its clarity.

AGATHON: When he tries to tell the others they don't believe him.

ALLEN: Well, no. He doesn't tell the others.

AGATHON: He doesn't?

ALLEN: No, he opens a meat market, he marries a dancer and dies of a cerebral hemorrhage at forty-two.

(They grab me and force the hemlock down. Here I usually wake up in a sweat and only some eggs and smoked salmon calm me down.)

The Kugelmass Episode

KUGELMASS, A PROFESSOR of humanities at City College, was unhappily married for the second time. Daphne Kugelmass was an oaf. He also had two dull sons by his first wife, Flo, and was up to his neck in alimony and child support.

"Did I know it would turn out so badly?" Kugelmass whined to his analyst one day. "Daphne had promise. Who suspected she'd let herself go and swell up like a beach ball? Plus she had a few bucks, which is not in itself a healthy reason to marry a person, but it doesn't hurt, with the kind of operating nut I have. You see my point?"

Kugelmass was bald and as hairy as a bear, but he had soul.

"I need to meet a new woman," he went on. "I need to have an affair. I may not look the part, but I'm a man who needs romance. I need softness, I need flirtation. I'm not getting younger, so before it's too late I want to make love in Venice, trade quips at '21,' and exchange coy glances over red wine and candlelight. You see what I'm saying?"

Dr. Mandel shifted in his chair and said, "An affair will solve nothing. You're so unrealistic. Your problems run much deeper."

"And also this affair must be discreet," Kugelmass continued. "I can't afford a second divorce. Daphne would really sock it to me."

"Mr. Kugelmass—"

"But it can't be anyone at City College, because Daphne also works there. Not that anyone on the faculty at C.C.N.Y. is any great shakes, but some of those coeds . . ."

"Mr. Kugelmass—"

"Help me. I had a dream last night. I was skipping through a meadow holding a picnic basket and the basket was marked 'Options.' And then I saw there was a hole in the basket."

"Mr. Kugelmass, the worst thing you could do is act out. You must simply express your feelings here, and together we'll analyze them. You have been in treatment long enough to know there is no overnight cure. After all, I'm an analyst, not a magician."

"Then perhaps what I need is a magician," Kugelmass said, rising from his chair. And with that he terminated his therapy.

A couple of weeks later, while Kugelmass and Daphne were moping around in their apartment one night like two pieces of old furniture, the phone rang.

"I'll get it," Kugelmass said. "Hello."

"Kugelmass?" a voice said. "Kugelmass, this is Persky."

"Who?"

"Persky. Or should I say The Great Persky?"

"Pardon me?"

"I hear you're looking all over town for a magician to bring a little exotica into your life? Yes or no?"

"Sh-h-h," Kugelmass whispered. "Don't hang up. Where are you calling from, Persky?"

Early the following afternoon, Kugelmass climbed three flights of stairs in a broken-down apartment house in the Bushwick section of Brooklyn. Peering through the darkness of the hall, he found the door he was looking for and pressed the bell. I'm going to regret this, he thought to himself.

Seconds later, he was greeted by a short, thin, waxy-looking man.

"*You're* Persky the Great?" Kugelmass said.

"The Great Persky. You want a tea?"

"No, I want romance. I want music. I want love and beauty."

"But not tea, eh? Amazing. O.K., sit down."

Persky went to the back room, and Kugelmass heard the sounds of boxes and furniture being moved around. Persky reappeared, pushing before him a large object on squeaky roller-skate wheels. He removed some old silk handkerchiefs that were lying on its top and blew away a bit of dust. It was a cheap-looking Chinese cabinet, badly lacquered.

"Persky," Kugelmass said, "what's your scam?"

"Pay attention," Persky said. "This is some beautiful effect. I developed it for a Knights of Pythias date last year, but the booking fell through. Get into the cabinet."

"Why, so you can stick it full of swords or something?"

"You see any swords?"

Kugelmass made a face and, grunting, climbed into the cabinet. He couldn't help noticing a couple of ugly rhinestones glued onto the raw plywood just in front of his face. "If this is a joke," he said.

"Some joke. Now, here's the point. If I throw any novel

into this cabinet with you, shut the doors, and tap it three times, you will find yourself projected into that book.''

Kugelmass made a grimace of disbelief.

"It's the emess," Persky said. "My hand to God. Not just a novel, either. A short story, a play, a poem. You can meet any of the women created by the world's best writers. Whoever you dreamed of. You could carry on all you like with a real winner. Then when you've had enough you give a yell, and I'll see you're back here in a split second.''

"Persky, are you some kind of outpatient?"

"I'm telling you it's on the level," Persky said.

Kugelmass remained skeptical. "What are you telling me—that this cheesy homemade box can take me on a ride like you're describing?"

"For a double sawbuck."

Kugelmass reached for his wallet. "I'll believe this when I see it," he said.

Persky tucked the bills in his pants pocket and turned toward his bookcase. "So who do you want to meet? Sister Carrie? Hester Prynne? Ophelia? Maybe someone by Saul Bellow? Hey, what about Temple Drake? Although for a man your age she'd be a workout.''

"French. I want to have an affair with a French lover."

"Nana?"

"I don't want to have to pay for it."

"What about Natasha in *War and Peace?*"

"I said French. I know! What about Emma Bovary? That sounds to me perfect."

"You got it, Kugelmass. Give me a holler when you've had enough." Persky tossed in a paperback copy of Flaubert's novel.

"You sure this is safe?" Kugelmass asked as Persky began shutting the cabinet doors.

"Safe. Is anything safe in this crazy world?" Persky rapped three times on the cabinet and then flung open the doors.

Kugelmass was gone. At the same moment, he appeared in the bedroom of Charles and Emma Bovary's house at Yonville. Before him was a beautiful woman, standing alone with her back turned to him as she folded some linen. I can't believe this, thought Kugelmass, staring at the doctor's ravishing wife. This is uncanny. I'm here. It's her.

Emma turned in surprise. "Goodness, you startled me," she said. "Who are you?" She spoke in the same fine English translation as the paperback.

It's simply devastating, he thought. Then, realizing that it was he whom she had addressed, he said, "Excuse me. I'm Sidney Kugelmass. I'm from City College. A professor of humanities. C.C.N.Y.? Uptown. I—oh, boy!"

Emma Bovary smiled flirtatiously and said, "Would you like a drink? A glass of wine, perhaps?"

She is beautiful, Kugelmass thought. What a contrast with the troglodyte who shared his bed! He felt a sudden impulse to take this vision into his arms and tell her she was the kind of woman he had dreamed of all his life.

"Yes, some wine," he said hoarsely. "White. No, red. No, white. Make it white."

"Charles is out for the day," Emma said, her voice full of playful implication.

After the wine, they went for a stroll in the lovely French countryside. "I've always dreamed that some mysterious stranger would appear and rescue me from the monotony of this crass rural existence," Emma said, clasping his hand. They passed a small church. "I love what you have on," she murmured. "I've never seen anything like it around here. It's so . . . so modern."

"It's called a leisure suit," he said romantically. "It was marked down." Suddenly he kissed her. For the next hour they reclined under a tree and whispered together and told each other deeply meaningful things with their eyes. Then Kugelmass sat up. He had just remembered he had to meet

Daphne at Bloomingdale's. "I must go," he told her. "But don't worry, I'll be back."

"I hope so," Emma said.

He embraced her passionately, and the two walked back to the house. He held Emma's face cupped in his palms, kissed her again, and yelled, "O.K., Persky! I got to be at Bloomingdale's by three-thirty."

There was an audible pop, and Kugelmass was back in Brooklyn.

"So? Did I lie?" Persky asked triumphantly.

"Look, Persky, I'm right now late to meet the ball and chain at Lexington Avenue, but when can I go again? Tomorrow?"

"My pleasure. Just bring a twenty. And don't mention this to anybody."

"Yeah. I'm going to call Rupert Murdoch."

Kugelmass hailed a cab and sped off to the city. His heart danced on point. I am in love, he thought, I am the possessor of a wonderful secret. What he didn't realize was that at this very moment students in various classrooms across the country were saying to their teachers, "Who is this character on page 100? A bald Jew is kissing Madame Bovary?" A teacher in Sioux Falls, South Dakota, sighed and thought, Jesus, these kids, with their pot and acid. What goes through their minds!

Daphne Kugelmass was in the bathroom-accessories department at Bloomingdale's when Kugelmass arrived breathlessly. "Where've you been?" she snapped. "It's four-thirty."

"I got held up in traffic," Kugelmass said.

Kugelmass visited Persky the next day, and in a few minutes was again passed magically to Yonville. Emma couldn't hide her excitement at seeing him. The two spent hours together, laughing and talking about their different backgrounds. Before Kugelmass left, they made love. "My

God, I'm doing it with Madame Bovary!" Kugelmass whispered to himself. "Me, who failed freshman English."

As the months passed, Kugelmass saw Persky many times and developed a close and passionate relationship with Emma Bovary. "Make sure and always get me into the book before page 120," Kugelmass said to the magician one day. "I always have to meet her before she hooks up with this Rodolphe character."

"Why?" Persky asked. "You can't beat his time?"

"Beat his time. He's landed gentry. Those guys have nothing better to do than flirt and ride horses. To me, he's one of those faces you see in the pages of *Women's Wear Daily*. With the Helmut Berger hairdo. But to her he's hot stuff."

"And her husband suspects nothing?"

"He's out of his depth. He's a lacklustre little paramedic who's thrown in his lot with a jitterbug. He's ready to go to sleep by ten, and she's putting on her dancing shoes. Oh, well . . . See you later."

And once again Kugelmass entered the cabinet and passed instantly to the Bovary estate at Yonville. "How you doing, cupcake?" he said to Emma.

"Oh, Kugelmass," Emma sighed. "What I have to put up with. Last night at dinner, Mr. Personality dropped off to sleep in the middle of the dessert course. I'm pouring my heart out about Maxim's and the ballet, and out of the blue I hear snoring."

"It's O.K., darling. I'm here now," Kugelmass said, embracing her. I've earned this, he thought, smelling Emma's French perfume and burying his nose in her hair. I've suffered enough. I've paid enough analysts. I've searched till I'm weary. She's young and nubile, and I'm here a few pages after Leon and just before Rodolphe. By showing up during the correct chapters, I've got the situation knocked.

Emma, to be sure, was just as happy as Kugelmass. She had been starved for excitement, and his tales of Broadway night life, of fast cars and Hollywood and TV stars, enthralled the young French beauty.

"Tell me again about O. J. Simpson," she implored that evening, as she and Kugelmass strolled past Abbé Bournisien's church.

"What can I say? The man is great. He sets all kinds of rushing records. Such moves. They can't touch him."

"And the Academy Awards?" Emma said wistfully. "I'd give anything to win one."

"First you've got to be nominated."

"I know. You explained it. But I'm convinced I can act. Of course, I'd want to take a class or two. With Strasberg maybe. Then, if I had the right agent—"

"We'll see, we'll see. I'll speak to Persky."

That night, safely returned to Persky's flat, Kugelmass brought up the idea of having Emma visit him in the big city.

"Let me think about it," Persky said. "Maybe I could work it. Stranger things have happened." Of course, neither of them could think of one.

"Where the hell do you go all the time?" Daphne Kugelmass barked at her husband as he returned home late that evening. "You got a chippie stashed somewhere?"

"Yeah, sure, I'm just the type," Kugelmass said wearily. "I was with Leonard Popkin. We were discussing Socialist agriculture in Poland. You know Popkin. He's a freak on the subject."

"Well, you've been very odd lately," Daphne said. "Distant. Just don't forget about my father's birthday. On Saturday?"

"Oh, sure, sure," Kugelmass said, heading for the bathroom.

"My whole family will be there. We can see the twins. And Cousin Hamish. You should be more polite to Cousin Hamish—he likes you."

"Right, the twins," Kugelmass said, closing the bathroom door and shutting out the sound of his wife's voice. He leaned against it and took a deep breath. In a few hours, he told himself, he would be back in Yonville again, back with his beloved. And this time, if all went well, he would bring Emma back with him.

At three-fifteen the following afternoon, Persky worked his wizardry again. Kugelmass appeared before Emma, smiling and eager. The two spent a few hours at Yonville with Binet and then remounted the Bovary carriage. Following Persky's instructions, they held each other tightly, closed their eyes, and counted to ten. When they opened them, the carriage was just drawing up at the side door of the Plaza Hotel, where Kugelmass had optimistically reserved a suite earlier in the day.

"I love it! It's everything I dreamed it would be," Emma said as she swirled joyously around the bedroom, surveying the city from their window. "There's F. A. O. Schwarz. And there's Central Park, and the Sherry is which one? Oh, there—I see. It's too divine."

On the bed there were boxes from Halston and Saint Laurent. Emma unwrapped a package and held up a pair of black velvet pants against her perfect body.

"The slacks suit is by Ralph Lauren," Kugelmass said. "You'll look like a million bucks in it. Come on, sugar, give us a kiss."

"I've never been so happy!" Emma squealed as she stood before the mirror. "Let's go out on the town. I want to see *Chorus Line* and the Guggenheim and this Jack Nicholson character you always talk about. Are any of his flicks showing?"

"I cannot get my mind around this," a Stanford professor said. "First a strange character named Kugelmass, and now she's gone from the book. Well, I guess the mark of a classic is that you can reread it a thousand times and always find something new."

• • • • •

The lovers passed a blissful weekend. Kugelmass had told Daphne he would be away at a symposium in Boston and would return Monday. Savoring each moment, he and Emma went to the movies, had dinner in Chinatown, passed two hours at a discothèque, and went to bed with a TV movie. They slept till noon on Sunday, visited SoHo, and ogled celebrities at Elaine's. They had caviar and champagne in their suite on Sunday night and talked until dawn. That morning, in the cab taking them to Persky's apartment, Kugelmass thought, It was hectic, but worth it. I can't bring her here too often, but now and then it will be a charming contrast with Yonville.

At Persky's, Emma climbed into the cabinet, arranged her new boxes of clothes neatly around her, and kissed Kugelmass fondly. "My place next time," she said with a wink. Persky rapped three times on the cabinet. Nothing happened.

"Hmm," Persky said, scratching his head. He rapped again, but still no magic. "Something must be wrong," he mumbled.

"Persky, you're joking!" Kugelmass cried. "How can it not work?"

"Relax, relax. Are you still in the box, Emma?"

"Yes."

Persky rapped again—harder this time.

"I'm still here, Persky."

"I know, darling. Sit tight."

"Persky, we *have* to get her back," Kugelmass whispered. "I'm a married man, and I have a class in three hours. I'm not prepared for anything more than a cautious affair at this point."

"I can't understand it," Persky muttered. "It's such a reliable little trick."

But he could do nothing. "It's going to take a little

while," he said to Kugelmass. "I'm going to have to strip it down. I'll call you later."

Kugelmass bundled Emma into a cab and took her back to the Plaza. He barely made it to his class on time. He was on the phone all day, to Persky and to his mistress. The magician told him it might be several days before he got to the bottom of the trouble.

"How was the symposium?" Daphne asked him that night.

"Fine, fine," he said, lighting the filter end of a cigarette.

"What's wrong? You're as tense as a cat."

"Me? Ha, that's a laugh. I'm as calm as a summer night. I'm just going to take a walk." He eased out the door, hailed a cab, and flew to the Plaza.

"This is no good," Emma said. "Charles will miss me."

"Bear with me, sugar," Kugelmass said. He was pale and sweaty. He kissed her again, raced to the elevators, yelled at Persky over a pay phone in the Plaza lobby, and just made it home before midnight.

"According to Popkin, barley prices in Kraków have not been this stable since 1971," he said to Daphne, and smiled wanly as he climbed into bed.

The whole week went by like that.

On Friday night, Kugelmass told Daphne there was another symposium he had to catch, this one in Syracuse. He hurried back to the Plaza, but the second weekend there was nothing like the first. "Get me back into the novel or marry me," Emma told Kugelmass. "Meanwhile, I want to get a job or go to class, because watching TV all day is the pits."

"Fine. We can use the money," Kugelmass said. "You consume twice your weight in room service."

"I met an Off Broadway producer in Central Park

yesterday, and he said I might be right for a project he's doing," Emma said.

"Who is this clown?" Kugelmass asked.

"He's not a clown. He's sensitive and kind and cute. His name's Jeff Something-or-Other, and he's up for a Tony."

Later that afternoon, Kugelmass showed up at Persky's drunk.

"Relax," Persky told him. "You'll get a coronary."

"Relax. The man says relax. I've got a fictional character stashed in a hotel room, and I think my wife is having me tailed by a private shamus."

"O.K., O.K. We know there's a problem." Persky crawled under the cabinet and started banging on something with a large wrench.

"I'm like a wild animal," Kugelmass went on. "I'm sneaking around town, and Emma and I have had it up to here with each other. Not to mention a hotel tab that reads like the defense budget."

"So what should I do? This is the world of magic," Persky said. "It's all nuance."

"Nuance, my foot. I'm pouring Dom Pérignon and black eggs into this little mouse, plus her wardrobe, plus she's enrolled at the Neighborhood Playhouse and suddenly needs professional photos. Also, Persky, Professor Fivish Kopkind, who teaches Comp Lit and who has always been jealous of me, has identified me as the sporadically appearing character in the Flaubert book. He's threatened to go to Daphne. I see ruin and alimony; jail. For adultery with Madame Bovary, my wife will reduce me to beggary."

"What do you want me to say? I'm working on it night and day. As far as your personal anxiety goes, that I can't help you with. I'm a magician, not an analyst."

By Sunday afternoon, Emma had locked herself in the bathroom and refused to respond to Kugelmass's

entreaties. Kugelmass stared out the window at the Woll-
man Rink and contemplated suicide. Too bad this is a low
floor, he thought, or I'd do it right now. Maybe if I ran
away to Europe and started life over . . . Maybe I could
sell the *International Herald Tribune,* like those young girls
used to.

The phone rang. Kugelmass lifted it to his ear mechani-
cally.

"Bring her over," Persky said. "I think I got the bugs
out of it."

Kugelmass's heart leaped. "You're serious?" he said.
"You got it licked?"

"It was something in the transmission. Go figure."

"Persky, you're a genius. We'll be there in a minute.
Less than a minute."

Again the lovers hurried to the magician's apartment,
and again Emma Bovary climbed into the cabinet with her
boxes. This time there was no kiss. Persky shut the doors,
took a deep breath, and tapped the box three times. There
was the reassuring popping noise, and when Persky
peered inside, the box was empty. Madame Bovary was
back in her novel. Kugelmass heaved a great sigh of relief
and pumped the magician's hand.

"It's over," he said. "I learned my lesson. I'll never
cheat again, I swear it." He pumped Persky's hand again
and made a mental note to send him a necktie.

Three weeks later, at the end of a beautiful spring afternoon, Persky answered his doorbell. It was Kugelmass,
with a sheepish expression on his face.

"O.K., Kugelmass," the magician said. "Where to this
time?"

"It's just this once," Kugelmass said. "The weather is
so lovely, and I'm not getting any younger. Listen, you've
read *Portnoy's Complaint?* Remember The Monkey?"

"The price is now twenty-five dollars, because the cost

of living is up, but I'll start you off with one freebie, due to all the trouble I caused you."

"You're good people," Kugelmass said, combing his few remaining hairs as he climbed into the cabinet again. "This'll work all right?"

"I hope. But I haven't tried it much since all that unpleasantness."

"Sex and romance," Kugelmass said from inside the box. "What we go through for a pretty face."

Persky tossed in a copy of *Portnoy's Complaint* and rapped three times on the box. This time, instead of a popping noise there was a dull explosion, followed by a series of crackling noises and a shower of sparks. Persky leaped back, was seized by a heart attack, and dropped dead. The cabinet burst into flames, and eventually the entire house burned down.

Kugelmass, unaware of this catastrophe, had his own problems. He had not been thrust into *Portnoy's Complaint*, or into any other novel, for that matter. He had been projected into an old textbook, *Remedial Spanish*, and was running for his life over a barren, rocky terrain as the word *tener* ("to have")—a large and hairy irregular verb—raced after him on its spindly legs.

My Speech to the Graduates

MORE than any other time in history, mankind faces a crossroads. One path leads to despair and utter hopelessness. The other, to total extinction. Let us pray we have the wisdom to choose correctly. I speak, by the way, not with any sense of futility, but with a panicky conviction of the absolute meaninglessness of existence which could easily be misinterpreted as pessimism. It is not. It is merely a healthy concern for the predicament of modern man. (Modern man is here defined as any person born after Nietzsche's edict that "God is dead," but before the hit recording "I Wanna Hold Your Hand.") This "predicament" can be stated one of two ways, though certain linguistic philosophers prefer to reduce it to a mathematical equation where it can be easily solved and even carried around in the wallet.

Put in its simplest form, the problem is: How is it possible to find meaning in a finite world given my waist and shirt size? This is a very difficult question when we realize that science has failed us. True, it has conquered many diseases, broken the genetic code, and even placed human beings on the moon, and yet when a man of eighty is left in a room with two eighteen-year-old cocktail waitresses nothing happens. Because the real problems never change. After all, can the human soul be glimpsed through a microscope? Maybe—but you'd definitely need one of those very good ones with two eyepieces. We know that the most advanced computer in the world does not have a brain as sophisticated as that of an ant. True, we could say that of many of our relatives but we only have to put up with them at weddings or special occasions. Science is something we depend on all the time. If I develop a pain in the chest I must take an X-ray. But what if the radiation from the X-ray causes me deeper problems? Before I know it, I'm going in for surgery. Naturally, while they're giving me oxygen an intern decides to light up a cigarette. The next thing you know I'm rocketing over the World Trade Center in bed clothes. Is this science? True, science has taught us how to pasteurize cheese. And true, this can be fun in mixed company—but what of the H-bomb? Have you ever seen what happens when one of those things falls off a desk accidentally? And where is science when one ponders the eternal riddles? How did the cosmos originate? How long has it been around? Did matter begin with an explosion or by the word of God? And if by the latter, could He not have begun it just two weeks earlier to take advantage of some of the warmer weather? Exactly what do we mean when we say, man is mortal? Obviously it's not a compliment.

Religion too has unfortunately let us down. Miguel de Unamuno writes blithely of the "eternal persistence of consciousness," but this is no easy feat. Particularly when reading Thackeray. I often think how comforting life must have been for early man because he believed in a powerful, benevolent Creator who looked after all things. Imagine his disappointment when he saw his wife putting on weight. Contemporary man, of course, has no such peace of mind. He finds himself in the midst of a crisis of faith. He is what we fashionably call "alienated." He has seen the ravages of war, he has known natural catastrophes, he has been to singles bars. My good friend Jacques Monod spoke often of the randomness of the cosmos. He believed everything in existence occurred by pure chance with the possible exception of his breakfast, which he felt certain was made by his housekeeper. Naturally belief in a divine intelligence inspires tranquillity. But this does not free us from our human responsibilities. Am I my brother's keeper? Yes. Interestingly, in my case I share that honor with the Prospect Park Zoo. Feeling godless then, what we have done is made technology God. And yet can technology really be the answer when a brand new Buick, driven by my close associate, Nat Zipsky, winds up in the window of Chicken Delight causing hundreds of customers to scatter? My toaster has never once worked properly in four years. I follow the instructions and push two slices of bread down in the slots and seconds later they rifle upward. Once they broke the nose of a woman I loved very dearly. Are we counting on nuts and bolts and electricity to solve our problems? Yes, the telephone is a good thing— and the refrigerator—and the air conditioner. But not every air conditioner. Not my sister Henny's, for instance. Hers makes a loud noise and still doesn't cool. When the man comes over to fix it, it gets worse. Either that or he tells her she needs a new one. When she complains, he says not to bother him. This man is truly alienated. Not only is he alienated but he can't stop smiling.

The trouble is, our leaders have not adequately prepared us for a mechanized society. Unfortunately our politicians are either incompetent or corrupt. Sometimes both on the same day. The Government is unresponsive to the needs of the little man. Under five-seven, it is impossible to get your Congressman on the phone. I am not denying that democracy is still the finest form of government. In a democracy at least, civil liberties are upheld. No citizen can be wantonly tortured, imprisoned, or made to sit through certain Broadway shows. And yet this is a far cry from what goes on in the Soviet Union. Under their form of totalitarianism, a person merely caught whistling is sentenced to thirty years in a labor camp. If, after fifteen years, he still will not stop whistling, they shoot him. Along with this brutal fascism we find its handmaiden, terrorism. At no other time in history has man been so afraid to cut into his veal chop for fear that it will explode. Violence breeds more violence and it is predicted that by 1990 kidnapping will be the dominant mode of social interaction. Overpopulation will exacerbate problems to the breaking point. Figures tell us there are already more people on earth than we need to move even the heaviest piano. If we do not call a halt to breeding, by the year 2000 there will be no room to serve dinner unless one is willing to set the table on the heads of strangers. Then they must not move for an hour while we eat. Of course energy will be in short supply and each car owner will be allowed only enough gasoline to back up a few inches.

Instead of facing these challenges we turn instead to distractions like drugs and sex. We live in far too permissive a society. Never before has pornography been this rampant. And those films are lit so badly! We are a people who lack defined goals. We have never learned to love. We lack leaders and coherent programs. We have no spiritual center. We are adrift alone in the cosmos wreaking monstrous violence on one another out of frustration and pain. Fortunately, we have not lost our sense of proportion. Summing up, it is clear the future holds great opportunities. It also holds pitfalls. The trick will be to avoid the pitfalls, seize the opportunities, and get back home by six o'clock.

The Diet

ONE DAY, for no apparent reason, F. broke his diet. He had gone to lunch at a café with his supervisor, Schnabel, to discuss certain matters. Just what "matters," Schnabel was vague about. Schnabel had called F. the night before, suggesting that they should meet for lunch. "There are various questions," he told him over the phone. "Issues that require resolutions. . . . It can all wait, of course. Perhaps another time." But F. was seized with such a gnawing anxiety over the precise nature and tone of Schnabel's invitation that he insisted they meet immediately.

"Let's have lunch tonight," he said.

"It's nearly midnight," Schnabel told him.

"That's O.K.," F. said. "Of course, we'll have to break into the restaurant."

"Nonsense. It can wait," Schnabel snapped, and hung up.

F. was already breathing heavily. What have I done, he

thought. I've made a fool of myself before Schnabel. By Monday it will be all over the firm. And it's the second time this month I've been made to appear ridiculous.

Three weeks earlier, F. had been discovered in the Xerox room behaving like a woodpecker. Invariably, someone at the office was ridiculing him behind his back. Sometimes, if he turned around rapidly, he would discover thirty or forty coworkers inches away from him with tongues outstretched. Going to work was a nightmare. For one thing, his desk was in the rear, away from the window, and whatever fresh air did reach the dark office was breathed by the other men before F. could inhale it. As he walked down the aisle each day, hostile faces peered at him from behind ledgers and appraised him critically. Once, Traub, a petty clerk, had nodded courteously, and when F. nodded back Traub fired an apple at him. Previously, Traub had obtained the promotion that was promised to F., and had been given a new chair for his desk. F.'s chair, by contrast, had been stolen many years ago, and because of endless bureaucracy he could never seem to requisition another. Since then he stood at his desk each day, hunched over as he typed, realizing the others were making jokes about him. When the incident occurred, F. had asked for a new chair.

"I'm sorry," Schnabel told him, "but you'll have to see the Minister for that."

"Yes, yes, certainly," F. agreed, but when it came time to see the Minister the appointment was postponed. "He can't see you today," an assistant said. "Certain vague notions have arisen and he is not seeing anyone." Weeks went by and F. repeatedly tried to see the Minister, to no avail.

"All I want is a chair," he told his father. "It's not so much that I mind stooping to work, but when I relax and put my feet up on the desk I fall over backward."

"Hogwash," his father said unsympathetically. "If they thought more of you, you'd be seated by now."

"You don't understand!" F. screamed. "I've tried to see the Minister, but he's always busy. And yet when I peep in his window I always see him rehearsing the Charleston."

"The Minister will never see you," his father said, pouring a sherry. "He has no time for weak failures. The truth is, I hear Richter has two chairs. One to sit on at work and one to stroke and hum to."

Richter! F. thought. That fatuous bore, who carried on an illicit love affair for years with the burgomaster's wife, until she found out! Richter had formerly worked at the bank, but certain shortages occurred. At first he had been accused of embezzling. Then it was learned he was eating the money. "It's roughage, isn't it?" he asked the police innocently. He was thrown out of the bank and came to work at F.'s firm, where it was believed that his fluent French made him the ideal man to handle the Parisian accounts. After five years, it became obvious that he couldn't speak a word of French but was merely mouthing nonsense syllables in a fake accent while pursing his lips. Although Richter was demoted, he managed to work his way back into the boss's favor. This time, he convinced his employer that the company could double its profits by merely unlocking the front door and allowing customers to come in.

"Quite a man, this Richter," F.'s father said. "That's why he will always get ahead in the business world, and you will always writhe in frustration like a nauseating, spindly-legged vermin, fit only to be squashed."

F. complimented his father for taking the long view, but later that evening he felt unaccountably depressed. He resolved to diet and make himself look more presentable. Not that he was fat, but subtle insinuations about town had led him to the inescapable notion that in certain circles he might be considered "unpromisingly portly." My father is right, F. thought. I am like some disgusting beetle. No wonder when I asked for a raise Schnabel sprayed me with Raid! I am a wretched, abysmal insect, fit for universal loathing. I deserve to be trampled to death, torn limb from limb by wild animals. I should live under the bed in the dust, or pluck my eyes out in abject shame. Definitely tomorrow I must begin my diet.

That night, F. was the dreamer of euphoric images. He saw himself thin and able to fit into smart new slacks—the kind that only men with certain reputations could get away with. He dreamed of himself playing tennis grace-fully, and dancing with models at fashionable spots. The dream ended with F. strutting slowly across the floor of the Stock Exchange, naked, to the music of Bizet's "Toreador's Song," saying, "Not bad, eh?"

He awoke the next morning in a state of bliss and pro-ceeded to diet for several weeks, reducing his weight by sixteen pounds. Not only did he feel better but his luck seemed to change.

"The Minister will see you," he was told one day.

Ecstatic, F. was brought before the great man and appraised.

"I hear you're into protein," the Minister said.

"Lean meats and, of course, salad," F. responded. "That is to say, an occasional roll—but no butter and cer-tainly no other starches."

"Impressive," the Minister said.

"Not only am I more attractive but I've greatly reduced the chance of heart attack or diabetes," F. said.

"I know all that," the Minister said impatiently.

"Perhaps now I could get certain matters attended to," F. said. "That is, if I maintain my current trim weight."

"We'll see, we'll see," the Minister said. "And your coffee?" he continued suspiciously. "Do you take it with half-and-half?"

"Oh, no," F. told him. "Skim milk only. I assure you, sir, all my meals are now completely pleasureless experiences."

"Good, good. We'll talk again soon."

That night F. terminated his engagement to Frau Schneider. He wrote her a note explaining that with the sharp drop in his triglyceride level plans they had once made were now impossible. He begged her to understand and said that if his cholesterol count should ever go above one hundred and ninety he would call her.

Then came the lunch with Schnabel—for F., a modest repast consisting of cottage cheese and a peach. When F. asked Schnabel why he had summoned him, the older man was evasive. "Merely to review various alternatives," he said.

"*Which* alternatives?" F. asked. There were no outstanding issues that he could think of, unless he was not remembering them.

"Oh, I don't know. Now it's all becoming hazy and I've quite forgotten the point of the lunch."

"Yes, but I feel you're hiding something," F. said.

"Nonsense. Have some dessert," Schnabel replied.

"No, thank you, Herr Schnabel. That is to say, I'm on a diet."

"How long has it been since you've experienced custard? Or an éclair?"

"Oh, several months," F. said.

"You don't miss them?" Schnabel asked.

"Why, yes. Naturally, I enjoy consummating a meal by ingesting a quantity of sweets. Still, the need for discipline . . . You understand."

"Really?" Schnabel asked, savoring his chocolate-covered pastry, so that F. could feel the man's enjoyment. "It's a pity you're so rigid. Life is short. Wouldn't you like to sample just a bite?" Schnabel was smiling wickedly. He proffered F. a morsel on his fork.

F. felt himself becoming dizzy. "Look here," he said, "I suppose I could always go back on my diet tomorrow."

"Of course, of course," Schnabel said. "That makes splendid sense."

Though F. could have resisted, he succumbed instead. "Waiter," he said, trembling, "an éclair for me, too."

"Good, good," Schnabel said. "That's it! Be one of the boys. Perhaps if you had been more pliable in the past, matters that should have been long resolved would now be finalized—if you know what I mean."

The waiter brought the éclair and placed it before F. F. thought he saw the man wink at Schnabel, but he couldn't be sure. He began eating the gooey dessert, thrilled by every luscious mouthful.

"Nice, isn't it?" Schnabel asked with a knowing smirk. "It's full of calories, of course."

"Yes," F. muttered, wild-eyed and shaking. "It will all go directly to my hips."

"Put it on in your hips, do you?" Schnabel asked.

F. was breathing hard. Suddenly remorse flooded every channel of his body. God in Heaven, what have I done! he thought. I've broken the diet! I've consumed a pastry, knowing full well the implications! Tomorrow I will have to let out my suits!

"Is something wrong, sir?" the waiter asked, smiling along with Schnabel.

"Yes, what is it?" Schnabel asked. "You look as if you've just committed a crime."

"Please, I can't discuss it now! I must have air! Can you get this check, and I'll get the next one."

"Certainly," Schnabel said. "I'll meet you back at the office. I hear the Minister wants to see you about certain charges."

"What? What charges?" F. asked.

"Oh, I don't know exactly. There've been some rumors. Nothing definite. A few questions the authorities need answered. It can wait, of course, if you're still hungry, Tubby."

F. bolted from the table and ran through the streets to his home. He threw himself on the floor before his father and wept. "Father, I have broken my diet!" he cried. "In a moment of weakness, I ordered dessert. Please forgive me! Mercy, I beg of you!"

His father listened calmly and said, "I condemn you to death."

"I knew you'd understand," F. said, and with that the two men embraced and reaffirmed their determination to spend more of their free time working with others.

The Lunatic's Tale

MADNESS is a relative state. Who can say which of us is truly insane? And while I roam through Central Park wearing moth-eaten clothes and a surgical mask, screaming revolutionary slogans and laughing hysterically, I wonder even now if what I did was really so irrational. For, dear reader, I was not always what is popularly referred to as "a New York street crazy," pausing at trash cans to fill my shopping bags with bits of string and bottle caps. No, I was once a highly successful doctor living on the upper East Side, gadding about town in a brown Mercedes, and bedecked dashingly in a varied array of Ralph Lauren tweeds. Hard to believe that I, Dr. Ossip Parkis, once a familiar face at theatre openings, Sardi's, Lincoln Center, and the Hamptons, where I boasted great wit and a formidable backhand, am now sometimes seen roller skating unshaven down Broadway wearing a knapsack and a pinwheel hat.

The dilemma that precipitated this catastrophic fall

from grace was simply this. I was living with a woman whom I cared for very deeply and who had a winning and delightful personality and mind; rich in culture and humor and a joy to spend time with. But (and I curse Fate for this) she did not turn me on sexually. Concurrently, I was sneaking crosstown nightly to rendezvous with a photographer's model called Tiffany Schmeederer, whose blood-curdling mentality was in direct inverse proportion to the erotic radiation that oozed from her every pore. Undoubtedly, dear reader, you have heard the expression, "a body that wouldn't quit." Well Tiffany's body would not only not quit, it wouldn't take five minutes off for a coffee break. Skin like satin, or should I say like the finest of Zabar's novy, a leonine mane of chestnut hair, long willowy legs and a shape so curvaceous that to run one's hands over any portion of it was like a ride on the Cyclone. This is not to say the one I roomed with, the scintillating and even profound Olive Chomsky, was a slouch physiognomywise. Not at all. In fact she was a handsome woman with all the attendant perquisites of a charming and witty culture vulture and, crudely put, a mechanic in the sack. Perhaps it was the fact that when the light hit Olive at a certain angle she inexplicably resembled my Aunt Rifka. Not that Olive actually *looked* like my mother's sister. (Rifka had the appearance of a character in Yiddish folklore called the Golem.) It was just that some vague similarity existed around the eyes, and then only if the shadows fell properly. Perhaps it was this incest taboo or perhaps it was just that a face and body like Tiffany Schmeederer's comes along every few million years and usually heralds an ice age or the destruction of the world by fire. The point is, my needs required the best of two women.

It was Olive I met first. And this after an endless string of relationships wherein my partner invariably left something to be desired. My first wife was brilliant, but had no sense of humor. Of the Marx Brothers, she was convinced the amusing one was Zeppo. My second wife was beautiful, but lacked real passion. I recall once, while we were making love, a curious optical illusion occurred and for a split second it almost looked as though she was moving. Sharon Pflug, whom I lived with for three months, was too hostile. Whitney Weisglass was too accommodating. Pippa Mondale, a cheerful divorcée, made the fatal mistake of defending candles shaped like Laurel and Hardy.

Well-meaning friends fixed me up with a relentless spate of blind dates, all unerringly from the pages of H. P. Lovecraft. Ads, answered out of desperation, in the *New York Review of Books*, proved equally futile as the "thirtyish poetess" was sixtyish, the "coed who enjoys Bach and Beowulf" looked like Grendel, and the "Bay Area bisexual" told me I didn't quite coincide with either of her desires. This is not to imply that now and again an apparent plum would not somehow emerge: a beautiful woman, sensual and wise with impressive credentials and winning ways. But, obeying some age-old law, perhaps from the Old Testament or Egyptian *Book of the Dead, she* would reject *me*. And so it was that I was the most miserable of men. On the surface, apparently blessed with all the necessities for the good life. Underneath, desperately in search of a fulfilling love.

Nights of loneliness led me to ponder the esthetics of perfection. Is anything in nature actually "perfect" with the exception of my Uncle Hyman's stupidity? Who am I to demand perfection? I, with my myriad faults. I made a list of my faults, but could not get past: 1) Sometimes forgets his hat.

Did anyone I know have a "meaningful relationship"? My parents stayed together forty years, but that was out of spite. Greenglass, another doctor at the hospital, married a woman who looked like a Feta cheese "because she's kind." Iris Merman cheated with any man who was registered to vote in the tri-state area. Nobody's relationship could actually be called happy. Soon I began to have nightmares.

I dreamed I visited a singles bar where I was attacked by a gang of roving secretaries. They brandished knives and forced me to say favorable things about the borough of Queens. My analyst counseled compromise. My rabbi said, "Settle, settle. What about a woman like Mrs. Blitzstein? She may not be a great beauty, but nobody is better at smuggling food and light firearms in and out of a ghetto." An actress I met, who assured me her real ambition was to be a waitress at a coffeehouse, seemed promising, but during one brief dinner her single response to everything I said was, "That's zalid." Then one evening, in an effort to unwind after a particularly trying day at the hospital, I attended a Stravinsky concert alone. During intermission I met Olive Chomsky and my life changed.

Olive Chomsky, literate and wry, who quoted Eliot and played tennis and also Bach's "Two Part Inventions" on the piano. And who never said, "Oh, wow," or wore anything marked Pucci or Gucci or listened to country and western music or dialogue radio. And incidentally, who was always willing at the drop of a hat to do the unspeakable and even initiate it. What joyful months spent with her till my sex drive (listed, I believe, in the *Guinness Book of World Records*) waned. Concerts, movies, dinners, weekends, endless wonderful discussions of everything from Pogo to Rig-Veda. And never a gaffe from her lips. Insights only. Wit too! And of course the appropriate hostility toward all deserving targets: politicians, television, face-lifts, the architecture of housing projects, men in leisure suits, film courses, and people who begin sentences with "basically."

Oh, curse the day that a wanton ray of light coaxed

forth those ineffable facial lines bringing to mind Aunt
Rifka's stolid visage. And curse the day also that at a loft
party in Soho, an erotic archetype with the unlikely name
of Tiffany Schmeederer adjusted the top of her plaid wool
kneesock and said to me with a voice resembling that of a
mouse in the animated cartoons, "What sign are you?"
Hair and fangs audibly rising on my face in the manner of
the classic lycanthropic, I felt compelled to oblige her with
a brief discussion of astrology, a subject rivaling my intellectual interest with such heavy issues as est, alpha waves,
and the ability of leprechauns to locate gold.

Hours later I found myself in a state of waxy flexibility
as the last piece of bikini underpants slid noiselessly to the
floor around her ankles while I lapsed inexplicably into the
Dutch National Anthem. We proceeded to make love in the
manner of The Flying Wallendas. And so it began.

Alibis to Olive. Furtive meetings with Tiffany. Excuses
for the woman I loved while my lust was spent elsewhere.
Spent, in fact, on an empty little yo-yo whose touch and
wiggle caused the top of my head to dislodge like a frisbee
and hover in space like a flying saucer. I was forsaking my
responsibility to the woman of my dreams for a physical
obsession not unlike the one Emil Jannings experienced in
The Blue Angel. Once I feigned illness, asking Olive to
attend a Brahms Symphony with her mother so that I
could satisfy the moronic whims of my sensual goddess
who insisted I drop over to watch "This Is Your Life" on
television, "because they're doing Johnny Cash!" Yet, after
I paid my dues by sitting through the show, she rewarded
me by dimming the rheostats and transporting my libido
to the planet Neptune. Another time I casually told Olive I
was going out to buy the papers. Then I raced seven blocks
to Tiffany's, took the elevator up to her floor, but, as luck
would have it, the infernal lift stuck. I paced like a caged

cougar between floors, unable to satisfy my flaming desires and also unable to return home by a credible time. Released at last by some firemen, I hysterically concocted a tale for Olive featuring myself, two muggers and the Loch Ness monster.

Fortunately, luck was on my side and she was sleeping when I returned home. Olive's own innate decency made it unthinkable to her that I would deceive her with another woman, and while the frequency of our physical relations had fallen off, I husbanded my stamina in such a manner as to at least partially satisfy her. Constantly ridden with guilt, I offered flimsy alibis about fatigue from overwork, which she bought with the guilelessness of an angel. In truth, the whole ordeal was taking its toll on me as the months went by. I grew to look more and more like the figure in Edvard Munch's "The Scream."

Pity my dilemma, dear reader! This maddening predicament that afflicts perhaps a good many of my contemporaries. Never to find all the requirements one needs in a single member of the opposite sex. On one hand, the yawning abyss of compromise. On the other, the enervating and reprehensible existence of the amorous cheat. Were the French right? Was the trick to have a wife and also a mistress, thereby delegating responsibility for varied needs between two parties? I knew that if I proposed this arrangement openly to Olive, understanding as she was, the chances were very good I would wind up impaled on her British umbrella. I grew weary and depressed and contemplated suicide. I held a pistol to my head, but at the last moment lost my nerve and fired in the air. The bullet passed through my ceiling, causing Mrs. Fitelson in the apartment overhead to leap straight upward onto her bookshelf and remain perched there throughout the high holidays.

Then one night it all cleared up. Suddenly, and with a

clarity one usually associates with LSD, my course of action became apparent. I had taken Olive to see a revival of a Bela Lugosi film at the Elgin. In the crucial scene, Lugosi, a mad scientist, switches the brain of some un-lucky victim with that of a gorilla, both being strapped to operating tables during an electrical storm. If such a thing could be devised by a screenwriter in the world of fiction, surely a surgeon of my ability could, in real life, accom-plish the same thing.

Well, dear reader, I won't bore you with the details which are highly technical and not easily understood by the lay mentality. Suffice it to say that one dark and stormy night a shadowy figure might have been observed smug-gling two drugged women (one with a shape that caused men to drive their cars up on the sidewalk) into an unused operating room at Flower Fifth Avenue. There, as bolts of lightning crackled jaggedly through the sky, he performed an operation done before only in the world of celluloid fantasy, and then by a Hungarian actor who would one day turn the hickey into an art form.

The result? Tiffany Schmeederer, her mind now ex-isting in the less spectacular body of Olive Chomsky, found herself delightfully free from the curse of being a sex object. As Darwin taught us, she soon developed a keen intelligence, and while not perhaps the equal of Hannah Arendt's, it did permit her to recognize the follies of astrol-ogy and marry happily. Olive Chomsky, suddenly the pos-sessor of a cosmic topography to go with her other superb gifts, became my wife as I became the envy of all around me.

The only hitch was that after several months of bliss with Olive that was the equal of anything in the *Arabian Nights*, I inexplicably grew dissatisfied with this dream woman and developed instead a crush on Billie Jean Za-pruder, an airline stewardess whose boyish, flat figure and

Alabama twang caused my heart to do flip-flops. It was at this point that I resigned my position at the hospital, donned my pinwheel hat and knapsack and began skating down Broadway.

Reminiscences: Places and People

BROOKLYN: TREE-LINED STREETS. The Bridge. Churches and cemeteries everywhere. And candy stores. A small boy helps a bearded old man across the street and says, "Good Sabbath." The old man smiles and empties his pipe on the boy's head. The child runs crying into his house. . . . Stifling heat and humidity descend on the borough. Residents bring folding chairs out onto the street after dinner to sit and talk. Suddenly it begins to snow. Confusion sets in. A vender wends his way down the street selling hot pretzels. He is set upon by dogs and chased up a tree. Unfortunately for him, there are more dogs at the top of the tree.

"Benny! Benny!" A mother is calling her son. Benny is sixteen but already has a police record. When he is twenty-six, he will go to the electric chair. At thirty-six, he will be hanged. At fifty, he will own his own dry-cleaning store. Now his mother serves breakfast, and because the family is too poor to afford fresh rolls he spreads marmalade on the *News*.

Ebbets Field: Fans line Bedford Avenue in hopes of retrieving home-run balls hit over the right-field wall. After eight scoreless innings, there is a roar from the crowd. A ball sails over the wall, and eager fans jostle for it! For some reason, it is a football—no one knows why. Later that season, the owner of the Brooklyn Dodgers will trade his shortstop to Pittsburgh for a left fielder, and then he will trade himself to Boston for the owner of the Braves and his two youngest children.

Sheepshead Bay: A leathery-faced man laughs heartily and hauls up his crab traps. A giant crab seizes the man's nose between his claws. The man is no longer laughing. His friends pull him from one side while the crab's friends pull from the other. It is no use. The sun sets. They are still at it.

New Orleans: A jazz band stands in the rain at a cemetery playing mournful hymns as a body is lowered into the earth. Now they strike up a spirited march and begin the parade back to town. Halfway there, someone realizes they have buried the wrong man. What's more, they weren't even close. The person they buried was not dead, or even sick; in fact, he was yodelling at the time. They return to the cemetery and exhume the poor man, who threatens to sue, although they promise to let him have his suit cleaned and send them the bill. Meanwhile, no one knows which person is actually dead. The band continues to play while each of the onlookers is buried in turn, on the theory that the deceased will go down the smoothest. Soon it becomes apparent that no one has died, and now it is too late to get a body, because of the holiday rush.

It is Mardi Gras. Creole food everywhere. Crowds in costume jam the streets. A man dressed as a shrimp is thrown into a steaming pot of bisque. He protests, but no one believes he is not a crustacean. Finally he produces a driver's license and is released.

Beauregard Square is teeming with sightseers. Once Marie Laveau practiced voodoo here. Now an old Haitian "conjure man" is selling dolls and amulets. A policeman tells him to move on, and an argument begins. When it is over, the policeman is four inches tall. Outraged, he still tries to make an arrest, but his voice is so high that no one can understand him. Presently a cat crosses the street, and the policeman is forced to run for his life.

Paris: Wet pavements. And lights—everywhere there are lights! I come upon a man at an outdoor café. It is André Malraux. Oddly, he thinks that I am André Malraux. I explain that he is Malraux and I am just a student. He is relieved to hear this, as he is fond of Mme. Malraux and would hate to think she is my wife. We talk of serious things, and he tells me that man is free to choose his own fate and that not until he realizes that death is part of life can he really understand existence. Then he offers to sell me a rabbit's foot. Years later, we meet at a dinner, and again he insists that I am Malraux. This time, I go along with it and get to eat his fruit cocktail.

Autumn. Paris is crippled by another strike. Now it is the acrobats. No one is tumbling, and the city comes to a standstill. Soon the strike spreads to include jugglers, and then ventriloquists. Parisians regard these as essential services, and many students become violent. Two Algerians are caught practicing handstands and their heads are shaved.

A ten-year-old girl with long brown curls and green eyes hides a plastic explosive device in the Minister of the Interior's chocolate mousse. With the first bite, he passes through the roof of Fouquet's and lands unharmed in Les Halles. Now Les Halles is no more.

• • • • •

Through Mexico by auto: The poverty is staggering. Clusters of sombreros evoke the murals of Orozco. It is over a hundred degrees in the shade. A poor Indian sells me a fried-pork enchilada. It tastes delicious, and I wash it down with some ice water. I feel a slight queasiness in the stomach and then start speaking Dutch. Suddenly a mild abdominal pain causes me to snap over like a book slamming shut. Six months later, I awake in a Mexican hospital completely bald and clutching a Yale pennant. It has been a fearful experience, and I am told that when I was delirious with fever and close to death's door I ordered two suits from Hong Kong.

I recuperate in a ward full of many wonderful peasants, several of whom will later become close friends. There is Alfonso, whose mother wanted him to be a matador. He was gored by a bull and then later gored by his mother. And Juan, a simple pig farmer who could not write his name but somehow managed to defraud I.T.T. out of six million dollars. And old Hernández, who had ridden beside Zapata for many years, until the great revolutionary had him arrested for constantly kicking him.

Rain. Six straight days of rain. Then fog. I sit in a London pub with Willie Maugham. I am distressed, because my first novel, *Proud Emetic*, has been coolly received by the critics. Its one favorable notice, in the *Times*, was vitiated by the last sentence, which called the book "a miasma of asinine clichés unrivalled in Western letters."

Maugham explains that while this quote can be interpreted many ways, it might be best not to use it in the print ads. Now we stroll up Old Brompton Road, and the rains come again. I offer my umbrella to Maugham and he takes it, despite the fact he already has an umbrella. Maugham now carries two open umbrellas while I run along beside him.

"One must never take criticism too seriously," he tells

me. "My first short story was harshly denounced by one particular critic. I brooded and made caustic remarks about the man. Then one day I reread the story and realized he had been correct. It *was* shallow and badly constructed. I never forgot the incident, and years later, when the Luftwaffe was bombing London, I shone a light on the critic's house."

Maugham pauses to buy and open a third umbrella. "In order to be a writer," he continues, "one must take chances and not be afraid to look foolish. I wrote *The Razor's Edge* while wearing a paper hat. In the first draft of *Rain*, Sadie Thompson was a parrot. We grope. We take risks. All I had when I began *Of Human Bondage* was the conjunction 'and.' I knew a story with 'and' in it could be delightful. Gradually the rest took shape."

A gust of wind lifts Maugham off his feet and slams him into a building. He chuckles. Maugham then offers the greatest advice anyone could give to a young author: "At the end of an interrogatory sentence, place a question mark. You'd be surprised how effective it can be."

Nefarious Times We Live In

YES. I CONFESS. It was I, Willard Pogrebin, mild mannered and promising at one time in life, who fired a shot at the President of the United States. Fortunately for all concerned, a member of the onlooking crowd jostled the Luger in my hand causing the bullet to ricochet off a McDonald's sign and lodge in some bratwurst at Himmelstein's Sausage Emporium. After a light scuffle in which several G-men laced my trachea into a reef knot, I was subdued and carted off for observation.

How did it happen that I had come to this, you ask? Me, a character with no pronounced political convictions; whose childhood ambition was to play Mendelssohn on the cello or perhaps dance on point in the great capitals of the world? Well, it all began two years ago. I had just been medically discharged from the army, the results of certain scientific experiments performed on me without my knowledge. More precisely, a group of us had been fed roast chicken stuffed with lysergic acid, in a research program designed to determine the quantity of LSD a man can ingest before he attempts to fly over the World Trade Center. Developing secret weapons is of great importance to the Pentagon and the previous week I had been shot with a dart whose drugged tip caused me to look and talk exactly like Salvador Dali. Cumulative side effects took their toll on my perception and when I could no longer tell the difference between my brother Morris and two soft-boiled eggs, I was discharged.

Electroshock therapy at the Veterans Hospital helped although wires got crossed with a behavioral psychology lab and I along with several chimpanzees all performed *The Cherry Orchard* together in perfect English. Broke and alone upon my release, I recall hitchhiking west and being picked up by two native Californians: a charismatic young man with a beard like Rasputin's and a charismatic young woman with a beard like Svengali's. I was exactly what they were looking for, they explained, as they were in the process of transcribing the Kaballah on parchment and had run out of blood. I tried to explain that I was en route to Hollywood seeking honest employment but the combination of their hypnotic eyes and a knife the size of a sculling oar convinced me of their sincerity. I recall being driven to a deserted ranch where several mesmerized young women force fed me organic health foods and then tried to emboss the sign of the pentagram on my forehead with a soldering iron. I then witnessed a black mass in which hooded adolescent acolytes chanted the words, "Oh wow," in Latin. I also recall being made to take peyote and cocaine and eat a white substance that came from boiled cactus, which caused my head to revolve completely around like a radar dish. Further details escape me, although my mind was clearly affected as two months later I was arrested in Beverly Hills for trying to marry an oyster.

Upon my release from police custody I longed for some inner peace in an attempt to preserve what remained of my precarious sanity. More than once I had been solicited by ardent proselytizers on the street to seek religious salvation with the Reverend Chow Bok Ding, a moon-faced charismatic, who combined the teachings of Lao-Tze with the wisdom of Robert Vesco. An esthetic man who renounced all worldly possessions in excess of those owned by Charles Foster Kane, the Reverend Ding explained his two modest goals. One was to instill in all his followers the values of prayer, fasting, and brotherhood and the other was to lead them in a religious war against the NATO countries. After attending several sermons, I noticed that Reverend Ding thrived on robotlike fealty and any diminution of divine fervor met with raised eyebrows. When I mentioned that it seemed to me the Reverend's followers were being systematically turned into mindless zombies by a fraudulent megalomaniac, it was taken as criticism. Moments later I was led swiftly by my lower lip into a devotional shrine, where certain minions of the Reverend who resembled Sumo wrestlers suggested I rethink my position for a few weeks with no petty distractions like food or water. To further underscore the general sense of disappointment with my attitude, a fist full of quarters was applied to my gums with pneumatic regularity. Ironically, the only thing that kept me from going insane was the constant repeating of my private mantra, which was "Yoicks." Finally, I succumbed to the terror and began to hallucinate. I recall seeing Frankenstein stroll through Covent Gardens with a hamburger on skis.

Four weeks later I awoke in a hospital reasonably O.K. except for a few bruises and the firm conviction that I was Igor Stravinsky. I learned the Reverend Ding had been sued by a fifteen-year-old Maharishi over the question of which of them was actually God and therefore entitled to free passes to Loew's Orpheum. The issue was finally resolved with the help of the Bunco Squad and both gurus

400

were apprehended as they tried to beat it across the border
to Nirvana, Mexico.

By this time, although physically intact, I had developed the emotional stability of Caligula and hoping to
rebuild my shattered psyche, I volunteered for a program
called PET—Perlemutter's Ego Therapy, named after its
charismatic founder, Gustave Perlemutter. Perlemutter
had been a former bop saxophonist and had come to psy-
chotherapy late in life but his method had attracted many
famous film stars who swore that it changed them much
more rapidly and in a deeper way than even the astrology
column in *Cosmopolitan*.

A group of neurotics, most of whom had struck out
with more conventional treatment, were driven to a pleas-
ant rural spa. I suppose I should have suspected something from the barbed wire and the Dobermans but
Perlemutter's underlings assured us that the screaming we
heard was purely primal. Forced to sit upright in hard-
backed chairs with no relief for seventy-two straight hours,
our resistance gradually crumpled and it was not long
before Perlemutter was reading us passages from *Mein
Kampf*. As time passed it was clear that he was a total psy-
chotic whose therapy consisted of sporadic admonitions to
"cheer up."

Several of the more disillusioned ones tried to leave
but to their chagrin found the surrounding fences electri-
fied. Although Perlemutter insisted he was a doctor of the
mind, I noticed he kept receiving phone calls from Yassir
Arafat and were it not for a last minute raid on the prem-
ises by agents of Simon Wiesenthal there is no telling what
might have happened.

Tense and understandably cynical by the turn of
events, I took up residence in San Francisco, earning
money in the only way I now could, by agitating at Berke-
ley and informing for the FBI. For several months I sold
and resold bits of information to federal agents, mostly

concerning a CIA plan to test the resiliency of New York
City residents by dropping potassium cyanide in the reservoir. Between this and an offer to be dialogue coach on a
snuff porn movie, I could just make ends meet. Then one
evening, as I opened my door to put out the garbage, two
men leaped stealthily from the shadows and draping a furniture pad over my head, hustled me off in the trunk of a
car. I remember being jabbed with a needle and before I
blacked out hearing voices comment that I seemed heavier
than Patty but lighter than Hoffa. I awakened to find myself in a dark closet where I was forced to undergo total
sensory deprivation for three weeks. Following that I was
tickled by experts and two men sang country and western
music to me until I agreed to do anything they wanted. I
cannot vouch for what ensued as it is possible it was all a
result of my brainwashing but I was then brought into a
room where President Gerald Ford shook my hand and
asked me if I would follow him around the country and
take a shot at him now and then, being careful to miss. He
said it would give him a chance to act bravely and could
serve as a distraction from genuine issues, which he felt
unequipped to deal with. In my weakened condition I
agreed to anything. Two days later the incident at Himmelstein's Sausage Emporium occurred.

A Giant Step for Mankind

LUNCHING yesterday on chicken in ichor—a house specialty at my favorite midtown restaurant—I was forced to listen to a playwright acquaintance defend his latest opus against a set of notices that read like a Tibetan *Book of the Dead*. Drawing tenuous connections between Sophocles' dialogue and his own, Moses Goldworm wolfed down his vegetable cutlet and raged like Carrie Nation against the New York theatre critics. I, of course, could do nothing more than offer a sympathetic ear and assure him that the phrase "a dramatist of zero promise" might be interpreted in several ways. Then, in the split second it takes to go from calm to bedlam, the Pinero manqué half rose from his seat, suddenly unable to speak. Frantically waving his arms and clutching his throat, the poor fellow turned a shade of blue invariably associated with Thomas Gainsborough.

"My God, what is it?" someone screamed, as

silverware clattered to the floor and heads turned from every table.

"He's having a coronary!" a waiter yelled.

"No, no, it's a fit," said a man at the booth next to me.

Goldworm continued to struggle and wave his arms, but with ever-diminishing style. Then, as various mutually exclusive remedies were advanced in anxious falsettos by sundry well-meaning hysterics in the room, the playwright confirmed the waiter's diagnosis by collapsing to the floor like a sack of rivets. Crumpled in a forlorn heap, Goldworm seemed destined to slip away before an ambulance could arrive, when a six-foot stranger possessing the cool aplomb of an astronaut strode to stage center and said in dramatic tones, "Leave everything to me, folks. We don't need a doctor—this is not a cardiac problem. By clutching his throat, this fellow has made the universal sign, known in every corner of the world, to indicate that he is choking. The symptoms may appear to be the same as those of a man suffering from a heart attack, but this man, I assure you, can be saved by the Heimlich Maneuver!"

With that, the hero of the moment wrapped his arms around my companion from behind and lifted him to an upright position. Placing his fist just under Goldworm's sternum, he hugged sharply, causing a side order of bean curd to rocket out of the victim's trachea and carom off the hat rack. Goldworm came to apace and thanked his savior, who then directed our attention to a printed notice, supplied by the Board of Health, affixed to the wall. The poster described the aforementioned drama with perfect fidelity. What we had witnessed was indeed "the universal choking signal," conveying the victim's tripartite plight: (1) Cannot speak or breathe, (2) Turns blue, (3) Collapses. The diagnostic signs on the notice were followed by clear directions on the administration of the lifesaving procedure: the selfsame abrupt hug and resulting airborne protein we had witnessed, which had relieved Goldworm of the awkward formalities of the Long Goodbye.

A few minutes later, strolling home on Fifth Avenue, I wondered if Dr. Heimlich, whose name is now so firmly placed in the national consciousness as the discoverer of the marvellous maneuver I had just seen performed, had any idea of how close he had once come to being scooped by three still utterly anonymous scientists who had worked for months on end in search of a cure for the same perilous mealtime trauma. I also wondered if he knew of the existence of a certain diary kept by an unnamed member of the pioneer trio—a diary that came into my possession at auction quite by mistake, because of its similarity in heft and color to an illustrated work entitled "Harem Slaves," for which I had bid a trifling eight weeks' salary. Following are some excerpts from the diary, which I set down here purely in the interest of science:

JANUARY 3. Met my two colleagues today for the first time and found them both enchanting, although Wolfsheim is not at all as I had imagined. For one thing, he is heavier than in his photo (I think he uses an old one). His beard is of a medium length but seems to grow with the irrational abandon of crabgrass. Add to this thick, bushy brows and beady eyes the size of microbes, which dart about suspiciously behind spectacles the thickness of bulletproof glass. And then there are the twitches. The man has accumulated a repertoire of facial tics and blinks that demand nothing less than a complete musical score by Stravinsky. And yet Abel Wolfsheim is a brilliant scientist whose work on dinner-table choking has made him a legend the world over. He was quite flattered that I was familiar with his paper on Random Gagging, and he confided to me that my once skeptically regarded theory, that hiccupping is innate, is now commonly accepted at M.I.T.

If Wolfsheim is eccentric-looking, however, the other

member of our triumvirate is exactly what I had expected from reading her work. Shulamith Arnolfini, whose experiments with recombinant DNA led to the creation of a gerbil that could sing "Let My People Go," is British in the extreme—predictably tweedy, with her hair skun in a bun, and with horn-rimmed glasses resting halfway down a beak nose. Furthermore, she possesses a speech impediment so audibly juicy that to be near her when she pronounces a word like "sequestered" is equivalent to standing at the center of a monsoon. I like them both and I predict great discoveries.

JANUARY 5. Things did not get under way as smoothly as I had hoped, for Wolfsheim and I have had a mild disagreement over procedure. I suggested doing our initial experiments on mice, but he regards this as unnecessarily timid. His idea is to use convicts, feeding them large chunks of meat at five-second intervals, with instructions not to chew before swallowing. Only then, he claims, can we observe the dimensions of the problem in its true perspective. I took issue on moral grounds, and Wolfsheim became defensive. I asked him if he felt science was above morality, and took issue with his equating humans and hamsters. Nor did I agree with his somewhat emotional assessment of me as a "unique moron." Fortunately, Shulamith took my side.

JANUARY 7. Today was a productive one for Shulamith and me. Working around the clock, we induced strangulation in a mouse. This was accomplished by coaxing the rodent to ingest healthy portions of Gouda cheese and then making it laugh. Predictably, the food went down the wrong pipe, and choking occurred. Grasping the mouse firmly by the tail, I snapped it like a small whip, and the morsel of cheese came loose. Shulamith and I made voluminous notes on the experiment. If we can transfer the tailsnap procedure to humans, we may have something. Too early to tell.

FEBRUARY 15. Wolfsheim has developed a theory that he insists on testing, although I find it simplistic. He is convinced that a person choking on food can be saved by (his words) "giving the victim a drink of water." At first I thought he was joking, but his intense manner and wild eyes indicated a definite commitment to the concept. Clearly, he has been up for days toying with this notion, and in his laboratory glasses of water filled to various levels were everywhere. When I responded skeptically, he accused me of being negative, and began twitching like a disco dancer. You can tell he hates me.

FEBRUARY 27. Today was a day off, and Shulamith and I decided to motor to the countryside. Once we were out in nature, the whole concept of choking seemed so far away. Shulamith told me that she had been married before, to a scientist who had pioneered a study of radioactive isotopes, and whose entire body vanished in mid-conversation while he was testifying before a Senate committee. We talked about our personal preferences and tastes and discovered that we were both fond of the same bacteria. I asked Shulamith how she would feel if I kissed her. She said, "Swell," giving me the full moist spray peculiar to her speech problem. I have come to the conclusion that she is quite a beautiful woman, particularly when viewed through an X-ray-proof lead screen.

MARCH 1. I now believe Wolfsheim is a madman. He tested his "glass of water" theory a dozen times, and in no case did it prove effective. When I told him to stop wasting valuable time and money, he bounced a petri dish off the bridge of my nose, and I was forced to hold him at bay with the Bunsen burner. As always, when work becomes more difficult frustrations mount.

MARCH 3. Unable to obtain subjects for our dangerous experiments, we have been forced to cruise restaurants and cafeterias, hoping to work rapidly should we be lucky enough to find someone in distress. At the Sand Souci Deli,

I tried lifting a Mrs. Rose Moscowitz by her ankles and shaking her, and although I managed to dislodge a monstrous chunk of kasha, she seemed ungrateful. Wolfsheim suggested that we might try slapping choke victims on the back, and pointed out that important back-slapping concepts had been suggested to him by Fermi at a symposium on digestion in Zurich thirty-two years ago. A grant to explore this was refused, however, when the government decided in favor of nuclear priorities. Wolfsheim, incidentally, has turned out to be a rival in my affair with Shulamith, and confessed affection for her yesterday in the biology lab. When he tried to kiss her, she hit him with a frozen monkey. He is a very complex and sad man.

MARCH 18. At Marcello's Villa today we chanced upon a Mrs. Guido Bertoni in the act of choking on what was later identified as either cannelloni or a Ping-Pong ball. As I had foreseen, slapping her on the back did not help. Wolfsheim, unable to part with the old theories, tried administering a glass of water, but unfortunately seized it from the table of a gentleman well placed in the cement and contracting community, and all three of us were escorted out of the service entrance and up against a lamppost, over and over.

APRIL 2. Today Shulamith raised the notion of a pincers —that is, some form of long tweezers or forceps to extract food that falls into the windpipe. Each citizen would carry one such instrument on his person and be educated in its use and handling by the Red Cross. In eager anticipation, we drove to Belknap's Salt of the Sea to remove a badly wedged crabcake from the esophagus of a Mrs. Faith Blitzstein. Unfortunately, the gasping woman became agitated when I produced the formidable tweezers, and sank her teeth into my wrist, causing me to drop the instrument down her throat. Only the quick action of her husband, Nathan, who held her above the ground by her hair and raised and lowered her like a yo-yo, prevented a fatality.

APRIL 11. Our project is coming to a close—unsuccessfully, I am sorry to say. Funding has been cut off, our foundation board having decided that the remaining money might be more profitably spent on some joy-buzzers. After I received the news of our termination, I had to have fresh air to clear my head, and as I walked alone at night by the Charles River I couldn't help reflecting on the limits of science. Perhaps people are *meant* to choke now and then when they eat. Perhaps it is all part of some unfathomable cosmic design. Are we so conceited as to think research and science can control everything? A man swallows too large a bite of steak, and gags. What could be simpler? What more proof is needed of the exquisite harmony of the universe? We will never know all the answers.

APRIL 20. Yesterday afternoon was our last day, and I chanced upon Shulamith in the Commissary, where she was glancing over a monograph on the new herpes vaccine and gobbling a matjes herring to tide her over till dinnertime. I approached stealthily from the rear and, seeking to surprise her, quietly placed my arms around her, experiencing at that moment the bliss that only a lover feels. Instantly she began choking, a portion of herring having lodged suddenly in her gullet. My arms were still around her, and, as fate would have it, my hands were clasped just under her sternum. Something—call it blind instinct, call it scientific luck—made me form a fist and snap it back against her chest. In a trice, the herring became disengaged, and a moment later the lovely woman was as good as new. When I told Wolfsheim about this, he said, "Yes, of course. It works with herring, but will it work with ferrous metals?"

I don't know what he meant and I don't care. The project is ended, and while it is perhaps true that we have failed, others will follow in our footsteps and, building upon our crude preliminary work, will at last succeed. Indeed, all of us here can foresee the day when our children, or certainly our grandchildren, will live in a world where no individual, regardless of race, creed, or color, will ever be fatally overcome by his own main course. To end on a personal note, Shulamith and I are going to marry, and until the economy begins to brighten a little she and Wolfsheim and I have decided to provide a much-needed service and open up a really first-class tattoo parlor.

The Shallowest Man

S ITTING around the delicatessen, discussing shallow
people we had known, Koppelman brought up the
name of Lenny Mendel. Koppelman said Mendel
was positively the shallowest human he'd ever come
across, bar none, and then proceeded to relate the following story.

For years there was a weekly poker game amongst
roughly the same personnel. It was a small stakes game
played for fun and relaxation at a rented hotel room. The
men bet and bluffed, ate and drank, and talked of sex and
sports and business. After a while (and no one could pin-
point the exact week) the players began to notice that one
of them, Meyer Iskowitz, was not looking too well. When
they commented on it, Iskowitz pooh-poohed the whole
thing.

"I'm fine, I'm fine," he said. "Whose bet?"

But as a few months passed he grew progressively
worse looking and when he didn't show up to play one

week the message was that he had checked into the hospital with hepatitis. Everyone sensed the ominous truth and so it was not a complete surprise three weeks later when Sol Katz phoned Lenny Mendel at the TV show where he worked and said, "Poor Meyer has cancer. The lymph nodes. A bad kind. It's already spread over his body. He's up at Sloan-Kettering."

"How horrible," Mendel said, shaken and suddenly depressed as he sipped weakly from his malted on the other end of the phone.

"Sol and I went to see him today. Poor guy has no family. And he looks awful. He was always robust too. Oy, what a world. Anyhow, it's Sloan-Kettering. 1275 York and visiting hours are twelve to eight."

Katz hung up, leaving Lenny Mendel in a gloomy mood. Mendel was forty-four and healthy as far as he knew. (Suddenly he was qualifying his self-assessment so as not to jinx himself.) He was only six years younger than Iskowitz and though the two were not terribly close they had shared many laughs over cards once a week for five years. The poor man, Mendel thought. I guess I should send some flowers. He instructed Dorothy, one of the secretaries at NBC, to call the florist and handle the details. The news of Iskowitz's imminent death weighed heavily over Mendel that afternoon, but what was beginning to gnaw at him and unnerve him even more was the unshakable realization that he would be expected to visit his poker crony.

What an unpleasant chore, Mendel thought. He felt guilty over his desire to avoid the whole business and yet he dreaded seeing Iskowitz under these circumstances. Of course Mendel understood that all men die and even took some comfort from a paragraph he had once come across in a book that said death is not in opposition to life but a natural part of it; yet when he actually focused on the fact of his own eternal annihilation it caused him to feel limitless panic. He was not religious and not a hero and not a stoic, and during the course of his day-to-day existence he didn't want to know from funerals or hospitals or terminal wards. If a hearse went by in the street the image might stay with him for hours. Now he pictured Meyer Iskowitz's wasted figure in front of him and himself awkwardly trying to make jokes or conversation. How he hated hospitals with their functional tile and institutional lighting. All that hush-hush, quiet atmosphere. And always too warm. Suffocating. And the lunch trays and the bedpans and the elderly and lame shuffling in white gowns through the halls, the heavy air saturated with exotic germs. And what if all the speculation of cancer being a virus is true? I should be in the same room as Meyer Iskowitz? Who knows if it's catching? Let's face it. What the hell do they know about this awful disease? Nothing. So one day they'll find that one of its admittedly myriad forms is transmitted by Iskowitz coughing on me. Or clasping my hand to his chest. The thought of Iskowitz expiring before his eyes horrified him. He saw his once hearty, now emaciated acquaintance (suddenly he was an acquaintance, not actually a friend) gasping a last breath and reaching out to Mendel saying, "Don't let me go— don't let me go!" Jesus, Mendel thought as his forehead beaded up with sweat. I don't relish visiting Meyer. And why the hell must I? We were never close. For God's sake, I saw the man once a week. Strictly for cards. We rarely exchanged more than a few words. He was a poker hand. In five years we never saw one another outside the hotel room. Now he's dying, and suddenly it's incumbent upon me to pay a visit. All of a sudden we're buddies. Intimate yet. I mean, for God's sake, he was tighter with every other person in that game. If anything, I was *least* close to him. Let them visit him. After all, how much traffic does a sick man need? Hell, he's dying. He wants quiet, not a parade of empty well-wishers. Anyhow I can't go today because there's a dress rehearsal. What do they think I am, a man of leisure? I've just been made associate producer. I got a million things on my mind. And the next few days are out too because it's the Christmas show and it's a madhouse here. So I'll do it next week. What's the big deal? The end of next week. Who knows? Will he even live till the end of next week? Well if he does I'll be there and if not, what the hell's the difference? If that's a hard line, well, then life's hard. Meanwhile the opening monologue on the show needs punching up. Topical humor. The show needs more topical humor. Not so many brand-name jokes.

Using one rationale or another, Lenny Mendel avoided visiting Meyer Iskowitz for two-and-a-half weeks. When his obligation rose more strongly to mind he felt very guilty and worse even yet when he caught himself half hoping that he would receive the news that it was over and Iskowitz had died, thereby getting him off the hook. It's a sure thing anyhow, he reasoned, so why not right away? Why should the man linger and suffer? I mean I know it sounds heartless, he thought to himself, and I know I'm weak, but some people can handle these things better than others. Visits to the dying that is. It's depressing. And like I don't have enough on my mind.

But the news of Meyer's death did not come. Only guilt-provoking remarks by his friends at the poker game.

"Oh, you haven't seen him yet? You really ought to. He gets so few visitors and he's so appreciative."

"He always looked up to you, Lenny."

"Yeah, he always liked Lenny."

"I know you must be very busy with the show but you should try and get up to see Meyer. After all, how much time does the man have left?"

"I'll go tomorrow," Mendel said, but when it came time he pushed it off again. The truth is, when he finally got up enough courage to make a ten-minute visit to the hospital it was more out of needing to have a self-image that he could live with rather than out of any compassion for Iskowitz. Mendel knew that if Iskowitz died and he had been too scared or disgusted to visit him, he might regret his cowardice and it would then all be irrevocable. I will hate myself for being spineless, he thought, and the others will know me for what I am—a self-centered louse. On the other hand, if I visit Iskowitz and act like a man, I will be a better person in my own eyes and in the eyes of the world. The point is that Iskowitz's need for comfort and companionship was not the force behind the visit.

Now the story takes a turn because we're discussing shallowness, and the dimensions of Lenny Mendel's record-breaking superficiality are just beginning to emerge. On a cold Tuesday evening at seven-fifty (so he couldn't visit more than ten minutes even if he wanted to) Mendel received from hospital security the laminated pass that allowed him access to room 1501 where Meyer Iskowitz lay alone in bed, surprisingly decent looking considering the stage to which his illness had advanced.

"How's it going, Meyer?" Mendel said weakly as he tried to maintain a respectable distance from the bed.

"Who's that? Mendel? Is that you, Lenny?"

"I been busy. Otherwise I'd have come sooner."

"Oh it's so nice of you to bother. I'm so glad to see you."

"How are you, Meyer?"

"How am I? I'm going to beat this thing, Lenny. Mark my words. I'm going to beat this thing."

"Sure you will, Meyer," Lenny Mendel said in a feeble voice, constricted by tension. "In six months you'll be back cheating at cards. Ha, ha, no seriously, you never cheated." Keep it light, Mendel thought, keep the one-liners coming. Treat him like he isn't dying, Mendel thought, recalling advice he had read on the subject. In the stuffy little room, Mendel imagined he was inhaling billows of the virulent cancer germs as they emanated from Iskowitz and multiplied in the warm air. "I bought you a *Post*," Lenny said, laying the offering down on the table.

"Sit, sit. Where you running? You just came," Meyer said warmly.

"I'm not running. It's just that the visiting instructions say to keep the visits short for the comfort of the patients."

"So what's new?" Meyer asked.

Resigned to chat the full time till eight, Mendel pulled up a chair (not too close) and tried to make conversation about cards, sports, headlines, and finances, always awkwardly conscious of the overriding, horrible fact that, despite Iskowitz's optimism, he would never be leaving this hospital alive. Mendel was perspiring and felt woozy. The pressure, the forced gaiety, the pervasive sense of disease and awareness of his own fragile mortality caused his neck to grow stiff and his mouth to dry up. He wanted to leave. It was already five after eight and he hadn't been asked to go. The visiting rules were lax. He squirmed in his seat as Iskowitz spoke softly of the old days and after five more depressing minutes Mendel thought he would faint. Then, just when it seemed he could stand it no longer, a momentous event occurred. The nurse, Miss Hill—the twenty-four-year-old, blond, blue-eyed nurse with her long hair and magnificently beautiful face—walked in and, fixing Lenny Mendel with a warm, ingratiating smile, said, "Visiting hours are over. You'll have to say goodbye." Right then Lenny Mendel, who had never seen a more exquisite creature in all his life, fell in love. It was as simple as that. He gaped, open-mouthed, with the stunned appearance of a man who had finally set eyes on the woman of his dreams. Mendel's heart virtually ached with an overwhelming feeling of the most profound longing. My God, he thought, it's like in a movie. And there was no question about it either, Miss Hill was absolutely adorable. Sexy and curvaceous in her white uniform, she had big eyes and lush, sensual lips. She had good, high cheekbones and

perfectly shaped breasts. Her voice was sweet and charming as she straightened up the sheets, teasing Meyer Iskowitz good-naturedly while she projected warm concern
for the sick man. Finally she picked up the food tray and
left, pausing only to wink at Lenny Mendel and whisper,
"Better go. He needs rest."

"This is your usual nurse?" Mendel asked Iskowitz after she was gone.

"Miss Hill? She's new. Very cheerful. I like her. Not
sour like some of the others here. Friendly as they come.
And a good sense of humor. Well, you better go. It was
such a pleasure seeing you, Lenny."

"Yeah, right. You too, Meyer."

Mendel rose in a daze and walked down the corridor
hoping to run into Miss Hill before he reached the elevators. She was nowhere to be found and when Mendel hit
the street with its cool night air he knew he would have to
see her again. My God, he thought, as he cabbed home
through Central Park, I know actresses, I know models,
and here a young nurse is more lovely than all the others
put together. Why didn't I speak to her? I should have
engaged her in conversation. I wonder if she's married?
Well no—not if it's *Miss* Hill. I should've asked Meyer
about her. Of course, if she's new . . . He ran through all
the "should-haves" imagining he blew some kind of big
chance but then consoled himself with the fact that at least
he knew where she worked and he could locate her again
when he regained his poise. It occurred to him that she
might finally prove unintelligent or dull like so many of
the beautiful women he met in show business. Of course
she is a nurse which could mean her concerns are deeper,
more humane, less egotistical. Or it could mean that if I
knew her better she'd be an unimaginative purveyor of
bedpans. No—life can't be that cruel. He toyed with the
notion of waiting for her outside the hospital but guessed

that her shifts would change and that he'd miss her. Also
that he might put her off if he accosted her.

He returned the following day to visit Iskowitz, bringing him a book called *Great Sport Stories,* which he felt
made his visit less suspicious. Iskowitz was surprised and
delighted to see him but Miss Hill was not on that night
and instead a virago named Miss Caramanulis floated in
and out of the room. Mendel could hardly conceal his
disappointment and tried to remain interested in what
Iskowitz had to say but couldn't. Iskowitz being a bit
sedated never noticed Mendel's distracted anxiousness to
leave.

Mendel returned the next day and found the heavenly
subject of his fantasies in attendance with Iskowitz. He
made some stammering conversation and when he was
about to leave did manage to get next to her in the corridor. Eavesdropping on her conversation with another
young nurse, Mendel seemed to get the impression that
she had a boyfriend and the two were going to see a musical the following day. Trying to appear casual as he waited
for the elevator, Mendel listened carefully to find out how
serious the relationship was but could never hear all the
details. He did seem to think she was engaged and while
she had no ring he thought he heard her refer to someone
as "my fiancé." He felt discouraged and imagined her the
adored partner of some young doctor, a brilliant surgeon
perhaps, with whom she shared many professional interests. His last impression as the elevator doors closed to
take him to street level was that of Miss Hill walking down
the corridor, chatting animatedly with the other nurse, her
hips swinging seductively and her laugh musically beautiful as it pierced the grim hush of the ward. I must have
her, Mendel thought, consumed by longing and passion,
and I must not blow it like I have so many others in the
past. I must proceed sensibly. Not too fast as is always my
problem. I must not act precipitously. I must find out more

about her. Is she indeed as wonderful as I imagine she is? And if so, how committed is she to the other person? And if he didn't exist, would I even then have a chance? I see no reason why if she's free that I couldn't court her and win her. Or even win her from this man. But I need time. Time to learn about her. Then time to work on her. To talk, to laugh, to bring what gifts I have of insight and humor to bear. Mendel was practically wringing his palms like a Medici prince and drooling. The logical plan is to see her as I visit Iskowitz and slowly, without pressing, build up points with her. I must be oblique. My hard sell, direct approach has failed me too often in the past. I must be restrained.

This decided, Mendel came to see Iskowitz every day. The patient couldn't believe his good fortune to have such a devoted friend. Mendel always brought a substantial and well thought out gift. One that would help him make a score in the eyes of Miss Hill. Pretty flowers, a biography of Tolstoy (he heard her mention how much she loved *Anna Karenina*), the poetry of Wordsworth, caviar. Iskowitz was stunned by the choices. He hated caviar and never heard of Wordsworth. Mendel did stop short of bringing Iskowitz a pair of antique earrings although he saw some he knew Miss Hill would adore.

The smitten suitor seized every opportunity to engage Iskowitz's nurse in conversation. Yes, she was engaged, he learned, but had trepidations about it. Her fiancé was a lawyer but she had fantasies of marrying someone more in the arts. Still, Norman, her beau, was tall and dark and gorgeous, a description that left the less physically prepossessing Mendel in a discouraged state. Mendel would always trumpet his accomplishments and observations to the deteriorating Iskowitz, in a voice loud enough to be heard by Miss Hill. He sensed that he might be impressing her but each time his position appeared strong, future plans with Norman entered the conversation. How lucky is this Norman, Mendel thought. He spends time with her, they laugh together, plan, he presses his lips to hers, he removes her nurse's uniform—perhaps not every stitch of it. Oh God! Mendel sighed, looking heavenward and shaking his head in frustration.

"You have no idea what these visits mean to Mr. Iskowitz," the nurse told Mendel one day, her delightful smile and big eyes making him go a hundred. "He has no family and most of his other friends have so little free time. My theory is, of course, that most people don't have the compassion or courage to spend lots of time with a terminal case. People write off the dying patient and prefer not to think about it. That's why I think your behavior is—well —magnificent."

Word of Mendel's indulgence of Iskowitz got around and at the weekly card game he was much beloved by the players.

"What you're doing is wonderful," Phil Birnbaum said to Mendel over poker. "Meyer tells me no one comes as regularly as you do and he says he thinks you even dress up for the occasion." Mendel's mind was fixed at that second on Miss Hill's hips, which he couldn't get out of his thoughts.

"So how is he? Is he brave?" Sol Katz asked.

"Is who brave?" Mendel asked in his reverie.

"Who? Who we talking about? Poor Meyer."

"Oh, er—yeah. Brave. Right," Mendel said, not even realizing he was at that moment holding a full house.

As the weeks passed, Iskowitz wasted away. Once, in a weakened condition, he looked up at Mendel who stood over him and muttered, "Lenny, I love you. Really." Mendel took Meyer's outstretched hand and said, "Thanks, Meyer. Listen, was Miss Hill in today? Huh? Could you speak up a little? It's hard to understand you." Iskowitz nodded weakly. "Uh-huh," Mendel said, "so what'd you guys talk about? Did my name come up?"

Mendel, of course, had not dared make a move for Miss Hill, finding himself in the awkward position of not wanting her ever to dream that he was there so frequently for any reason other than to see Meyer Iskowitz.

Sometimes, being at death's door would inspire the patient to philosophize and he would say things like, "We're here, we don't know why. It's over before we know what hit us. The trick is to enjoy the moment. To be alive is to be happy. And yet I believe God exists and when I look around me and see the sunlight streaming through the window or the stars come out at night, I know that He has some ultimate plan and that it's good."

"Right, right," Mendel would answer. "And Miss Hill? Is she still seeing Norman? Did you find out what I asked you? If you see her when they come to do those tests on you tomorrow, find out."

On a rainy April day Iskowitz died. Before expiring he told Mendel once again that he loved him and that Mendel's concern for him in these last months was the most touching and deepest experience he ever had with another human being. Two weeks later Miss Hill and Norman broke up and Mendel started dating her. They had an affair that lasted a year and then they went their separate ways.

"That's some story," Moscowitz said when Koppelman finished relating this tale about the shallowness of Lenny Mendel. "It goes to show how some people are just no damn good."

"I didn't get that out of it," Jake Fishbein said. "Not at all. The story shows how love of a woman enables a man to overcome his fears of mortality if only for a while."

"What are you talking about?" Abe Trochman chimed in. "The point of the story is that a dying man becomes the beneficiary of his friend's sudden adoration of a woman."

"But they weren't friends," Lupowitz argued. "Mendel went out of obligation. He returned out of self-interest."

"What's the difference?" Trochman said. "Iskowitz experienced a closeness. He died comforted. That it was motivated by Mendel's lust for the nurse—so?"

"Lust? Who said lust? Mendel, despite his shallowness, may have felt love for the first time in his life."

"What's the difference?" Bursky said. "Who cares what the point of the story is? If it even has a point. It was an entertaining anecdote. Let's order."

The Query

(The following is a one-act play based on an incident in the life of Abraham Lincoln. The incident may or may not be true. The point is I was tired when I wrote it.)

I

(Lincoln with boyish eagerness beckons George Jennings, his press secretary, into the room.)

JENNINGS: Mr. Lincoln, you sent for me?

LINCOLN: Yes, Jennings. Come in. Sit down.

JENNINGS: Yes, Mr. President?

LINCOLN: *(Unable to suppress a grin)* I want to discuss an idea.

JENNINGS: Of course, sir.

LINCOLN: Next time we have a conference for the gentlemen of the press . . .

JENNINGS: Yessir . . . ?

LINCOLN: When I take questions . . .

JENNINGS: Yes, Mr. President . . . ?

LINCOLN: You raise your hand and ask me: Mr. President, how long do you think a man's legs should be?

JENNINGS: Pardon me?

LINCOLN: You ask me: how long do I think a man's legs should be?

JENNINGS: May I ask why, sir?

LINCOLN: Why? Because I have a very good answer.

JENNINGS: You do?

LINCOLN: Long enough to reach the ground.

JENNINGS: Excuse me?

LINCOLN: Long enough to reach the ground. That's the answer! Get it? How long do you think a man's legs should be? Long enough to reach the ground!

JENNINGS: I see.

LINCOLN: You don't think it's funny?

JENNINGS: May I be frank, Mr. President?

LINCOLN: *(Annoyed)* Well, I got a big laugh with it today.

JENNINGS: Really?

LINCOLN: Absolutely. I was with the cabinet and some friends and a man asked it and I shot back that answer and the whole room broke up.

JENNINGS: May I ask, Mr. Lincoln, in what context did he ask it?

LINCOLN: Pardon me?

JENNINGS: Were you discussing anatomy? Was the man a surgeon or a sculptor?

LINCOLN: Why-er-no-I-I-don't think so. No. A simple farmer, I believe.

JENNINGS: Well, why did he want to know?

LINCOLN: Well, I don't know. All I know is he was someone who had requested an audience with me urgently . . .

JENNINGS: *(Concerned)* I see.

LINCOLN: What is it, Jennings, you look pale?

JENNINGS: It is a rather odd question.

LINCOLN: Yes, but I got a laugh off it. It was a quick answer.

JENNINGS: No one's denying that, Mr. Lincoln.

LINCOLN: A big laugh. The whole cabinet just broke up.

JENNINGS: And then did the man say anything?

LINCOLN: He said thank you and left.

JENNINGS: You never asked why he wanted to know?

LINCOLN: If you must know, I was too pleased with my answer. Long enough to reach the ground. It came out so fast. I didn't hesitate.

JENNINGS: I know, I know. It's just, well, this whole thing's got me worried.

II

(Lincoln and Mary Todd in their bedroom, middle of the night. She in bed, Lincoln pacing nervously.)

MARY: Come to bed, Abe. What's wrong?

LINCOLN: That man today. The question. I can't get it out of my mind. Jennings's opened a can of worms.

MARY: Forget it, Abe.

LINCOLN: I want to, Mary. Jesus, don't you think I want to? But those haunting eyes. Imploring. What could have prompted it? I need a drink.

MARY: No, Abe.

LINCOLN: Yes.

MARY: I said, no! You've been jittery lately. It's this   **433**
damn civil war.

LINCOLN: It's not the war. I didn't respond to the
human being. I was too preoccupied with getting
the quick laugh. I allowed a complex issue to elude
me just so I could get some chuckles from my cabinet. They hate me anyhow.

MARY: They love you, Abe.

LINCOLN: I'm vain. Still, it was a fast comeback.

MARY: I agree. Your answer was clever. Long
enough to reach his torso.

LINCOLN: To reach the ground.

MARY: No, you said it the other way.

LINCOLN: No. What's funny about that?

MARY: To me it's a lot funnier.

LINCOLN: That's funnier?

MARY: Sure.

LINCOLN: Mary, you don't know what you're talking about.

MARY: The image of legs rising to a torso . . .

LINCOLN: Forget it! Can we forget it! Where's the bourbon?

434

MARY: *(Withholding the bottle)* No, Abe. You won't drink tonight! I won't allow it!

LINCOLN: Mary, what's happened to us? We used to have such fun.

MARY: *(Tenderly)* Come here, Abe. There's a full moon tonight. Like the night we met.

LINCOLN: No, Mary. The night we met there was a waning moon.

MARY: Full.

LINCOLN: Waning.

MARY: Full.

LINCOLN: I'll get the almanac.

MARY: Oh Christ, Abe, forget it!

LINCOLN: I'm sorry.

MARY: Is it the question? The legs? Is it still that?

LINCOLN: What did he mean?

III

(The cabin of Will Haines and his wife. Haines enters after a long ride. Alice puts down her quilting basket and runs to him.)

ALICE: Well, did you ask him? Will he pardon Andrew?

WILL: *(Beside himself)* Oh, Alice, I did such a stupid thing.

ALICE: *(Bitterly)* What? Don't tell me he won't pardon our son?

WILL: I didn't ask him.

ALICE: You what!? You didn't ask him!?

WILL: I don't know what came over me. There he was, the President of the United States, surrounded by important people. His cabinet, his friends. Then someone said, Mr. Lincoln, this man has ridden all day to speak to you. He has a question to ask. All the while I was riding I had gone over the question in my mind. "Mr. Lincoln, sir, our boy Andrew made a mistake. I realize how serious it is to fall asleep on guard duty, but executing such a young man seems so cruel. Mr. President, sir, couldn't you commute his sentence?"

ALICE: That was the correct way to put it.

WILL: But for some reason, with all those folks staring at me, when the President said, "Yes, what is your question?" I said, "Mr. Lincoln, how long do you think a man's legs should be?"

ALICE: What?

WILL: That's right. That was my question. Don't ask me why it came out. How long do you think a man's legs should be?

ALICE: What kind of question is that?

WILL: I'm telling you, I don't know.

ALICE: His legs? How long?

WILL: Oh, Alice, forgive me.

ALICE: How long should a man's legs be? That's the stupidest question I've ever heard.

WILL: I know, I know. Don't keep reminding me.

ALICE: But why leg length? I mean, legs are not a subject that particularly interests you.

WILL: I was fumfering for words. I forgot my original request. I could hear the clock ticking. I didn't want to appear tongue-tied.

ALICE: Did Mr. Lincoln say anything? Did he answer?

WILL: Yes. He said, long enough to reach the ground.

ALICE: Long enough to reach the ground? What the hell does that mean?

WILL: Who knows? But he got a big laugh. Of course, those guys are disposed toward reacting.

ALICE: *(Suddenly turns)* Maybe you really didn't want Andrew pardoned.

WILL: What?

ALICE: Maybe down deep you don't want our son's sentence commuted. Maybe you're jealous of him.

WILL: You're crazy. I-I. Me? Jealous?

ALICE: Why not? He's stronger. He's smoother with pick and ax and hoe. He's got a feel for the soil like no man I've seen.

WILL: Stop it! Stop it!

ALICE: Let's face it, William, you're a lousy farmer.

WILL: *(Trembling with panic)* Yes, I admit it! I hate farming! The seeds all look alike to me! And the soil! I can never tell it apart from dirt! You, from the east, with your fancy schools! Laughing at me. Sneering. I plant turnips and corn comes up! You think that doesn't hurt a man!?

ALICE: If you would just fasten the seed packets to a little stick you'd know what you planted!

WILL: I want to die! Everything is going black!

(Suddenly there is a knock at the door and when Alice opens it, it is none other than Abraham Lincoln. He is haggard and red-eyed.)

LINCOLN: Mr. Haines?

WILL: President Lincoln . . .

LINCOLN: That question—

WILL: I know, I know . . . how stupid of me! It was all I could think of, I was so nervous.

(Haines falls on his knees weeping. Lincoln also weeps.)

LINCOLN: Then I was right. It was a non sequitur.

WILL: Yes, yes . . . forgive me . . .

LINCOLN: *(Weeping unashamedly)* I do, I do. Rise. Stand up. Your boy will be pardoned today. As will all boys who made a mistake be forgiven.

(Gathering the Haines family in his arms)

Your stupid question has caused me to reevaluate my life. For that I thank you and love you.

ALICE: We did some reevaluating too, Abe. May we call you . . . ?

LINCOLN: Yes, sure, why not? Do you guys have anything to eat? A man travels so many miles, at least offer him something.

(As they break out the bread and cheese the curtain falls.)

Fabrizio's: Criticism and Response

(An exchange in one of the more thought-provoking journals, in which Fabian Plotnick, our most high-minded restaurant critic, reviews Fabrizio's Villa Nova Restaurant, on Second Avenue, and, as usual, stimulates some profound responses.)

PASTA as an expression of Italian Neo-Realistic starch is well understood by Mario Spinelli, the chef at Fabrizio's. Spinelli kneads his pasta slowly. He allows a buildup of tension by the customers as they sit salivating. His fettuccine, though wry and puckish in an almost mischievous way, owes a lot to Barzino, whose use of fettuccine as an instrument of social change is known to us all. The difference is that at Barzino's the patron is led to expect white fettuccine and gets it. Here at Fabrizio's he gets green fettuccine. Why? It all seems so gratuitous. As customers, we are not prepared for the change. Hence, the green noodle does not amuse us. It's disconcerting in a way unintended by the chef. The linguine, on the other hand, is quite delicious and not at all didactic. True, there is a pervasive Marxist quality to it, but this is hidden by the sauce. Spinelli has been a devoted Italian Communist for years, and has had great success in espousing his Marxism by subtly including it in the tortellini.

441

I began my meal with an antipasto, which at first appeared aimless, but as I focused more on the anchovies the point of it became clearer. Was Spinelli trying to say that all life was represented here in this antipasto, with the black olives an unbearable reminder of mortality? If so, where was the celery? Was the omission deliberate? At Jacobelli's, the antipasto consists solely of celery. But Jacobelli is an extremist. He wants to call our attention to the absurdity of life. Who can forget his scampi: four garlic-drenched shrimp arranged in a way that says more about our involvement in Vietnam than countless books on the subject? What an outrage in its time! Now it appears tame next to Gino Finochi's (of Gino's Vesuvio Restaurant) Soft Piccata, a startling six-foot slice of veal with a piece of black chiffon attached to it. (Finochi always works better in veal than either fish or chicken, and it was a shocking oversight by *Time* when reference to him was omitted in the cover story on Robert Rauschenberg.) Spinelli, unlike these avant-garde chefs, rarely goes all the way. He hesitates, as with his spumoni, and when it comes, of course it is melted. There has always been a certain tentativeness about Spinelli's style—particularly in his treatment of Spaghetti Vongole. (Before his psychoanalysis, clams held great terror for Spinelli. He could not bear to open them, and when forced to look inside he blacked out. His early attempts at Vongole saw him dealing exclusively with "clam substitutes." He used peanuts, olives, and finally, before his breakdown, little rubber erasers.)

One lovely touch at Fabrizio's is Spinelli's Boneless Chicken Parmigiana. The title is ironic, for he has filled the chicken with extra bones, as if to say life must not be ingested too quickly or without caution. The constant removal of bones from the mouth and the depositing of them on the plate give the meal an eerie sound. One is reminded at once of Webern, who seems to crop up all the time in Spinelli's cooking. Robert Craft, writing about Stravinsky, makes an interesting point about Schoenberg's influence on Spinelli's salads and Spinelli's influence on Stravinsky's Concerto in D for Strings. In point of fact, the minestrone is a great example of atonality. Cluttered as it is with odd bits and pieces of food, the customer is forced to make noises with his mouth as he drinks it. These tones are arranged in a set pattern and repeat themselves in serial order. The first night I was at Fabrizio's, two patrons, a young boy and a fat man, were drinking soup simultaneously, and the excitement was such that they received a standing ovation. For dessert, we had tortoni, and I was reminded of Leibniz's remarkable pronouncement: "The Monads have no windows." How apropos! Fabrizio's prices, as Hannah Arendt told me once, are "reasonable without being historically inevitable." I agree.

To the Editors:
Fabian Plotnick's insights into Fabrizio's Villa Nova Restaurant are full of merit and perspicuity. The only point missing from his penetrating analysis is that while Fabrizio's is a family-run restaurant, it does not conform to the classic Italian nuclear-family structure but, curiously, is modeled on the homes of pre-Industrial Revolution middle-class Welsh miners. Fabrizio's relationships with his wife and sons are capitalistic and peer-group oriented. The sexual mores of the help are typically Victorian—especially the girl who runs the cash register. Working conditions also reflect English factory problems, and waiters are often made to serve eight to ten hours a day with napkins that do not meet current safety standards.

Dove Rapkin

To the Editors:
In his review of Fabrizio's Villa Nova, Fabian Plotnick called the prices "reasonable." But would he call Eliot's Four Quartets "reasonable"? Eliot's return to a more

primitive stage of the Logos doctrine reflects immanent reason in the world, but $8.50 for chicken tetrazzini! It doesn't make sense, even in a Catholic context. I refer Mr. Plotnick to the article in *Encounter* (2/58) entitled "Eliot, Reincarnation, and Zuppa Di Clams."

Eino Shmeederer

To the Editors:
What Mr. Plotnick fails to take into account in discussing Mario Spinelli's fettuccine is, of course, the size of the portions, or, to put it more directly, the quantity of the noodles. There are obviously as many odd-numbered noodles as all the odd- and even-numbered noodles combined. (Clearly a paradox.) The logic breaks down linguistically, and consequently Mr. Plotnick cannot use the word "fettuccine" with any accuracy. Fettuccine becomes a symbol; that is to say, let the fettuccine = x. Then $a = x/b$ (b standing for a constant equal to half of any entrée). By this logic, one would have to say: the fettuccine *is* the linguine! How ridiculous. The sentence clearly cannot be stated as "The fettuccine was delicious." It must be stated as "The fettuccine and the linguine are not the rigatoni." As Gödel declared over and over, "Everything must be translated into logical calculus before being eaten."

Prof. Word Babcocke
Massachusetts Institute of Technology

To the Editors:
I have read with great interest Mr. Fabian Plotnick's review of Fabrizio's Villa Nova, and find it to be yet another shocking contemporary example of revisionist history. How quickly we forget that during the worst era of the Stalinist purges Fabrizio's not only was open for business but enlarged its back room to seat more customers! No one there said anything about Soviet political repression. In fact, when the Committee to Free Soviet Dissidents peti-

tioned Fabrizio's to leave the gnocchi off the menu until the Russians freed Gregor Tomshinsky, the well-known Trotskyite short-order cook, they refused. Tomshinsky by then had compiled ten thousand pages of recipes, all of which were confiscated by the N.K.V.D.

"Contributing to the heartburn of a minor" was the pathetic excuse the Soviet court used to send Tomshinsky into forced labor. Where were all the so-called intellectuals at Fabrizio's then? The coat-check girl, Tina, never made the smallest attempt to raise her voice when coat-check girls all over the Soviet Union were taken from their homes and forced to hang up clothing for Stalinist hoodlums. I might add that when dozens of Soviet physicists were accused of overeating and then jailed, many restaurants closed in protest, but Fabrizio's kept up its usual service and even instituted the policy of giving free after-dinner mints! I myself ate at Fabrizio's in the thirties, and saw that it was a hotbed of dyed-in-the-wool Stalinists who tried to serve blinchiki to unsuspecting souls who ordered pasta. To say that most customers did not know what was going on in the kitchen is absurd. When somebody ordered scungilli and was handed a blintz, it was quite clear what was happening. The truth is, the intellectuals simply preferred not to see the difference. I dined there once with Professor Gideon Cheops, who was served an entire Russian meal, consisting of borscht, Chicken Kiev, and halvah —upon which he said to me, "Isn't this spaghetti wonderful?"

Prof. Quincy Mondragon
New York University

Fabian Plotnick *replies:*
Mr. Shmeederer shows he knows nothing of either restaurant prices or the "Four Quartets." Eliot himself felt $7.50 for good chicken tetrazzini was (I quote from an interview in *Partisan Review)* "not out of line." Indeed, in "The Dry

Salvages," Eliot imputes this very notion to Krishna, though not precisely in those words.

I'm grateful to Dove Rapkin for his comments on the nuclear family, and also to Professor Babcocke for his penetrating linguistic analysis, although I question his equation and suggest, rather, the following model:

(a) some pasta is linguine
(b) all linguine is not spaghetti
(c) no spaghetti is pasta, hence all spaghetti is linguine.

Wittgenstein used the above model to prove the existence of God, and later Bertrand Russell used it to prove that not only does God exist but He found Wittgenstein too short.

Finally, to Professor Mondragon. It is true that Spinelli worked in the kitchen of Fabrizio's in the nineteen-thirties —perhaps longer than he should have. Yet it is certainly to his credit that when the infamous House Un-American Activities Committee pressured him to change the wording on his menus from "Prosciutto and melon" to the less politically sensitive "Prosciutto and figs," he took the case to the Supreme Court and forced the now famous ruling "Appetizers are entitled to full protection under the First Amendment."

Retribution

THAT CONNIE CHASEN returned my fatal attraction toward her at first sight was a miracle unparalleled in the history of Central Park West. Tall, blond, high cheekboned, an actress, a scholar, a charmer, irrevocably alienated, with a hostile and perceptive wit only challenged in its power to attract by the lewd, humid eroticism her every curve suggested, she was the unrivaled desideratum of each young man at the party. That she would settle on me, Harold Cohen, scrawny, long-nosed, twenty-four-year-old, budding dramatist and whiner, was a *non sequitur* on a par with octuplets. True, I have a facile way with a one-liner and seem able to keep a conversation going on a wide range of topics, and yet I was taken by surprise that this superbly scaled apparition could zero in on my meager gifts so rapidly and completely.

"You're adorable," she told me, after an hour's energetic exchange while we leaned against a bookcase,

449

throwing back Valpolicella and finger foods. "I hope you're going to call me."

"Call you? I'd like to go home with you right now."

"Well great," she said, smiling coquettishly. "The truth is, I didn't really think I was impressing you."

I affected a casual air while blood pounded through my arteries to predictable destinations. I blushed, an old habit.

"I think you're dynamite," I said, causing her to glow even more incandescently. Actually I was quite unprepared for such immediate acceptance. My grape-fueled cockiness was an attempt to lay groundwork for the future, so that when I would indeed suggest the boudoir, let's say, one discreet date later, it would not come as a total surprise and violate some tragically established Platonic bond. Yet, cautious, guilt-ridden, worrier-victim that I am, this night was to be mine. Connie Chasen and I had taken to each other in a way that would not be denied and one brief hour later were thrashing balletically through the percales, executing with total emotional commitment the absurd choreography of human passion. To me, it was the most erotic and satisfying night of sex I had ever had, and as she lay in my arms afterward, relaxed and fulfilled, I wondered exactly how Fate was going to extract its inevitable dues. Would I soon go blind? Or become a paraplegic? What hideous vigorish would Harold Cohen be forced to pony up so the cosmos might continue in its harmonious rounds? But this would all come later.

The following four weeks burst no bubbles. Connie and I explored one another and delighted in each new discovery. I found her quick, exciting, and responsive; her imagination was fertile and her references erudite and varied. She could discuss Novalis and quote from the Rig-Veda. The verse of every song by Cole Porter, she knew by heart. In bed she was uninhibited and experimental, a true child of the future. On the minus side one had to be niggling to find fault. True she could be a tad temperamental. She inevitably changed her food order in a restaurant and always long after it was decent to do so. Invariably she got angry when I pointed out this was not exactly fair to waiter or chef. Also she switched diets every other day, committing with whole heart to one and then disregarding it in favor of some new, fashionable theory on weight loss. Not that she was remotely overweight. Quite the opposite. Her shape would have been the envy of a *Vogue* model, and yet an inferiority complex rivaling Franz Kafka's led her to painful bouts of self-criticism. To hear her tell it, she was a dumpy little nonentity, who had no business trying to be an actress, much less attempting Chekhov. My assurances were moderately encouraging and I kept them flowing, though I felt that if her desirability was not apparent from my obsessional glee over her brain and body, no amount of talk would be convincing.

Along about the sixth week of a wonderful romance, her insecurity emerged full blown one day. Her parents were having a barbecue in Connecticut and I was at last going to meet her family.

"Dad's great," she said worshipfully, "and great-looking. And Mom's beautiful. Are yours?"

"I wouldn't say beautiful," I confessed. Actually, I had a rather dim view of my family's physical appearance, likening the relatives on my mother's side to something usually cultured in a petri dish. I was very hard on my family and we all constantly teased each other and fought, but were close. Indeed, a compliment had not passed through the lips of any member during my lifetime and I suspect not since God made his covenant with Abraham.

"My folks never fight," she said. "They drink, but they're real polite. And Danny's nice." Her brother. "I mean he's strange but sweet. He writes music."

"I'm looking forward to meeting them all."

"I hope you don't fall for my kid sister, Lindsay."

"Oh sure."

"She's two years younger than me and so bright and sexy. Everyone goes nuts over her."

"Sounds impressive," I said. Connie stroked my face.

"I hope you don't like her better than me," she said in half-serious tones that enabled her to voice this fear gracefully.

"I wouldn't worry," I assured her.

"No? Promise?"

"Are you two competitive?"

"No. We love each other. But she's got an angel's face and a sexy, round body. She takes after Mom. And she's got this real high IQ and great sense of humor."

"You're beautiful," I said and kissed her. But I must admit, for the rest of that day, fantasies of twenty-one-year-old Lindsay Chasen did not leave my mind. Good Lord, I thought, what if she is this *Wunderkind?* What if she is indeed as irresistible as Connie paints her? Might I not be smitten? Weakling that I am, might not the sweet body scent and tinkling laugh of a stunning Connecticut WASP named Lindsay—Lindsay yet!—not turn this fascinated, though unpledged, head from Connie toward fresh mischief? After all, I had only known Connie six weeks and, while having a wonderful time with the woman, was not yet actually in love with her beyond all reason. Still, Lindsay would have to be pretty damn fabulous to cause a ripple in the giddy tempest of chuckles and lust that made these past three fortnights such a spree.

That evening I made love with Connie, but when I slept it was Lindsay who trespassed my dreams. Sweet little Lindsay, the adorable Phi Beta Kappa with the face of a movie star and the charm of a princess. I tossed and turned and woke in the middle of the night with a strange feeling of excitement and foreboding.

In the morning my fantasies subsided, and after breakfast Connie and I set off for Connecticut bearing wine and flowers. We drove through the fall countryside listening to Vivaldi on FM and exchanging our observations on that day's Arts and Leisure Section. Then, moments before we passed through the front gate of the Chasens' Lyme acreage, I once again wondered if I was about to be stupefied by this formidable kid sister.

"Will Lindsay's boyfriend be here?" I asked in a probing, guilt-strangled falsetto.

"They're finished," Connie explained. "Lindsay runs through one a month. She's a heartbreaker." Hmm, I thought, in addition to all else, the young woman is available. Might she really be more exciting than Connie? I found it hard to believe, and yet I tried to prepare myself for any eventuality. Any, of course, except the one that occurred that crisp, clear, Sunday afternoon.

Connie and I joined the barbecue, where there was much revelry and drinking. I met the family, one by one, scattered as they were amidst their fashionable, attractive cohorts and though sister Lindsay was indeed all Connie had described—comely, flirtatious, and fun to talk to—I did not prefer her to Connie. Of the two, I still felt much more taken with the older sister than the twenty-one-year-old Vassar grad. No, the one I hopelessly lost my heart to that day was none other than Connie's fabulous mother, Emily.

Emily Chasen, fifty-five, buxom, tanned, a ravishing pioneer face with pulled-back greying hair and round, succulent curves that expressed themselves in flawless arcs like a Brancusi. Sexy Emily, whose huge, white smile and chesty, big laugh combined to create an irresistible warmth and seductiveness.

What protoplasm in this family, I thought! What award-winning genes! Consistent genes too, as Emily Chasen seemed to be as at ease with me as her daughter was. Clearly she enjoyed talking with me as I monopolized her time, mindless of the demands of the other afternoon guests. We discussed photography (her hobby) and books. She was currently reading, with great delight, a book of Joseph Heller's. She found it hilarious and laughing fetchingly as she filled my glass said, "God, you Jews are truly exotic." Exotic? She should only know the Greenblatts. Or Mr. and Mrs. Milton Sharpstein, my father's friends. Or for that matter, my cousin Tovah. Exotic? I mean, they're nice but hardly exotic with their endless bickering over the best way to combat indigestion or how far back to sit from the television set.

Emily and I talked for hours of movies, and we discussed my hopes for the theatre and her new interest in making collages. Obviously this woman had many creative and intellectual demands that for one reason or another remained pent up within her. Yet clearly she was not unhappy with her life as she and her husband, John Chasen, an older version of the man you'd like to have piloting your plane, hugged and drank in lovey-dovey fashion. Indeed, in comparison to my own folks, who had been married inexplicably for forty years (out of spite it seemed), Emily and John seemed like the Lunts. My folks, naturally, could not discuss even the weather without accusations and recriminations just short of gunfire.

When it came time to go home I was quite sorry and left with dreams of Emily in complete command of my thoughts.

"They're sweet, aren't they?" Connie asked as we sped toward Manhattan.

"Very," I concurred.

"Isn't Dad a knockout? He's really fun."

"Umm." The truth was I had hardly exchanged ten sentences with Connie's dad.

"And Mom looked great today. Better than in a long time. She's been ill with the flu, too."

"She's quite something," I said.

"Her photography and collages are very good,"

Connie said. "I wish Dad encouraged her more instead of being so old-fashioned. He's just not fascinated by creativity in the arts. Never was."

"Too bad," I said. "I hope it hasn't been too frustrating for your mother over the years."

"It has," Connie said. "And Lindsay? Are you in love with her?"

"She's lovely—but not in your class. At least as far as I'm concerned."

"I'm relieved," Connie said laughingly and pecked me on the cheek. Abysmal vermin that I am, I couldn't, of course, tell her that it was her incredible mother that I wanted to see again. Yet even as I drove, my mind clicked and blinked like a computer in hopes of concocting some scheme to filch more time with this overpowering and wonderful woman. If you had asked me where I expected it to lead, I really couldn't have said. I knew only as I drove through the cold, night, autumn air that somewhere Freud, Sophocles, and Eugene O'Neill were laughing.

During the next several months I managed to see Emily Chasen many times. Usually it was in an innocent threesome with Connie, both of us meeting her in the city and taking her to a museum or concert. Once or twice I did something with Emily alone if Connie was busy. This delighted Connie—that her mother and lover should be such good friends. Once or twice I contrived to be where Emily was "by accident" and wound up having an apparently impromptu walk or drink with her. It was obvious she enjoyed my company as I listened sympathetically to her artistic aspirations and laughed engagingly at her jokes. Together we discussed music and literature and life, my observations consistently entertaining her. It was also obvious the idea of regarding me as anything more than just a new friend was not remotely on her mind. Or if it was, she certainly never let on. Yet what could I expect? I was living with her daughter. Cohabitating honorably in a

456 civilized society where certain taboos are observed. After all, who did I imagine this woman was anyhow? Some amoral vamp out of German films who would seduce her own child's lover? In truth, I'm sure I would have lost all respect for her if she did confess feelings for me or behave in any other way than untouchable. And yet I had a terrible crush on her. It amounted to genuine longing, and despite all logic I prayed for some tiny hint that her marriage was not as perfect as it seemed or that, resist as she might, she had grown fatally fond of me. There were times that I flirted with the notion of making some tepidly aggressive move myself, but banner headlines in the yellow press formed in my mind and I shrank from any action.

I wanted so badly, in my anguish, to explain these confused feelings to Connie in an above-board way and enlist her aid in making sense out of the painful tangle, but I felt to do so invited certain carnage. In fact, instead of this manly honesty, I nosed around like a ferret for bits and clues regarding Emily's feelings toward me.

"I took your mother to the Matisse exhibit," I said to Connie one day.

"I know," she said. "She had a great time."

"She's a lucky woman. Seems to be happy. Fine marriage."

"Yes." Pause.

"So, er—did she say anything to you?"

"She said you two had a wonderful talk afterwards. About her photography."

"Right." Pause. "Anything else? About me? I mean, I felt maybe I get overbearing."

"Oh God, no. She adores you."

"Yes?"

"With Danny spending more and more time with Dad, she thinks of you kind of like a son."

"Her son!?" I said, shattered.

"I think she would have liked a son who is as

interested in her work as you are. A genuine companion. More intellectually inclined than Danny. Sensitive to her artistic needs a little. I think you fulfill that role for her.''

That night I was in a foul mood and, as I sat home with Connie watching television, my body again ached to be pressed in passionate tenderness against this woman who apparently thought of me as nothing more dangerous than her boy. Or did she? Was this not just a casual surmise of Connie's? Might Emily not be thrilled to find out that a man, much younger than herself, found her beautiful and sexy and fascinating and longed to have an affair with her quite unlike anything remotely filial? Wasn't it possible a woman of that age, particularly one whose husband was not overly responsive to her deepest feelings, would welcome the attention of a passionate admirer? And might I not, mired in my own middle-class background, be making too much of the fact that I was living with her daughter? After all, stranger things happen. Certainly amongst temperaments gifted with profounder artistic intensity. I had to resolve matters and finally put an end to these feelings which had assumed the proportions of a mad obsession. The situation was taking too heavy a toll on me, and it was time I either acted on it or put it out of my mind. I decided to act.

Past successful campaigns suggested instantly the proper route to take. I would steer her to Trader Vic's, that dimly lit, foolproof Polynesian den of delights where dark, promising corners abounded and deceptively mild rum drinks quickly unchained the fiery libido from its dungeon. A pair of Mai Tai's and it would be anybody's ball game. A hand on the knee. A sudden uninhibited kiss. Fingers intertwined. The miraculous booze would work its dependable magic. It had never failed me in the past. Even when the unsuspecting victim pulled back with eyebrows arched, one could back out gracefully by imputing all to the effects of the island brew.

"Forgive me," I could alibi, "I'm just so zonked by this drink. I don't know what I'm doing."

Yes, the time for polite chitchat was over, I thought. I am in love with two women, a not terribly uncommon problem. That they happen to be mother and child? All the more challenging! I was becoming hysterical. Yet drunk with confidence as I was at that point, I must admit that things did not finally come off quite as planned. True, we did make it to Trader Vic's one cold February afternoon. We did also look in each other's eyes and waxed poetic about life while knocking back tall, foamy, white beverages that held minuscule wooden parasols lanced into floating pineapple squares—but there it ended. And it did so because, despite the unblocking of my baser urges, I felt that it would completely destroy Connie. In the end it was my own guilty conscience—or, more accurately, my return to sanity—that prevented me from placing the predictable hand on Emily Chasen's leg and pursuing my dark desires. That sudden realization that I was only a mad fantasizer who, in fact, loved Connie and must never risk hurting her in any way did me in. Yes, Harold Cohen was a more conventional type than he would have us believe. And more in love with his girl friend than he cared to admit. This crush on Emily Chasen would have to be filed and forgotten. Painful as it might be to control my impulses toward Connie's mom, rationality and decent consideration would prevail.

After a wonderful afternoon, the crowning moment of which would have been the ferocious kissing of Emily's large, inviting lips, I got the check and called it a day. We exited laughingly into the lightly blowing snow and, after walking her to her car, I watched her take off for Lyme while I returned home to her daughter with a new, deeper feeling of warmth for this woman who nightly shared my bed. Life is truly chaos, I thought. Feelings are so unpredictable. How does anyone ever stay married for forty years? This, it seems, is more of a miracle than the parting of the Red Sea, though my father, in his naïveté, holds the latter to be a greater achievement. I kissed Connie and confessed the depth of my affection. She reciprocated. We made love.

Dissolve, as they say in the movies, to a few months later. Connie can no longer have intercourse with me. And why? I brought it on myself like the tragic protagonist of a Greek play. Our sex began falling off insidiously weeks ago.

"What's wrong?" I'd ask. "Have I done something?"

"God no, it's not your fault. Oh hell."

"What? Tell me."

"I'm just not up to it," she'd say. "Must we *every* night?" The every night she referred to was in actuality only a few nights a week and soon less than that.

"I can't," she'd say guiltily when I'd attempt to instigate sex. "You know I'm going through a bad time."

"What bad time?" I asked incredulously. "Are you seeing someone else?"

"Of course not."

"Do you love me?"

"Yes. I wish I didn't."

"So what? Why the turnoff? And it's not getting better, it's getting worse."

"I can't do it with you," she confessed one night. "You remind me of my brother."

"What?"

"You remind me of Danny. Don't ask me why."

"Your brother? You must be joking!"

"No."

"But he's a twenty-three-year-old, blond WASP who works in your father's law practice, and I remind you of him?"

"It's like going to bed with my brother," she wept.

"O.K., O.K., don't cry. We'll be all right. I have to take

some aspirin and lie down. I don't feel well." I pressed my throbbing temples and pretended to be bewildered, but it was, of course, obvious that my strong relationship with her mother had in some way cast me in a fraternal role as far as Connie was concerned. Fate was getting even. I was to be tortured like Tantalus, inches from the svelte, tanned body of Connie Chasen, yet unable to lay a hand on her without, at least for the time being, eliciting the classical expletive, "Yuck." In the irrational assigning of parts that occurs in all of our emotional dramas, I had suddenly become a sibling.

Various stages of anguish marked the next months. First the pain of being rejected in bed. Next, telling ourselves the condition was temporary. This was accompanied by an attempt by me to be understanding, to be patient. I recalled not being able to perform with a sexy date in college once precisely because some vague twist of her head reminded me of my Aunt Rifka. This girl was far prettier than the squirrel-faced aunt of my boyhood, but the notion of making love with my mother's sister wrecked the moment irreparably. I knew what Connie was going through, and yet sexual frustration mounted and compounded itself. After a time, my self-control sought expression in sarcastic remarks and later in an urge to burn down the house. Still, I kept trying not to be rash, trying to ride out the storm of unreason and preserve what in all other ways was a good relationship with Connie. My suggestion for her to see a psychoanalyst fell on deaf ears, as nothing was more alien to her Connecticut upbringing than the Jewish science from Vienna.

"Sleep with other women. What else can I say?" she offered.

"I don't want to sleep with other women. I love you."

"And I love you. You know that. But I can't go to bed with you." Indeed I was not the type who slept around, for despite my fantasy episode with Connie's mother, I had never cheated on Connie. True, I had experienced normal daydreams over random females—this actress, that stewardess, some wide-eyed college girl—yet never would I have been unfaithful toward my lover. And not because I couldn't have. Certain women I had come in contact with had been quite aggressive, even predatory, but my loyalty had remained with Connie; doubly so, during this trying time of her impotence. It occurred to me, of course, to hit on Emily again, whom I still saw with and without Connie in innocent, companionable fashion, but I felt that to stoke up embers I had labored so successfully to dampen would only lead to everybody's misery.

This is not to say that Connie was faithful. No, the sad truth was, on at least several occasions, she had succumbed to alien wiles, bedding surreptitiously with actors and authors alike.

"What do you want me to say?" she wept one three A.M. when I had caught her in a tangle of contradicting alibis. "I only do it to assure myself I'm not some sort of a freak. That I still am able to have sex."

"You can have sex with anyone but me," I said, furious with feelings of injustice.

"Yes. You remind me of my brother."

"I don't want to hear that nonsense."

"I told you to sleep with other women."

"I've tried not to, but it looks as if I'm going to have to."

"Please. Do it. It's a curse," she sobbed.

It was truly a curse. For when two people love each other and are forced to separate because of an almost comical aberration, what else could it be? That I brought it on myself by developing a close relationship with her mother was undeniable. Perhaps it was my comeuppance for thinking I could entice and bed Emily Chasen, having already made whoopee with her offspring.

The sin of hubris, maybe. Me, Harold Cohen, guilty of

hubris. A man who has never thought of himself in an order higher than rodent, nailed for hubris? Too hard to swallow. And yet we did separate. Painfully, we remained friends and went our individual ways. True, only ten city blocks lay between our residences and we spoke every other day, but the relationship was over. It was then, and only then, that I began to realize how much I had really adored Connie. Inevitably bouts of melancholy and anxiety accentuated my Proustian haze of pain. I recalled all our fine moments together, our exceptional love-making, and in the solitude of my large apartment, I wept. I attempted to go out on dates, but again, inevitably, everything seemed flat. All the little groupies and secretaries that paraded through the bedroom left me empty; even worse than an evening alone with a good book. The world seemed truly stale and unprofitable; quite a dreary, awful place, until one day I got the stunning news that Connie's mother had left her husband and they were getting a divorce. Imagine that, I thought, as my heart beat faster than normal speed for the first time in ages. My parents fight like the Montagues and Capulets and stay together their whole lives. Connie's folks sip martinis and hug with true civility and, bingo, they're divorcing.

My course of action was now obvious. Trader Vic's. Now there could be no crippling obstacles in our path. Though it would be somewhat awkward as I had been Connie's lover, it held none of the overwhelming difficulties of the past. We were now two free agents. My dormant feelings for Emily Chasen, always smoldering, ignited once again. Perhaps a cruel twist of fate ruined my relationship with Connie, but nothing would stand in the way of my conquering her mother.

Riding the crest of the large economy-size hubris, I phoned Emily and made a date. Three days later we sat huddled in the dark of my favorite Polynesian restaurant, and loose from three Bahia's, she poured out her heart about the demise of her marriage. When she got to the part about looking for a new life with less restraint and more creative possibilities, I kissed her. Yes, she was taken aback but she did not scream. She acted surprised, but I confessed my feelings toward her and kissed her again. She seemed confused but did not bolt from the table, outraged. By the third kiss I knew she would succumb. She shared my feelings. I took her to my apartment and we made love. The following morning, when the effects of the rum had worn off, she still looked magnificent to me and we made love again.

"I want you to marry me," I said, my eyes glazed over with adoration.

"Not really," she said.

"Yes," I said. "I'll settle for nothing less." We kissed and had breakfast, laughing and making plans. That day I broke the news to Connie, braced for a blow that never came. I had anticipated any number of reactions ranging from derisive laughter to outright fury, but the truth was Connie took it in charming stride. She herself was leading an active social life, going out with several attractive men, and had experienced great concern over her mother's future when the woman had gotten divorced. Suddenly a young knight had emerged to care for the lovely lady. A knight who still had a fine, friendly relationship with Connie. It was a stroke of good fortune all around. Connie's guilt over putting me through hell would be removed. Emily would be happy. I would be happy. Yes, Connie took it all in casual, good-humored stride, natural to her upbringing.

My parents, on the other hand, proceeded directly to the window of their tenth-story apartment and competed for leaping space.

"I never heard of such a thing," my mother wailed, rending her robe and gnashing her teeth.

"He's crazy. You idiot. You're crazy," my father said, looking pale and stricken.

"A fifty-five-year-old *shiksa!?*" my Aunt Rose shrieked, lifting the letter opener and bringing it to her eyes.

"I love her," I protested.

"She's more than twice your age," Uncle Louie yelled.

"So?"

"So it's not done," my father yelled, invoking the Torah.

"His girl friend's mother he's marrying?" Aunt Tillie yelped as she slid to the floor unconscious.

"Fifty-five and a *shiksa*," my mother screamed, searching now for a cyanide capsule she had reserved for just such occasions.

"What are they, Moonies?" Uncle Louie asked. "Do they have him hypnotized!?"

"Idiot! Imbecile," Dad screamed. Aunt Tillie regained consciousness, focused on me, remembered where she was, and passed out again. In the far corner, Aunt Rose was down on her knees intoning Sh'ma Yisroel.

"God will punish you, Harold," my father yelled. "God will cleave your tongue to the roof of your mouth and all your cattle and kine shall die and a tenth of all thy crops shall wither and . . ."

But I married Emily and there were no suicides. Emily's three children attended and a dozen or so friends. It was held in Connie's apartment and champagne flowed. My folks could not make it, a previous commitment to sacrifice a lamb taking precedence. We all danced and joked and the evening went well. At one point, I found myself in the bedroom with Connie alone. We kidded and reminisced about our relationship, its ups and downs, and how sexually attracted I had been to her.

"It was flattering," she said warmly.

"Well, I couldn't swing it with the daughter, so I carried off the mother." The next thing I knew, Connie's tongue was in my mouth. "What the hell are you doing?" I said, pulling back. "Are you drunk?"

"You turn me on like you can't believe," she said, dragging me down on the bed.

"What's gotten into you? Are you a nymphomaniac?" I said, rising, yet undeniably excited by her sudden aggressiveness.

"I have to sleep with you. If not now, then soon," she said.

"Me? Harold Cohen? The guy who lived with you? And loved you? Who couldn't get near you with a ten-foot pole because I became a version of Danny? Me you're hot for? Your brother symbol?"

"It's a whole new ball game," she said, pressing close to me. "Marrying Mom has made you my father." She kissed me again and just before returning to the festivities said, "Don't worry, Dad, there'll be plenty of opportunities."

I sat on the bed and stared out the window into infinite space. I thought of my parents and wondered if I should abandon the theatre and return to rabbinical school. Through the half-open door I saw Connie and also Emily, both laughing and chatting with guests, and all I could mutter to myself as I remained a limp, hunched figure was an age-old line of my grandfather's which goes "Oy vey."

Confessions of a Burglar

(Following are excerpts from the soon to be published memoirs of Virgil Ives, who is currently serving the first of four consecutive ninety-nine-year sentences for various felonies. Mr. Ives plans on working with children when he gets out.)

S URE I STOLE. Why not? Where I grew up, you had to steal to eat. Then you had to steal to tip. Lots of guys stole fifteen per cent, but I always stole twenty, which made me a big favorite among the waiters. On the way home from a heist, I'd steal some pajamas to sleep in. Or if it was a hot night, I'd steal underwear. It was a way of life. I had a bad upbringing, you might say. My dad was always on the run from the cops and I never saw him out of disguise till I was twenty-two. For years, I thought he was a short, bearded man with dark glasses and a limp; actually, he was tall and blond and resembled Lindbergh. He was a professional bank robber, but sixty-five was the mandatory retirement age, so he had to get out. Spent his last few years in mail fraud, but the postal rates went up and he lost everything.

Mom was wanted, too. Of course in those days it wasn't the way it is now, with women demanding equal rights, and all. Back then, if a woman turned to crime the only opportunities open to her were blackmail and, once in a while, arson. Women were used in Chicago to drive get-away cars, but only during the drivers' strike, in 1926. Terrible strike. It lasted eight weeks, and whenever a gang pulled a job and ran out with the money they were forced to walk or take a cab.

I had a sister and two brothers. Jenny married money. Not an actual human being—it was a pile of singles. My brother Vic got in with a gang of plagiarists. He was in the middle of signing his name to "The Waste Land" when the feds surrounded the house. He got ten years. Some rich kid from a highfalutin family who signed Pound's "Cantos" got off on probation. That's the law for you. Charlie—that's my youngest brother—he's been a numbers runner, a fence, and a loan shark. Never could find himself. Eventually he was arrested for loitering. He loitered for seven years, till he realized it was not the kind of crime that brought in any money.

The first thing I ever stole was a loaf of bread. I was working for Rifkin's Bakery, where my job was to remove the jelly from doughnuts that had gone stale and transfer it to fresh goods. It was very exacting work, done with a rubber tube and a scalpel. If your hands shook, the jelly went on the floor and old man Rifkin would pull your hair. Arnold Rothstein, who we all looked up to, came in one day and said he wanted to get his hands on a loaf of bread but he absolutely refused to pay for it. He hinted that this was a chance for some smart kid to get into the rackets. I took that as a cue, and each day when I left I put one slice of rye under my coat, until after three weeks I had accumulated a whole loaf. On the way to Rothstein's office, I began to feel remorse, because even though I hated Rifkin his wife had once let me take home two seeds from a roll when my uncle was dying. I tried to return the bread, but I got caught while I was trying to figure out which loaf each slice belonged to. The next thing I knew, I was in Elmira Reformatory.

Elmira was a tough joint. I escaped five times. Once I tried to sneak out in the back of a laundry truck. The guards got suspicious, and one of them poked me with his stick and asked me what the hell I was doing lying around in a hamper. I looked him right in the eye and said, "I'm some shirts." I could tell he was dubious. He kept pacing back and forth and staring at me. I guess I got a little panicky. "I'm some *shirts*," I told him. "Some denim work shirts—blue ones." Before I could say another word, my arms and legs were manacled and I was back in stir.

I learned everything I knew about crime at Elmira: how to pick pockets, how to crack a safe, how to cut glass —all the fine points of the trade. For instance, I learned (and not even all professional criminals know this) that in the event of a shootout with the cops, the cops are always allowed the first two shots. It's just the way it's done. Then you return fire. And if a cop says, "We have the house surrounded, come out with your hands up," you don't just shoot wildly. You say, "I'd prefer not to," or "I'd rather not at this particular time." There's a right way to do these things, but today . . . Well, why go into all that?

For the next few years of my life I was the best damn burglar you ever saw. People talk about Raffles, but Raffles had his style and I had mine. I had lunch with Raffles' son once. Nice guy. We ate at the old Lindy's. He stole the pepper mill. I stole the silverware and napkins. Then he took the ketchup bottle. I took his hat. He got my umbrella and tiepin. When we left we kidnapped a waiter. It was quite a hall. The original Raffles began as a cat burglar. (I couldn't do that, because the whiskers make me sneeze.) He'd dress up in this beat-up cat suit and dart over rooftops. In the end, he was caught by two dogs from Scotland Yard dressed as dogs. I suppose you've heard of the Kissing Bandit? He'd break into a joint and rob the victim, and if it was a woman he'd kiss her. It was sad the way the law finally nailed him. He had two old dowagers tied up and he was prancing in front of them singing "Gimme a Little Kiss, Will Ya, Huh?" when he slipped on a footstool and fractured his pelvis.

Those boys made all the headlines, but I pulled off some capers that the police never did figure out. Once, I entered a mansion, blew the safe, and removed six thousand dollars while a couple slept in the same room. The husband woke up when the dynamite went off, but when I assured him that the entire proceeds would go to the Boys' Clubs of America he went back to sleep. Cleverly, I left behind some fingerprints of Franklin D. Roosevelt, who was President then. Another time, at a big diplomatic cocktail party, I stole a woman's diamond necklace while we were shaking hands. Used a vacuum cleaner on her—an old Hoover. Got her necklace and earrings. Later, when I opened the bag I found some false teeth there, which belonged to the Dutch Ambassador.

My most beautiful job, though, was when I broke into the British Museum. I knew that the entire floor of the Rare Gems Room was wired and the slightest pressure on it would set off an alarm. I was lowered in upside down by a rope from the skylight, so I wouldn't touch the ground. I came through neat as you please, and in a minute I was hovering over the famous Kittridge Diamonds in their display case. As I pulled out my glass cutter a little sparrow flew in through the skylight and landed on the floor. The alarm sounded and eight squad cars arrived. I got ten years. The sparrow got twenty to life. The bird was out in six months, on probation. A year later, he was picked up in Fort Worth for pecking Rabbi Morris Klugfein into a state of semiconsciousness.

What advice would I give the average homeowner to protect himself against burglars? Well, the first thing is to keep a light on in the house when you go out. It must be at least a sixty-watt bulb; anything less and the burglar will ransack the house, out of contempt for the wattage. Another good idea is to keep a dog, but this is not foolproof. Whenever I was about to rob a house with a dog in it, I threw in some dog food mixed with Seconal. If that didn't work, I'd grind up equal parts of chopped meat and a novel by Theodore Dreiser. If it happens that you are going out of town and must leave your house unguarded, it's a good idea to put a cardboard silhouette of yourself in the window. Any silhouette will do. A Bronx man once placed a cardboard silhouette of Montgomery Clift in his window and then went to Kutsher's for the weekend. Later, Montgomery Clift himself happened to walk by and saw the silhouette, which caused him great anxiety. He attempted to strike up a conversation, and when it failed to answer for seven hours Clift returned to California and told his friends that New Yorkers were snobbish.

If you surprise an intruder in the act of burglarizing your home, do not panic. Remember, he is as frightened as you are. One good device is to rob *him*. Seize the initiative and relieve the burglar of his watch and wallet. Then he can get into your bed while you make a getaway. Trapped by this defense, I once wound up living in Des Moines for six years with another man's wife and three children, and only left when I was fortunate enough to surprise another burglar, who took my place. The six years I lived with that family were very happy ones, and I often look back on them with affection, although there is also much to be said for working on a chain gang.

ABOUT THE AUTHOR

After he was rejected from both New York University and City College, Woody Allen turned to a professional writing career, at first for television and comedians. In 1964 he decided to become a comedian himself.

Woody Allen's first screenplay, written in 1964, was the enormously popular *What's New Pussycat?* He has written, directed, and often starred in numerous popular and critically acclaimed films, including: *Take the Money and Run, Bananas, Everything You Always Wanted to Know About Sex (But Were Afraid to Ask), Sleeper, Love and Death, Annie Hall, Manhattan, Stardust Memories, A Midsummer Night's Sex Comedy, Broadway Danny Rose, Zelig, Hannah and Her Sisters, Crimes and Misdemeanors, Interiors, The Purple Rose of Cairo, Radio Days, September, Alice, Bullets over Broadway, Manhattan Murder Mystery, Mighty Aphrodite,* and *Everyone Says I Love You.* In addition, Mr. Allen has written three plays, *Don't Drink the Water, Play It Again, Sam* (the latter starring himself in both the play and the subsequent film version), and *The Floating Lightbulb.*

Mr. Allen has written and appeared in his own television specials and has been a frequent contributor to *The New Yorker,* among other periodicals. His pieces have been collected in three books, *Getting Even, Without Feathers,* and *Side Effects,* which have been combined in this hardcover omnibus edition.